A SHORT, OFFHAND, KILLING AFFAIR

A SHORT, OFFHAND, KILLING AFFAIR

Soldiers and Social Conflict during the Mexican-American War

PAUL FOOS

THE UNIVERSITY OF NORTH CAROLINA PRESS
CHAPEL HILL AND LONDON

Designed by Geoff Halber {OLD MAN HALBER'S}
Set in Adobe Jenson and Aquiline types
by Tseng Information Systems, Inc.

Manufactured in the United States of America

*The paper in this book meets the guidelines
for permanence and durability of the Committee
on Production Guidelines for Book Longevity
of the Council on Library Resources.*

Library of Congress Cataloging-in-Publication Data
Foos, Paul W.
A short, offhand, killing affair : soldiers and social
conflict during the Mexican-American War /
by Paul Foos.
    p. cm.
Includes bibliographical references and index.
ISBN 0-8078-2731-2 (cloth : alk. paper) —
ISBN 0-8078-5405-0 (pbk. : alk. paper)
1. United States. Army — History — Mexican War,
1846–1848.   2. Mexican War, 1846–1848 — Social
aspects.   3. Soldiers — United States — Social
conditions — 19th century.   4. United States.
Army — Military life — History — 19th century.
5. Mexican War, 1846–1848 — Influence.   I. Title.
E409.2 .F66   2002
973.6′28 — dc21   2001059757

CLOTH   06 05 04 03 02   5 4 3 2 1
PAPER   06 05 04 03 02   5 4 3 2 1

for LISA

Contents

Tables, Illustrations, & Map

A SHORT, OFFHAND, KILLING AFFAIR

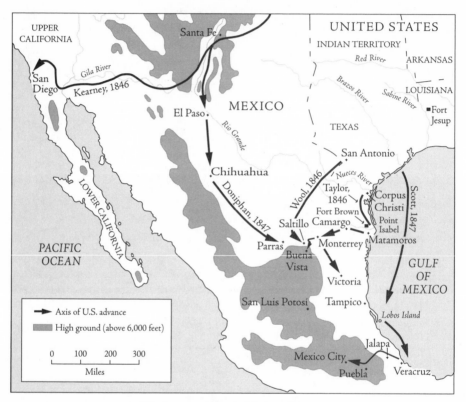

UPPER
CALIFORNIA

San
Diego

Gila River

Kearney, 1846

PACIFIC
OCEAN

LOWER CALIFORNIA

Santa Fe

El Paso

MEXICO

Rio Grande

Chihuahua

Doniphan, 1847

Wool, 1846

Saltillo

Parras

Buena
Vista

San Luis Potosí

UNITED STATES

INDIAN TERRITORY

Red River

ARKANSAS

Brazos River

Sabine River

LOUISIANA

Fort
Jesup

TEXAS

San Antonio

Nueces River

Taylor,
1846

Corpus
Christi

Fort Brown
Camargo

Point
Isabel

Monterrey

Matamoros

Scott, 1847

Victoria

Tampico

GULF
OF
MEXICO

Lobos Island

Jalapa

Mexico City

Puebla

Veracruz

➤ Axis of U.S. advance

High ground (above 6,000 feet)

0   100   200   300
Miles

U.S. Army campaigns in Mexico, 1846–1847

Introduction

"A Mexican mob is not that short, offhand, killing affair that it is in the 'far west' of the United States; . . . it is rather an uproarious meeting, a somewhat irregular procession, arranged with a certain decency, and executed more from love of plunder than thirst of blood."[1] Thus did an American doctor from Missouri summarize his treatment at the hands of a would-be lynch mob—and, by implication, the entire experience of the Mexican-American War. Adolphus Wislizenus meant to disparage Mexicans with his comments, showing a preference for more decisive, American modes of action. This is somewhat odd, given that he owed his life to the decision of a patriotic Mexican mob to demonstrate rather than to execute. Wislizenus and a small group of Americans set out on an exploratory and trading journey in 1846 and were caught in Chihuahua shortly after the outbreak of war. They were neither killed nor plundered, but held for a few months until American troops arrived.

It was not at all unusual for Americans to offer broad generalizations about Mexico and its people during the 1840s, and for those statements to reflect strong prejudices about race, religion, and nationality. American supporters of the Mexican War wished to see Mexicans as inherently flawed, their society sliding toward dissolution, thus creating an opening for Americans to take control.

The experience of many soldiers in Mexico, however, led them to harsh criticisms of their own officers and comrades. Ohio volunteer Orlando John Hodge saw his fellow privates whipped and executed for infractions of discipline when he served along the Rio Grande in 1847; he complained that his officers wasted their time drinking and gambling and even fighting duels. Hodge returned home convinced that military discipline, based in class privilege, was more hateful than any racial or national enemy.[2]

An Arkansas soldier, John Palmer, was befriended by Mexican rancheros and sought to settle in northern Mexico as a landowner. His plans were set awry by the hostility of both lower-class Mexicans and soldiers in the Arkansas regiment who were denied similar opportunities to seize the fruits of manifest destiny.[3]

In the late 1840s the United States faced deep racial and ethnic divisions, leading ultimately to civil war. The war of 1846–48 provided Americans with a venue to confront their own internal conflicts as they fought a war heavily promoted by politicians and the press in the name of white, Anglo-Saxon supremacy.

Although the war directly affected only a small minority of the citizens of the United States, it produced storms of controversy, changed the political and social climate, and inspired decisive action and much commentary from those who served in the military or helped recruit armies for Mexico.

Through first-person recollections of Mexican-American War participants like Adolphus Wislizenus, Orlando John Hodge, John Palmer, and others, this book examines alternative perspectives on the war. For the most part, diaries and letters from the Mexican War are steeped in romantic, heroic rhetoric. Accounts that focus on issues of desertion, actual relations with Mexicans, soldiers' rights, and the perplexing religious, political, and racial notions that composed "manifest destiny" are of great importance in discerning the untold history of this war. Rather than providing an exhaustive or comprehensive history of the Mexican-American conflict, this book serves to enhance the existing body of work on the subject by analyzing newly uncovered and long-ignored sources. As much as possible these sources offer commentary that eschews the heroic mode so common in personal and public accounts of the 1840s.

Another central concern here is the reclamation of the points of view of the laboring population that drifted in and out of military service in this era. The sources for this aspect of the Mexican War are fragmentary at best but important nonetheless. Most commentary by or about the nascent working class during this period comes from the antiwar, antislavery, and labor press. Unfortunately, many of these reformers were determinedly middle class in outlook (with a few important exceptions). They often dismissed soldiers as pawns of slave owners and politicians. A close look at soldiers' acts and words reveals much that is brutal and racist but also provides thoughtful reflections on issues of democracy, race relations, and the emerging capitalist society. Some soldiers were infused with the spirit of manifest destiny, whereas others were troubled by implications of racial war and by the divisions it produced among white Americans. Grass-roots discontent with the American war played a crucial part in limiting U.S. gains. The annexation of Texas, New Mexico, and Upper California represented a shortfall of the goals of manifest destiny, a political program that aimed for continental and even hemispheric mastery.

Much historical writing on the 1846–48 war has focused on political debate over the expansion of slavery and the stirring up of sectional conflict. Although these issues are vital, in hindsight the stupendous catastrophe of the American Civil War has obscured some of the more important national and international struggles that were aggravated by the Mexican-American conflict.

The Mexican War was a pivotal event in westward expansion and, as such, was critical in shaping the new exploitive social relations that would characterize "free labor" and American capitalism in the nineteenth and twentieth centuries. The experiences of Americans in Mexico expose the colossal weight of racism as a determinant of Americans' thought and actions but also reveal the perplexing ways in which soldiers and others confused issues of race, ethnicity, religion, and economic status, making damning judgments based on peculiar configurations of personal experience, prejudice, and received propaganda.

Clearly, racism pervaded American popular thought and freighted almost every word and action. However, individuals made their own judgments about the meaning of race. The naked opportunism of the 1846–48 war, the class conflict that the army brought with it to Mexico, and face-to-face experience with the Mexican people would bring about changed racial thinking: some individuals and groups became more exploitive than ever, but others rejected the cant of racial destiny.

The experiences of Americans as occupiers of Mexico shook the foundations of Jacksonian ideas and practices, particularly the principle of herrenvolk democracy, which envisioned landed equality for whites, with servile subject races.[4] The limits of populist, Democratic ideology were reached in recruiting and mobilization of troops, when hierarchy and exploitation of whites became the norm rather than the exception. In 1847, after the initial war enthusiasm had waned, recruiters scoured jails and low taverns seeking men to "volunteer" under coercion.

The territorial gains of the Mexican War were significant, though the boundless optimism of manifest destiny was not sated. Disturbing social and political divisions intensified in the aftermath of the war. The shortfall of manifest destiny was a bitter pill, in an optimistic era, when many Americans thought that republicanism was the universal tonic for oppressed and divided nations of Latin America and Europe. Democratic Party propagandists dared to dream of an Americanized hemisphere and world. The retreat to "free soil"—a white man's empire upon "empty" lands—was a fallback position and turned American disputes over race and slavery inward, compressing and inflaming them.

Soldiers in Mexico often rebelled against their increasingly disciplined, waged role, subordinate to national and commercial interests. The loosely organized volunteers decided at the company level to collect the wages of manifest destiny in the form of looting and racial atrocity, or simply to return home. The regular army subjected immigrant and poor soldiers to harsh discipline. These men deserted the service in large numbers, most seeking nonmilitary employment, with a small but significant minority joining the Mexican army to fight against their nominal countrymen.

The years from 1835 to 1845 encompassed several invasions, occupations, and wars involving Mexico and the short-lived Republic of Texas—which was, in essence, an American creation. Also deeply involved were migrants, speculators, and mercenaries from the United States. These conflicts revolved around American desires to expand trade, agriculture, and political sovereignty. The aggressive activity in the Old Southwest of the United States and northern Mexico in these years set the stage for war and annexation. New Orleans occupied a central position in the commercial and military campaigns against Mexico; the city was a staging area for the occupation and seizure of Texas, for land speculators, and for depredations upon Mexican commerce. When national elites were ready and willing, in the 1840s, to back southward expansion, entrepreneurs and adventurers in New Orleans had already established procedures and rationales for doing so.

In 1846 the administration of President James K. Polk, elected on a pro-expansion platform, moved purposefully to acquire territory in western North America, putting diplomatic and military pressure on Great Britain and the Republic of Mexico. In the spring of that year, Polk accepted a diplomatic compromise with Britain over the Oregon Territory, and mobilized armies and warships in provocative forward movements to the Rio Grande and Upper California. Polk's initiatives evoked military resistance from Mexico, a nation that had never recovered economically from a long and devastating revolutionary era, and which was in a chronic state of political and social turmoil. During 1846 and 1847, armed forces of the United States seized control of the Mexican provinces of Upper California and New Mexico and northeastern Mexico as far south as the Sierra Madre range.

An American expeditionary force that landed at Veracruz on the Gulf Coast in January 1847 conquered and occupied the economic and population centers of the nation, including the capital, Mexico City. During 1847 and 1848, American officers and soldiers acted as an occupation force, setting up civil administration and battling partisan guerrilla activity.

The coalition of forces that elected James K. Polk to the presidency in 1844 explicitly sought free trade and territorial expansion. In the short term, these goals achieved some measure of success but soon reached immovable barriers. In discussing the expansionist propaganda of the Democrats of the 1840s, historians often view its grandiose vision of manifest destiny as exaggerated and hyperbolic—the effusions of overzealous editors and unrepresentative politicians.[5] A look at the responsible political figures, however, does not reveal them as having goals significantly more modest than those of James Gordon Bennett, Moses Beach, John L. O'Sullivan, or other enthusiastic spokesmen for hemispheric domination.[6]

Early in the war, Polk expressed his desire to take not only California and New Mexico but also the Mexican provinces north of the Sierra Madre range;[7] however, Polk had to remain acutely sensitive to public opinion, electoral politics, and the vicissitudes of the war. In mid-1846, as the war got underway, Polk sought to appease the northern wing of the Democratic Party by denying any plans to take Mexican territory. Ex-president Martin Van Buren and other northern Democrats were ready to split the party rather than endorse a war for the extension of slavery.[8] By August of 1846 the president was saying privately to advisors and party members that the settlement of the war must include purchase of Mexican territory. This raised a storm among Democrats who opposed the expansion of slavery, and resulted in Pennsylvania representative David Wilmot's famous proviso to the $2 million war appropriation bill. Antislavery politicians, wary of opposing funding for American troops in the field, consoled themselves with Wilmot's demand that "neither slavery nor involuntary servitude shall ever exist in any part of said territory."[9]

By late 1847 the U.S. president was exasperated with the dilatoriness of the Mexican Congress in settling the war, and with the continuing guerrilla warfare against the North American occupiers. Polk and his most influential advisors, discussed a range of options in dictating a peace to Mexico, including annexation of Mexico north of the twenty-sixth parallel, dismemberment of that nation, or establishment of an American protectorate.[10]

Treasury secretary Robert J. Walker was a consistent voice for annexation, and Polk was generally sympathetic to his views. But the president reluctantly accepted the terms of Ambassador Nicholas Trist's settlement—the basis for the Treaty of Guadalupe Hidalgo—taking only New Mexico and California; Polk was politically strapped, with a Whig majority in Congress, and Whig war heroes vying for the presidency. Polk realized that Congress was likely to deny him funding to continue the war, and that this might lead to an even less favorable treaty.[11] On March 10 the Senate, after secret debate, voted 38 to 14 to ratify the treaty, with a majority of the northern senators voting in opposition. A motion to include a Wilmot Proviso clause in the treaty was defeated.[12]

Following the precedent of Anglo-Texan settlers of the 1830s and 1840s, the peace settlement of 1848 marked a continuation of colonization in the Mexican cession. Anglo entrepreneurs intermarried with landed Mexicans, slowly insinuating themselves into the old agrarian system. In later decades, the coming of the railroad and capitalist agriculture transformed this process; Anglos flooded into Texas and the Mexican cession after the Civil War and established firm social and economic dominance.[13]

In the areas of northern and central Mexico from which the United States withdrew in 1848, the Mexican propertied classes were not uncongenial to such an arrangement, but smallholders and laborers resisted it fiercely. Their steady war of attrition sapped the will of would-be conquerors. On the American side, common soldiers realized that their part in conquest would be as wage-earning guardians of the propertied classes, Mexican and Anglo, with their "glory" collected in the form of atrocities against the poor and dispossessed. This was a betrayal of recruiting promises: a demoralized soldiery tended toward desertion and riot.

Much of the historical scholarship on the Mexican War has stressed the enthusiasm for the war in the southern and frontier states as opposed to the tepid or negative reception Polk's call for volunteers received in the Northeast. The initial crush of volunteering in the South and West was indeed disproportionate: as a result of this enthusiasm of 1846 Tennessee received the soubriquet, "the Volunteer State."

This led to a perception, now somewhat discredited, that the Mexican War laid the groundwork for the sectional divisions of the Civil War.[14] Popular enthusiasm, at the outset of the war, was indeed greater in the western states, but some of the evidence that follows shows that enthusiasm was quite shallow and short-lived. Historians have noted that a large majority of Mexican War recruits enlisted in southern and western state regiments.

This is true, but as shown in table 2 (in chapter 7), a little over a year into the war regular army and volunteer enlistment figures were almost even. The regular army was preponderantly drawn from the Northeast.

Scholars of the Mexican-American War have been hard-pressed to remain objective in the face of the contentious politics of the 1840s, using them—intentionally or unintentionally—as a sounding board for latter day political debates. The expansionist imperative of manifest destiny has been curiously echoed by contemporary scholars. A recent book went so far as to state that the policies of the 1840s made the United States "coextensive with the entire continent." U.S. historians of a nationalistic bent have viewed the outcome of the war as a triumphant moment for the United States: writing during the Vietnam era, Jack Bauer portrayed the Mexican War as an exemplary "limited war" that persisted despite widespread unpopularity and restored vigor to the nation's economy.[15]

Liberal scholars, from the era of the Civil War through the Cold War, have highlighted the resistance to territorial acquisition on the part of prominent Whigs and antislavery politicians such as Joshua Giddings, Daniel Webster, Abraham Lincoln, David Wilmot, and others. This school of historical scholarship stresses the importance of elite dissent in reining in the imperial ambitions of Polk and company; it portrays nonelites and popular opinion as putty in the hands of expansionist propagandists. The historian John S. Schroeder concluded that, in 1846–48: "Americans and their servants in government were more concerned with the reality of territory than with the abstractions of republican virtue, and the antiwar movement was swept aside by the relentless tide of expansionism. . . . Ebullient and determined to realize their territorial destiny, most Americans did not understand, nor did they care about the broad implications of an aggressive war."[16]

However, the nature of warfare and occupation in Mexico and the hierarchy of the military was odious to American soldiers in many ways: they *did* care, they *did* understand, although they, perhaps, did not speak the language of formal diplomacy or politics. Other Americans whose lives were touched by the recruiting drives, or who were caught up in the politics of slavery had a great deal to say about the war and its implications.

In using the military as a lens through which to view American society and thought in the 1840s, it will be crucial to understand the two opposing poles of military organization and philosophy, the regular army and the volunteer militia. The first two chapters of this book provide extensive background information on the nature of military service in the early republic and on the often schizophrenic ways in which Americans thought about the military—as the lowest sort of common labor and as the most vaunted civic duty.

Chapter 1 examines regular army life in the years leading up to the Mexican War, placing the lowly regular soldier in the context of other proletarian occupations. The U.S. Army camps in South Texas in 1845 were rife with internal conflicts that reflected the problems of creating large-scale organizations in a society based upon individualistic principles. Chapter 2 sketches the historical importance of armed volunteers to the republic and looks at the ways in which the militia system was contested social and political terrain in the mid-1840s. Although volunteering served republican theory as a great social leveler, emerging class and political interests tried to remold volunteering to suit their needs.

Chapters 3 and 4 examine Mexican War recruiting in the United States, focusing on various locales to illustrate the conflicts that arose between the volunteers' expectations and the reality of military service. The rhetoric of recruiters emphasized manifest destiny, yet Americans responded to the volunteer mobilization in surprising and individualized ways. The war mobilization receives an in-depth look in two locales; in Boston and New York City, the volunteer ethic was subsumed to the machinations of political and economic leaders, and working class and ethnic groups maintained spirited, though often sporadic, resistance to this process.

Chapters 5 and 6 shift to wartime Mexico and show soldiers interacting and fighting both among themselves and with Mexican soldiers and civilians. The promises of manifest destiny are contrasted with the actual experience of volunteer and regular soldiers. In the absence of any significant fulfillment of the recruiters' promises, individual soldiers acted to forward their own interests. Mexican War soldiers, like soldiers in countless other wars, acted out personal, organizational, and societal frustrations through atrocities on Mexican civilians. Rather than dismiss this as simply an inevitable consequence of wartime, chapter 6 dissects some of the situations in which American soldiers lashed out against Mexicans, and analyzes what these actions reflect about the situation of Americans in Mexico. The chapter also takes a look at Mexican society, with its own racial and class divisions, and the important ways in which Mexicans resisted and transformed the conditions of war and occupation.

Chapter 7 addresses the winding down of the war in northeastern Mexico and examines some individual soldiers who attempted to fulfill the promises of land and wealth in Mexico. The stories of these soldiers and the debates in Congress over annexing large areas of Mexico south of the Rio Grande outline the human and political limits of manifest destiny.

The final chapter looks at the homecomings of (mainly northern) soldiers and the ways in which they brought their experiences with the military and with Mexico into the political arena, creating shock waves for the political system, particularly for the Democratic leadership that sent them on their mission. The institution of the citizen-soldier, transformed in the Mexican War, was to experience a troubled career in succeeding decades.

CHAPTER 1

The Regular Army and Antebellum Labor
SERVICE AND SERVITUDE

The regular army—that is, the United States Army—bore the brunt of the Mexican War fighting and also, as an institution that many Americans mistrusted, received more than its share of criticism; journalists and politicians reserved most of their praise for volunteer soldiers. Republican tradition saw regular army soldiers as excessively servile, an institutional anomaly in a democratic society. Going beyond the rhetoric, it is essential to examine how the regular army functioned during the Mexican War era, and how the army both reflected, and was an integral part of, the labor system of antebellum America. Individuals and social practices passed in and out of military life during wartime and peacetime; the regular army retained archaic forced labor conditions but also was an innovator in modern management and organization techniques. This chapter examines the situation of laboring Americans in the 1840s and shows how the U.S. Army was an integral part of that society.

The most striking feature of military life in the Mexican War was the sharp distinction between regular and volunteer organizations. It was not so much that they were composed of different men; in fact, as the Mexican War progressed over its relatively short span, the two branches of service came to resemble each other in significant ways. The self-conception of the soldiers and the differing standards of discipline marked the two branches as distinct. Regular army officers were notoriously quick to resort to the lash or other humiliating physical punishments against miscreant soldiers. In the volunteer regiments, soldiers elected their officers, and expected to be treated as citizens, if not heroes. The politicians who launched the Mexican War celebrated the volunteer soldier as the bulwark of national policy, but the despised regulars were the chief instrument of those same politicians in launching and prosecuting the Mexican War.

Wage Labor in the Antebellum Period

Employment-at-will was as yet an emerging concept in the 1840s, and wage work was often synonymous with binding contracts for a year or six months. This sort of arrangement was prevalent in textile factories and for agricultural laborers. In the textile mills of southern New England, increasing production and high demand for labor led to greater mobility among operatives and a tendency for employers to forgive workers' breaking of contracts. These workers came from a variety of rural, urban, and immigrant backgrounds, and their skills were in demand by both small and large manufacturers. The late 1840s and early 1850s were a transitional time for textile labor. The millowners built their fortunes upon the labor of rural New Englanders, the mill "girls" of Lowell and, in "Slater" type mills, entire families from neighboring farm communities. There had always been a significant component of immigrant labor, particularly skilled operatives from the British Isles, but in the late 1840s booming immigration transformed the demographics of the mill population.[1]

While archaic forms of bound labor—except slavery—were fading away in the 1840s, manufacturers and employees negotiated newer forms of wage labor in the American workplace. In the antebellum era wage earners became a large segment of society, and their legal and economic rights the subject of great contention. Important Whig thinkers, notably Abraham Lincoln, viewed wage labor as a temporary station for free laborers: in a free economy, according to Lincoln, opportunities for economic self-sufficiency were available to all.[2] In the 1840s this opportunity was limited for lower-class natives and immigrants. A mobile and restless laboring class moved from construction and mining, to manufacturing work, farm labor, and, sometimes, military service. Some native-born Americans also drifted into wage work, to supplement family farms, or as a result of failed artisan and entrepreneurial endeavors.

Immigration softened up the labor market, and helped textile capitalists fend off worker demands for a ten-hour day and an end to speed ups and wage cuts. The Irish who poured into the New England mills were not necessarily docile employees: militant strikes and political demonstrations continued through the 1850s.[3] But the growing association of immigrant and waged status acted to stigmatize labor in the minds of natives, creating further divisions among workers.

Large capital projects like railroads and canals also had a work force saturated with immigrant labor. Natives began to shun this type of work in the 1830s; wages and working conditions deteriorated despite militant strikes and organization. Large canal projects in the first half of the nineteenth century, enjoying a surfeit of laborers, treated them as waged servants. The canals were typically joint private-state projects, with funding coming from contractors, investors, and state bonds. Like regular soldiers, common laborers on canals and railroads were increasingly isolated from native, middling society. The historian Peter Way observes that "republican freemen soon lost their appetite for canalling, making it one of the first truly lumpen proletarian professions in North America." Centers of mining, canal, and railroad labor, like military camps, were set apart from the rest of society and tended toward internal conflicts; except in cases of strikes they were isolated from friendly or unfriendly encounters with the rest of society. Canal workers' daily lives were consumed with backbreaking labor, drinking, and the rough-and-tumble sociability of the camps.[4]

By the 1840s as canal investment and construction fell off dramatically, lower profits for contractors prompted a new system of subcontracting, in which contractors extracted their profits in advance and the subcontractors drove the workers ever harder to squeeze marginal returns from their labor. The scarcity of work in the depression years after 1837 meant that benefits like free food or whiskey were eliminated. On the Illinois and Michigan canal, wages dropped from forty dollars a month in 1836 to sixteen dollars in 1843. This was barely double the wage of the common soldier and included fewer extra compensations. Employers broke a strike on the I&M in 1847, and many workers drifted off to farm labor. These sort of floating laborers were also prime candidates for military recruiters.[5]

Although the regular army and canal labor drew from the same desperate and despised labor force, the evolution of group action, through strikes, during the 1830s and 1840s on canal projects smashed the kind of paternalism and individual coercion that persisted in the regular military. Gone were the head shavings and corporal punishment on the diggings; but canal laborers lost wages, benefits, and control over their work environment; the soldiers' lot remained servile, with continued personal degradation, but some guarantees of income and sustenance. While manufacturing workers and, increasingly, laborers rejected the designation "servant," the regular soldier found himself mired in servitude.[6] His officers routinely called on him to act as valet or manservant.

The Mexican War brought into conflict various theories on how a repub-

15

lican military should compose and comport itself, and in that instance the regular army with all its archaic customs was superior for the task of fighting the war but inferior for creating a broad political coalition around the war.

Some critics of the Mexican War advocated an end to military servility along with an end to slavery. Abolitionists and peace advocates championed free labor, not necessarily on terms of full equality but with the elimination of vile relics like flogging. The lash was the crowning symbol of servility, and its use upon whites in civil society was disgusting to those who both advocated and opposed slavery.[7]

In 1843 Congressman (later Senator) John Hale put forward legislation calling for the abolition of flogging in the navy, but it was rejected by the House. Hale labored against significant opposition from the navy and politicians for the next seven years. Hale and other antiflogging advocates argued that American citizens should not be subjected to the lash: the opposing camp retorted that most sailors were recent immigrants and thus not capable of appreciating democratic society. An antiflogging bill passed Congress narrowly in 1850. Herman Melville's *White Jacket*, a fictional narrative of service in the U.S. Navy, was published the same year and included fifty pages of condemnation of the lash. Popular sentiment against corporal punishment had reached a peak in the North, where it was also under attack or defunct in factories, farms, and prisons.[8] Flogging in the army remained legal until 1861 and seems to have fallen drastically out of favor in the Civil War, despite the persistence of other brutal punishments, such as bucking and gagging.[9]

William Lloyd Garrison's antislavery paper, the *Liberator*, commented on reports of Massachusetts officers flogging volunteer soldiers during the Mexican War. An editorial dismissed the indignation of the Boston press over the flogging incidents as hypocritical: "Flogging is as essential to the discipline of an army, as to that of a plantation. And it is as absurd for people who hold to armies and to fighting, to find fault with military flogging as it is for those who justify Slavery, to make wry faces about slave-flogging." Furthermore, said the *Liberator*, it was quite logical to impose slave-driving methods when the army was "in the field for the purpose of extending the domain of the whip-power."[10]

Political spokesmen with a working-class and immigrant constituency were more likely than abolitionists to offer principled objections to corporal punishment. Democratic editor Walt Whitman commented on an incident in 1846, in which a sea captain flogged a German immigrant for some refractory conduct on shipboard, "as if he were a seaman." The German sued with the help of an emigrant society and won damages from the captain. Americans despised tyranny in social relations, whether they blamed the rapacity of the tyrant or the servility of the oppressed. Clearly, public indignation seized upon these cases of corporal discipline of free individuals, not voluntarily bound to any sort of labor contract, while the lot of seamen, laborers, and soldiers was a more ambiguous one, deplorable, but perhaps necessary, and involving some degree of consent. Immigration and unruly masses in the cities spurred class violence as urban police forces routinely inflicted beatings for "disorderly conduct."[11]

Manufacturing operatives and laborers were subject less and less to punitive violence in the workplace in this period; with a swelling labor supply, however, work rules and industrial discipline, the brutality of foremen and overseers, and dangerous, unhealthy work conditions all served to impose increasing degrees of violence on the working classes, albeit not administered with the unrepublican means of flogging.[12] In the regular army, soldiers were precluded from organizing to better their lot: individual desertion remained the most common means of redress for soldiers, and the quest for more independent, better-paid employment the incentive for desertion.

Corpus Christi, 1845: The Regular Army to the Front

In June 1845 about 4,000 regular army soldiers under General Zachary Taylor landed near Corpus Christi, Texas. President Polk ordered them to this position to back up the newly annexed state's tenuous claims to the territory between the Rio Grande and the Nueces River. These troops remained in this inhospitable location until March 1846, when they moved forward to the bank of the Rio Grande, across from the Mexican town of Matamoros. In that month, skirmishes with Mexican troops, in the disputed region between the Nueces River and the Rio Grande, gave President Polk the pretext for declaring war. "American blood" had been shed on "American soil." By the time of these fateful skirmishes Polk had already sent a military expedition overland to California and instituted a naval blockade of the Rio Grande.[13] The small group of regulars in South Texas was the first wave of an invading army that would eventually include 90,000 men, as many as 43,000 of whom were in service at one given time.

During the months before the declaration of war Taylor's regular soldiers experienced extremes of hardship and disease. Dysentery and fevers raged through the camp until one-sixth of the men were on sick report, and about one-half suffered from some degree of infirmity. The tents provided by the Quartermaster's Corps were worn and rotten and had been condemned by a board of survey. The border region suffered from frequent "northers," fierce storms that could drop the temperature from ninety degrees to below freezing in a matter of hours. The men slept in mud and cold water, the quartermaster having neglected to provide floors for the tents.[14]

Corpus Christi at this time was composed mainly of the ranch of Henry L. Kinney. In 1845 the ranch was a major trade depot surrounded by fortified works and manned by a private army. "Colonel" Kinney and his partner, a Mr. Aubrey, were the beneficiaries of a vast trade; they brought in huge droves of horses and mules laden with Mexican "saddles and bridles, Mexican blankets and silver, and in return take back the common unbleached [cotton goods] and tobacco." Mexican teamsters took care of transporting these goods back and forth across the border. A Texas Ranger estimated the value of trade passing through Corpus Christi to be $2 million in 1848.[15]

When the troops arrived the ranch was "as quiet and peaceful as a village in New England." But soon hordes of liquor sellers, gamblers, prostitutes, pimps, "all the cut-throats, thieves and murderers of the United States and Texas" congregated in an improvised shantytown around Kinney's ranch. These professional camp followers robbed, assaulted, and murdered soldiers, and General Taylor was unable to do much to disperse them, it being a point of military law that civilian crimes be handled by a civil authority. The soldiers, too, were constrained from taking vengeance against the camp followers, by the disciplinary strictures of their service.[16]

It should be noted, however, that in another instance, a few years after the Mexican War, when residents of a Texas border town pursued a campaign of harassment against U.S. soldiers, the soldiers retaliated clandestinely. After breaking up a filibustering ring in Rio Grande City, U.S. soldiers faced beatings and reprisals from citizens.[17]

A correspondent in the town reported that this "was something that they were not disposed to submit to; so about a dozen of them, without the knowledge of their officers, provided themselves with good stout *shillalahs,* walked into town," attacked the responsible parties, "and ran them completely out of town."[18]

Whether or not the regulars at Corpus Christi retaliated against their persecutors, their officers praised the good order of the troops, under the difficult circumstances. However, hard times in the camp persisted and a small but steady flow of desertions continued in the prewar months. The men suffered from a lack of wood for fires, and there were no beasts of burden or carts with which to gather wood. The sparse grasslands provided little but mesquite in any event, and gathering wood was a time-consuming and exhausting chore. In addition, mounted troops were provided with no fodder for their horses, and so they were ordered to cut their own from the surrounding dry scrub. The recruits "neglected drill and training to attack the prairie with scythes."[19]

For regulars the Mexican War was quite literally a "waged" war: unfortunately the service offered very little of wages or honor; the wages, in fact, were the same as those paid to volunteers. Infantry privates were paid $7.00 a month plus $3.50 for clothing, and with bread and other staples provided. During the Mexican War paymasters were often abysmally tardy in reaching the troops, though the regulations of the service required soldiers to be paid at least every two months.[20] In the interim a network of sutlers extended credit to enlisted men, and they charged generally twice the market rate. Sutlers were independent merchants, sometimes former soldiers, who followed the army and were officially commissioned by a regiment.

A U.S. Army lieutenant, present on the Rio Grande in the months leading up to the outbreak of war, denounced the harsh conditions for officers and men. He accused the War Department and the administration of depraved indifference toward the troops. Not having seen a paymaster in many months, they were compelled to borrow from "Shylocks in search of victims that pollute the camp." In addition, throughout the Mexican War campaigns sickness was pervasive and often permanently debilitating or fatal. In this particular situation, "sick soldiers, directed by their surgeons to return to the United States, had either to remain and die, or to submit to *being shaved* by unfeeling villains in their pension certificates and pay accounts, though the law requires the pay-masters to cash them in specie." When the long-awaited payday arrived, a muster and general inspection were held, and on that solemn occasion the "paymaster having seated himself at the head of the table, the commander of the troop or squadron places himself on his right, while the sutler, with his books, occupies the left hand. The men are then called in according to their rank, if noncommissioned officers, and alphabetically if privates." Officers were on an honor system to disburse their own salaries from available funds, which if nonexistent, were supplemented by borrowing from their better-off colleagues. The temptations for foraging and outright robbery were great; regular soldiers were closely guarded and swiftly punished for such offenses.[21]

Officers

Regular army officers were not necessarily antidemocratic but were devoted to discipline in defense of the state. Except during wartime the regular army remained tiny in the nineteenth century. Between 1815 and 1861 the professionalization of officers's education and a small but steady demand for commissioned military men produced a distinct military subculture in the United States. The army was making great strides in technology and scientific methods. The U.S. Military Academy provided one of the best scientific educations available and operated to a great extent as a meritocracy. Army officers during peacetime were often isolated from the larger society, but where they did interact with civilians they were welcomed into the homes and society of the wealthy. An officer's education was a perfectly acceptable entrée as a gentleman despite his relatively meager salary. The slow and arduous process of promotion frustrated many officers — especially when civilians liberally partook of titles like "colonel" and "major" which were dispensed by state authorities for militia duty.[22] Upon leaving the service, army officers tended toward careers as civil engineers, merchants, or farmers.

While in army service, officers specialized in a particularly heavy-handed, and almost ceaseless form of personnel management. The conditions of army camps threw officers into almost constant personal contact with enlisted men, a group composed largely of their social and economic inferiors. A U.S. Army officer, writing in 1848, unapologetically called the discipline in his service "the most arbitrary in the world," adding that it was "necessarily so," to prevent the sort of conditions that were actively sought after in the volunteer regiments:

American citizens, grown up in jealousy of their rights and privileges; prompt to defend them with the right arm and with their voice, would make the army one scene of struggle and one great debating society. The question of abstract right and wrong is therefore never mentioned or even thought of by military men, who restrict their researches altogether to discovering what the rules and articles of war and the customs of the service permit and forbid.[23]

Army officers took absolute authority as their prerogative and attempted to enforce it even though their troops were often a drunken and unruly mob. In the antebellum period as many as one-third of the men on enlistment rolls had deserted the service. The majority of West Point cadets left the academy qualified for careers in engineering, and in the 1840s this suited them for increasingly managerial roles in canal and railroad construction—often supervising the same sort of men whom they had overseen in the military.[24]

The officer had his subordinates, noncommissioned officers, to deal personally with the men, but very often these were as unreliable as the privates, and again and again the role of the army officer was that of wielding his sword or sidearm against drunken and rebellious soldiers. The regular officer's sword was far from a ceremonial adornment. Courts of inquiry in the Mexican War era regularly showed leniency to officers who injured or killed unruly soldiers, even when they acted rashly or peevishly.[25] Courts-martial regularly doled out whippings and other corporal punishments and ritual humiliations to common soldiers, and this severity maintained the unbridgeable social gulf between officer and enlisted man.

Regular officers felt a need to defend their branch of the service, particularly during wartime, when they were dying in far greater numbers than volunteer officers. The army explicitly prohibited officers from publishing their own accounts of battles, but many did so regardless, using surrogates, or, in the case of politically connected volunteer officers, publishing self-aggrandizing accounts of battles, with little concern that they would be disciplined.

One regular officer criticized the inflated claims of volunteers soon after the battle of Monterrey. He asserted that the hard-fought victory had been entirely "effected by General Worth's division of regulars, with the assistance of Col. Hays' of [Texas] Rangers acting as light troops. The other two divisions did nothing whatever but waste their blood like water and inspire the enemy with confidence."[26] In the press the regulars were commonly derided as "hirelings" and the volunteers lauded as invincible "citizen soldiers," but in a strategic assault on one of the world's most heavily fortified cities, the real value of professionalism and discipline came clearly to light.[27] The U.S. Army sought to establish itself on a par with European military organizations, and had made important strides in the training of officers, technology, and the production of weapons. In a society with revolutionary origins, even a small degree of power granted to an officer class and its obedient minions provoked fears of both aristocracy and servile revolt. The army moved ahead with its modernization, but against much resistance and criticism, and thus remained limited in size, too small to contemplate a war with Britain but perfect for taking on a weak foe like Mexico.

Common Soldiers

George Ballentine, a Scottish immigrant, arrived in New York in 1845. A handloom weaver from Paisley, he was unable to make ends meet during the sluggish economic times of the mid-1840s. Ballentine joined the army after several weeks of tramping the streets of New York City looking for employ-ment and consulting colleagues on the prospects for work in his trade.

Unemployment was the recruiting officer's best friend in an economy which was chaotic in the decade after the crash of 1837. Even at the height of the war workers complained that wartime production was monopolized by a few big contractors who jobbed out piecework to skilled workers at very low rates. A New York labor correspondent noted in February 1847 that "nearly every kind of trade or employment is inert or dead, except those re-quired to furnish army and navy supplies, which are monopolized by a few wire-pullers."[28] Only shipbuilding and related trades were hiring regularly. In addition, wartime inflation was draining workers' pocketbooks.

George Ballentine had served in the British army, and with his experience of military discipline and hardships, the army was an acceptable alternative. Nonetheless, he found the food and living conditions abominable at Gov-ernors Island in New York and at subsequent posts in the South. Soldiers were left to their own devices at times to find food and bedding. They could supplement their miserable rations at a sutler's store, which offered goods at inflated prices and extended credit against a soldiers pay. During 1845 and 1846 Ballentine spent most of his time stationed at posts in Florida drilling and maintaining fortifications. The nights in Florida were occupied in aim-less fashion, drinking being the sole—and almost constant—preoccupation of the soldiers. Officially forbidden, but winked at by the officers, "the illicit trade in whiskey to the soldiers is carried on by blacks, at the time employed in repairs on the fort. . . . They were young, healthy and intelligent-looking Negroes, speaking remarkably good English with great fluency, better than most of the soldiers at the fort." The slaves sold the whiskey at a 100 per-cent markup. They themselves were rented to the service for about twenty dollars a month.[29]

Ballentine's infantry regiment shipped out for Mexico in mid-1846 and served under General Scott in the landing at Veracruz and the push to Mexico City.[30] Ballentine adapted to wartime service better than most; he saw combat in some of the most grueling battles of the war and produced a remarkably detailed and sensitive account of his experiences. An experienced soldier, he was able to weather the hardships of army life in peace and war. Vast numbers of his comrades fared less well, rejecting the service entirely or running afoul of its disciplinary structures.

Regular army recruits tended to come from the eastern states and were more heavily immigrant than the volunteer forces, which were preponderantly from the South and West. The General Recruiting Service was an arm of the U.S. military that operated throughout the country. A sample of its records for 1840-49 showed 40 percent of recruits to be immigrants; 35 percent could not sign their own names; their average age was about twenty-five. In 1850-51 over 70 percent of regular recruits were immigrants. An artillery company in one of the new regular army regiments raised in 1847 remained less than half full after months of recruiting in New York and Philadelphia. It filled the remaining fifty positions in the company by selecting from a crew of ditch diggers outside of Fort Monroe, Virginia. This group was entirely Irish and German according to a recruit in the regiment.[31]

For recruiters the best place to secure enlistments was in the northeastern cities and adjacent towns. Their ideal candidate was a sturdy Yankee farmer, but laborers and new immigrants were in the majority. A military doctor examined 316 soldiers at various army bases in 1842, and found half to be from New York and Pennsylvania; 155 were native-born and 161 were immigrants.[32]

Recruits from the northern New England states were "famous for desertion" according to one officer, especially New Hampshire men. Citizens of the Granite State often harbored deserters and even forcibly resisted the military authorities in their attempts to capture absconding recruits. Northern Vermont was a booming area for recruitment; it served as a depot for deserters from British posts in Canada. These men were professional soldiers, and notorious drinkers and brawlers.[33] The War Department instructed recruiting officers to secure discharge papers from any men they suspected of having been in the British service, a requirement that was often ignored. Despite the poor material out of which the army was composed, a large cohort of applicants failed to make the grade, with about one-third being rejected in 1846. The leading causes of rejection were age, habitual drunkenness, and inability to speak English.[34]

Nonetheless, all these conditions existed to a large degree within the service. The routine of army life during peacetime consisted of tedious drudgery, shut away in outposts that had been left behind by the advance of the frontier. A typical recruit complained that when he "enlisted for a soldier . . . I never was told that I would be called on to make roads, build bridges, quarry stone, burn brick and lime, carry the hod, cut wood, hew timber, construct it into rafts and float it to the garrison . . . etc., etc., etc."[35]

Recruits were continually reminded that they occupied a static and inferior position in society. Regular army soldiers, like many civilian agricultural and industrial workers, signed contractual agreements for specified lengths of time. But work contracts were generally for one year or less; the soldier signed on for five, and a deserter was subject to immediate imprisonment upon apprehension. Yet, desertion and flight, the only way out for the soldier, were frequently resorted to. Even when the economy was sluggish, the army had trouble recruiting and keeping soldiers, and a poor, immigrant soldiery was the inevitable result. In 1847 the army dropped its prohibition against nonnaturalized recruits, after struggling unsuccessfully for several years to enforce it. The long-feared army of foreign mercenaries materialized, with a small balance composed of natives as socially and economically marginalized as the immigrants.[36]

Paradoxically, civilian critics of the army, adherents to Jacksonian ideology, saw this fighting force drawn largely from the laboring classes as "nonproducers," in that they were not partnered with the soil or the workbench in the ways celebrated in popular thought.[37] Their service to the state often consisted of building the most practical structures and infrastructure—for example, fortifications and roads. But it was not the sort of work that brought honor to the individual nor bound him to the community. Regular army soldiers sought out ways even within the confines of the service to capture the kind of heroic and entrepreneurial paths that were open to others—even though the army tried to keep them isolated as much as possible from mainstream society, with its expectations of political and economic rights.

Such was the status of army recruits that a large part of their social interaction with U.S. society was with slaves and other laborers hired by the army: "rented" slaves were at least separated from the direct paternalism of their owners, and, as observed by Ballentine, could engage in various economic activities. The soldiers, on the other hand, were in a close paternal relationship with their officers and were subject at any time to perform any task requested of them, or to endure corporal punishment.

In a society where contractual servitude was rapidly being done away with soldiers occupied an archaic status in a rapidly changing society. The army retained its paternalistic responsibility for soldiers but treated them more like prisoners than workers. Soldiers opted for desertion when better economic opportunities presented, but most stayed in barracks under a numbing regime of labor, threats of corporal punishment, and heavy drinking. The military promised to care for the health of its recruits, but medical care, food, shelter, and other necessities were often inadequate or nonexistent, offering further inducement to desert.

Officers imposed cruel and bizarre corporal punishments for various minor offenses. A favorite practice was bucking, that is, tying a soldier in a cramped position, with a wooden pole running under his knees and through his elbows; he could be left like this for hours, sometimes at intervals over several consecutive days. Deserters and other serious offenders were made to wear iron collars with spikes, or a ball and chain, *and* subjected to hard labor. Desertion during wartime was punishable by hanging, but more commonly by a combination of branding, flogging, and imprisonment.[38]

The problem of desertion was greater in peacetime than during war, even though the Mexican War had the highest rate of desertion of any American war. Ballentine attributed the high desertion rate to the miserable conditions and the dashed expectations of soldiers. Some soldiers, however, were more calculating, using the service for transportation to choice frontier areas. In 1849 and 1850, as the excitement over California gold reached a frenzy, desertions emptied entire barracks in the West. In any given year of the antebellum era, up to one-third of the men on service rosters had in fact deserted.[39]

Catholics and the Regular Army

The regular army spearheaded the most grueling fighting, in General Winfield Scott's 1847 drive to Mexico City. This fact received little recognition in contemporary reportage of the war, except in the Catholic press. The volunteer forces were, on the other hand, lionized as an effective example of republican soldiers defending their country's honor in time of peril. Discrimination against Catholics was the semiofficial policy of the military, and changes came only informally, mainly at the behest of generals concerned about morale.[40] The *Catholic Herald* of Philadelphia complained of such violations of civil rights, particularly in response to nativists's charges that Protestant soldiers were being forced to submit to Catholic ritual. The exact reverse, in fact, was the more usual case.

Military authorities jailed a Lieutenant John O'Brien in 1845 for refusing to attend Protestant religious service, as was mandated in his army division. The case against him was sustained before the military courts; President Tyler finally pardoned O'Brien. The exceptional case of a Catholic officer was one that stirred controversy in government and the press; for most private soldiers official laissez-faire was the rule of thumb. Catholic soldiers attended churches in Mexican communities, unable to find any such service offered by the military.[41]

As Taylor and the regulars moved into Texas in 1845 a simmering problem of Catholic disaffection in the army deepened, aggravated by contact of Catholic soldiers with their coreligionists in the border region. The Catholic press in the United States generally supported the war, and many Catholics loyal to the Democratic Party were firmly behind militant expansionism. American Catholics in Mexico, however, experienced discrimination from their countrymen, and ambivalence about the justness of the American invasion. The direct appeals of Mexicans to Catholics to join their cause was a direct challenge to the legitimacy of an army that sanctioned religious discrimination.

It was common practice to compel soldiers to attend religious service in the army, the chaplain invariably being a Protestant. The blatant unconstitutionality of this practice was slyly evaded in the article of war that "earnestly recommended" rather than compelled officers and enlisted men to attend divine service. This article was still in effect during the Mexican War despite the controversy over the O'Brien case, and the reliance of the Polk administration and the Democratic Party on Catholic voters.[42]

One soldier observed a connection between religious persecution and desertion in the months just before the war, when General Taylor's "Army of Occupation" was posted on the Rio Grande across from Matamoros. This was a period of heavy desertion during which the nucleus of the San Patricio Battalion—American deserters who fought for Mexico—absconded from the service, including its commander John Reilly. Taylor ordered deserters shot if caught crossing the river and sentries killed some deserters in the water. This same soldier described the "mutinous spirit" prevailing in the army, on the part of the "two thirds" of the troops professing the Catholic religion. The officers compelled the men, every Sunday, "to attend the sermons of a Presbyterian minister, whose words are mainly directed to insulting, calumniating and abusing the Catholic Church. We know nevertheless, that one of the articles of the Constitution declares that every man is free to worship God in accordance to the dictates of his own conscience; and if so how is it that soldiers are denied that right."[43]

Apparently the army was not a magnet for talented and forward-looking clergy — nor doctors, according to accounts of horrible conditions in military hospitals. In any event, the harshness and intolerance of the clergy helped maintain nativist ill-will.[44] These bigoted chaplains alienated Catholic soldiers and retarded any socialization into or identification with American society.

Soon after the war began, in the spring of 1846, President Polk sent two Catholic priests as chaplains to the U.S. Army. Father Rey was fluent in Spanish and was murdered by guerrillas in early 1847. The other Catholic chaplain whom Polk sent to minister to the U.S. Army was Father John McElroy, a Jesuit priest and missionary in Maryland. McElroy and Rey's appointment raised storms of protest from nativist elements in the Democratic Party, but Polk and the Washington *Union* managed to downplay these tales of Jesuit conspiracies. Father McElroy served for a year in Mexico and was widely praised by Protestants who witnessed his preaching and ministering to the sick.[45]

McElroy, age sixty-five at the time of his appointment to Mexico, was "a tough farm boy from Ulster who had come to the United States in 1803, served as a Jesuit lay brother for nine years, and then struggled through the Jesuit program of studies as a scholastic until he was ordained to the priesthood in 1817."[46] McElroy had served similar ministries in the past, as an itinerant priest to Irish Catholic laborers along the Chesapeake and Ohio canal diggings. In Maryland Father McElroy was supported by the Protestant builders and contractors and often dined with these canal worthies. More important, McElroy helped the builders to maintain labor peace along the diggings, using his influence with the men to head off strikes and mutinies.[47] In Mexico he would serve a similar role mediating between Protestant "managers," and Catholic "workers."

McElroy was an ideal figure to mediate nativist animosities in the army. Like other prominent figures in the American church, notably Bishop John

Hughes of New York, McElroy made loyalty to the nation a high priority and sought to lay to rest any notions of contradictions between religious principle and patriotic action.

Catholic soldiers found Mexican churches to be a refuge, offering familiarity and sometimes friendliness. Rural priests were often active in resistance and guerrilla activities, this segment of the clergy having a long tradition of militant activism in the struggles for independence.[48] In remote areas of the Rio Grande, Mexican Catholic priests rode a circuit and preached to mixed congregations of soldiers and civilians. Whatever tolerance was shown came from conscientious officers, whose professionalism encompassed obedience through good morale and mutual respect, rather than terror and humiliation.[49]

There was a large and growing body of Catholic officers in the army, many of whom served with distinction in the Mexican War. One such officer, Julius P. Garesché, came from a wealthy Haitian planter family that had fallen on hard times since emigrating to the United States He graduated from West Point a few years before the outbreak of war. Garesché's devout Catholicism—he had studied for the priesthood at Georgetown University—led him to oppose the Mexican War silently, despite the official support of the American Catholic Church for the war effort. He did not volunteer for combat; nonetheless, his sense of duty led him to accept assignment to Mexico when called upon.[50]

Garesché maintained a dignified and pious demeanor, even toward the lowly recruits. On one occasion a drunken Virginia volunteer officer made a disgraceful spectacle of himself at a military funeral and unwarrantedly offered insult to Garesché, calling him a liar. Garesché was in torment, knowing that he was open to charges of cowardice if he did not reply in some way. He felt that he was in a particularly doubtful position, torn between honor and his religion. "He had never had an occasion to show his courage on the field of battle, he had not volunteered in the War, he was a Regular Army Officer . . . and the one who had insulted him was a Volunteer, what therefore would be thought of him?" Garesché finally resolved to horsewhip the offender, but his fellow officers prevented him from carrying out the retaliation. Other Virginians eventually came to Garesché and apologized for their comrade, acknowledging him to be a cowardly wretch.[51]

The irony of Garesché's intimidation by the volunteer is that the former's association with the U.S. military was a badge of shame, while the volunteer's membership in a loose-knit band of ruffians gave him considerable freedom to abuse others. Garesché eventually rallied, with the backing of his own peers, and the withdrawal of the support of the Virginia volunteers for their abusive comrade.

The army was in many respects a haven for Catholics in the United States, offering, at least for officers, opportunities denied them in other professions.

The 1840s produced curious groupings and blending of contractual servitude, "Irishness" and Catholicism. The facts and mythology of these concepts elicited violent reactions from Americans who defined themselves in opposition to servility. This behavior was by no means confined to the military. However, the immersion of this struggle over work and culture in a complex racial war inflamed distinctions among Americans. It was essential to the stability and self-esteem of an "American"'s self-conception that those who occupied a category of subcitizenship be identified and kept in place.

CHAPTER 2

Citizens' Militias in the United States

Militias and the Mexican War

In the Mexican War the word "volunteer" came to mean something quite different than it did under peacetime militia conditions. President James K. Polk's original war bill of May 13, 1846, called for 50,000 volunteers, with requisitions on almost all the states. The calls were answered with great enthusiasm, especially in southern and western states, with many times more volunteers presenting themselves than were needed. The first troops were drawn from Texas and Louisiana, as three- and six-month volunteers. Many of these were abruptly ordered returned to their homes as the volunteer bill in its final form required a minimum enlistment of twelve months; anything less was considered a great inconvenience to the government, which was responsible for transporting the men to and from Mexico.[1]

In the initial enthusiasm many new volunteer companies were formed, and existing volunteer state militia companies paraded in full regalia. But the existing volunteer militia system of the United States did not provide a great deal of the manpower for the war. By 1846 there was great controversy over the role and purpose of volunteer militias in the republic. These militias were theoretically the bedrock of republicanism, with deep roots in Anglo-American society. But when President Polk called on the states to fight a volunteer's war, it became apparent that the militia system had in many instances become defunct or largely ceremonial in function; in other instances, existing militia companies were too democratic, established in the name of ethnic or working-class solidarity. In all instances, the invasion of a foreign country required a coordinated national effort. The concept of voluntarism was honored in rhetoric, and the government had to carefully honor the forms of a citizens' militia while not allowing the volunteer to obstruct the efficient functioning of armies in the field.

Polk's war bill of May 1846 called for volunteers to be organized and officered according to the militia regulations of the various states, but to be under the command of the federal government, not the individual governors. Several Whig governors and state legislatures, opponents of Mr. Polk's war, argued that the mobilization was a violation of the constitutional provisions for calling out the militia "to execute the laws of the Union, suppress insurrections, and repel invasions"; this was a foreign war, and a war of invasion. The volunteers were thus exclusively *federal* troops, and the states had no responsibility to finance them. Senator Daniel Webster, in a shrewd dissent to the president's war policy, called on Polk to assert his constitutional authority and call on the militias, if this was indeed a foreign invasion. In that case the governors would be bound to make a compulsory draft on the militias. It was clear, Webster said, that the volunteers were directly in the service of the federal government and should be officered and paid by that authority. Webster sought to place responsibility for the war directly in the hands of the president. Without the patriotic enthusiasm, community spirit, and local patronage of the volunteer companies, the war would have lost a great deal of its political momentum.[2]

The volunteers of 1846 came to recruiting depots with expectations engendered by militia traditions: they expected to elect their own officers, to serve in companies with men from their own community and from similar social and ethnic backgrounds. They hoped to negotiate at least some of the terms of their service, by negotiation with the state, and by voting within their companies.

The volunteers expected full rights as citizens, including the right to proffer or withdraw their membership in the group as they saw fit. The only unforgivable offense was betrayal of one's comrades in time of danger or hardship.

One Richmond volunteer company presented its captain with a series of resolutions declaring the volunteers' intention to behave as—and to be treated as—citizens. These resolutions were arrived at in a meeting of the company, independent of its officers; while recognizing the "strict regard to subordination and discipline that becomes good citizens," the volunteers also asserted that "in our intercourse with each other, we will indulge those amicable and friendly feelings which ought to possess the breasts of men who expect to serve their country together in a foreign land."

In presenting these resolutions to their captain, and requesting that he publish them, that officer was publicly subjected to community standards.[3] A subtext of this message was that the virtue and manliness of the volunteers themselves made them good, bad, or indifferent soldiers, not blind obe-dience to the orders of a military martinet.

Leading political figures felt compelled to praise the volunteers even if they opposed the Mexican War, and supporters of the president found it expedient to criticize his policies when he gave preference to regular over volunteer soldiers. In early 1847 a bill went before Congress to increase the army by forming ten new regiments of the regular army, to be dissolved at war's end. This legislation provided a podium in both houses to lionize the volunteers, even though a solid majority lined up behind the president's bill for more regulars. The comments of these representatives and senators con-tain a range of popular clichés about citizen-soldiers and slightly varying in-terpretations of those clichés which revealed class biases — which Americans were worthy of basic citizenship, and what constituted free labor in a mili-tary context.

It was generally accepted among the elite political class that regular sol-diers constituted a servile and degraded class of men, who fought for pay and not out of patriotism. This distinction was maintained in political speech even though the terms of service, including pay, length of enlistment,[4] land bounties, and direct subjection to the federal government were (theo-retically) identical in both volunteer and regular services.

Senator Atchinson spoke in favor of the increase of the army but favored new volunteer rather than regular regiments.

> A citizen did not feel that he lost his rights when he volunteered. He did not feel that he had expatriated himself, and merged in the soldier the character of the citizen. The volunteer was not impelled by the same mo-tive to enter the service as the regular soldier. He volunteered not with a view to pecuniary gain and the hope of pecuniary reward. It was not mere employment that he sought. He was actuated by a different spirit. He vol-unteered because he felt it to be his duty as a citizen and a patriot to enter the public service. He went because he was emulous of distinction.

These motives were contrasted with those of the "regulars," who fought only for money.[5]

The Meaning of Militia Organization in the Republic

Republican theory and tradition had celebrated volunteer militias and ar-mies since Roman times, as the symbol and bulwark of popular governments. In the United States a consistent strain of political philosophy had borne this idea from Renaissance thinkers to the pamphleteers of the English Civil War, and through the American Revolution.

Niccolò Machiavelli laid some of the groundwork for republican thinking about militias in *L'arte della guerra*. Machiavelli maintained that professional soldiers were not fully citizens of the republic, in that their fixed interest in war and their lack of a stake in civil society allowed them to pursue war to its furthest extent, apart from the interest of the state. On the other hand, an individual who pursued only commercial interests, and would not agree to be a part-time soldier, was also a poor citizen. It was only the citizen-soldier, with both civic and private interests who would make an effective defender of the state. Military *virtú*—that is, fortitude and courage—and political virtue were thus inseparable.[6]

In seventeenth-century England republican political thinkers once again excoriated the "standing army" as the right arm of despotism and corruption. Cromwell's New Model Army of the 1640s established new standards for armed service. The royal armies of Europe had traditionally been conscripted from among jailbirds and paupers. The parliamentarians in the English Civil War made voluntarism the political foundation for the revolution.[7]

As the New Model Army went to and fro across the country it picked up soldiers from city and countryside, and the army became a leading forum and exponent of political debate. Chaplains within the army preached on political topics to mixed audiences of civilians and soldiers, and common soldiers took up the role of preacher. The revolutionary soldiers called for limits on the size of individual property holdings and refused to disband after the war was won in 1647. Spokesmen for the common soldiers, called "Agitators," demanded a universal franchise, including soldiers but excluding "servants and beggars."[8] Even these revolutionary volunteers wished to maintain a barrier against those without property or wages—those too dependent on the wealth of others to maintain republican independence.

Cromwell won the backing of conservatives when he put down the radical soldiers and reestablished hierarchical military rule. A citizens' army remained an important republican ideal, however; with the restoration of 1660 the army disbanded and returned its loyalty to the king, only with the stipulation that the county militia system be restored. The militias themselves were placed in the hands of local gentry, their "natural leaders."[9]

The "country" strain of republican thought continued to praise the people's militia into the eighteenth century, and this idea crossed the Atlantic with the pamphlets of John Trenchard and Thomas Gordon. But with the expansion of British commerce, new justifications for state-controlled military, particularly naval power, were presented forcefully by "court" thinkers, like Charles Davenant. Not Rome, but Venice was the model for an expansive republic, which combined civic virtue with growth and with new territory for plantations.[10]

But even an influential "country" theorist, James Harrington, recognized the impetus to republican virtue inherent in an expanding agrarian sphere, a sphere for citizen-warriors, who could remove themselves from the purview of corrupt central governments and selfish commercial interests. Such expansionist views translated well from imperial Britain to revolutionary North America, and, as the political scientist J. G. A. Pocock comments, "Americans gazing beyond the Appalachians could—with the aid of a little contemplated genocide—share the same vision."[11]

As a sovereign nation, born in military struggle, the young United States soon developed a centralized military structure, incorporating both citizens' militias and "professionals" in the pay of the federal government. As early as revolutionary times Americans distrusted professional soldiers as corrupt, and their experience with an occupying British soldiery served to enshrine this distrust in political rhetoric. In the dire necessity of revolutionary times it was acknowledged, not quite accurately as it turned out, that professional soldiers were a necessary evil, that their regimentation, and their vices, made them more effective fighters.[12]

In a war of resistance, fought on native soil and using guerrilla tactics, the volunteer and part-time soldier indeed served the republic well. Even more salient was the political and social force of class alliances, which put arms in the hands of the lower classes fighting for the patriot cause. The federal militia act of 1792 established a people's army, with universal service for white males—although it was an institution almost perpetually in decline and subject to contradictions. Within the politics of deference of the early republic, and in the populist electoral arena of the Jacksonian era, this vision of an armed white citizenry figured enormously in the social equation.[13]

Even when there was no need for armed men to defend the republic, it was politically essential that citizens brandish their arms, and it was often necessary to create situations where white men of yeoman and mechanic—or higher—status could exert violence for supposedly patriotic causes. In skirmishes or massacres directed at groups of Native Americans in the path of European settlement; in putting down tenant revolts; in nativist riots; and in volunteer mobilizations for the wars of the first half of the nineteenth century, small constituencies of free men were bound together through excessive, poorly directed, or counterproductive violence. This was also the means through which they defined their relationship to the federal government.

Despite the voluntarist rhetoric, the federal government relied on the regular army for whatever effective military action was needed. The regulars proved their value to Jeffersonians by enforcing the embargo against Britain in 1808, and by serving as the bulwark of military operations in the War of 1812.[14]

As Pocock notes, the Kentucky riflemen who stood by Andrew Jackson at the battle of New Orleans in 1815 were a defining image of Democratic politics, more useful as a symbol than as actual defenders of the republic. "[T]he myths of Jackson and the other frontier heroes were in part consciously manufactured by not invisible image-makers; that Jackson was a planter and not a frontiersman, who won his victory at New Orleans by artillery and not rifle fire. . . ."

While European leaders were formulating statist theories of warfare on behalf of the republic, the Jacksonian ethic based its growing economic and territorial nationalism on a military structure that was civic and revered democratic decision making.[15]

In addition to the bearing of arms, an essential component of citizenship was the universal holding of, or at least access to, land. In popular thought land represented independence—that is, economic status sufficient to resist coercion by elites. The prominence of agrarian political movements, even among urban workers, is evidence of the deeply ingrained importance of the ideals through which Americans saw themselves and the republic. The very existence of a frontier of armed, freeholding, white men was a vital ideological concept, celebrated in everyday social and political life, in holiday ceremonies, election day rhetoric, in fraternal orders, and political clubs. The idea of freeholder equality transcended the political spectrum from radical to conservative in the 1840s and became a substitute for tangible political and economic democracy.[16] The frontier was the repository of great hopes, and served as a unifying force in political culture. But, as we shall see, the practice of military expansionism served to sharpen political and economic conflicts within the polity.

Militia as Police

As mentioned earlier, universal militia service was an institution in decline almost from its inception. From 1815 to 1846 the United States was not at war with any foreign power, and so the role of militias as defenders of the hearth came under scrutiny, particularly in eastern areas not threatened by Indian attack

The irrelevancy of uniformed militia in dealing with urban disorder had been apparent for several years and was a factor in reforms of the police force of Boston to provide controls over the unruly classes. The change from an old-style "watch" to police came in the wake of the 1837 Broad Street Riot, in which fire companies attacked an Irish funeral procession. The conflict mushroomed until a mob of 15,000 attacked Irish in their homes along the street. The ineffectiveness of the militia in quelling the riot was widely re-marked upon. A city council report criticized the Irish for "retaining their native ways" but concluded that there was no room for hostility to immi-grants in a free nation with high wages and a chronic shortage of labor. Both the police and fire departments underwent extensive reforms. The firemen were stripped of their "volunteer" status and fired, and a smaller, paid force formed. The dismissed firemen formed Boston's first anti-Catholic news-paper, the *American*, "which for somewhat less than a year attacked alter-nately the Irish and the *'paid patriots'* who replaced them."[17]

The police were reorganized as a "preventive" force, which historian Roger Lane has labeled as "criminal police." According to Lane, the "new police force dealt brutally and arbitrarily with the lower classes. . . . Respect-able citizens, who occasionally had run-ins with the police protested, but the system blithely defended its adequacy for dealing with the lower orders." The police did little in the way of enforcing the liquor laws and civic health and safety ordinances, generally leaving merchants and artisans in peace.[18]

While losing some of their police functions, militias retained a strong so-cial role for a variety of groups; one of those functions was ethnic violence. In 1837, the year of the Broad Street Riot, the Boston City Guards militia com-pany attacked the (Irish) Montgomery Guards at a general muster, with the help of a civilian mob. The city government forced the Montgomery Guards to disband two years later, and nativist agitation remained high in the early 1840s, culminating with the election of a nativist mayor, T. A. Davis, in 1845.[19]

By the time of the Mexican War, a handful of Irish militia companies remained active in Boston; they were inspired by the stirrings of nationalist activity in Ireland. By and large, though, most working people were happy to be legally free of militia duty, and the flourishing companies were those organized (but not necessarily manned) by upper- and middle-class militiamen. Massachusetts subsidized this volunteer system to the tune of $35,000 a year.

In times of peace also, the efficacy of volunteer militias was debatable. In 1844 the militias did nothing to prevent the violence and destruction in Irish sections of Philadelphia. The New York *Journal of Commerce* noted that in an 1845 abolition riot in that city the militia had proved useless, and that an equal number of armed police officers would have better served the purpose of keeping order.[20]

An editorialist in Boston expressed similar opinions about the militia in his city:

> The expenses of the Massachusetts Volunteer Militia for the year 1846 amounted to more than $32,500. . . . If a number of individuals wish to dress themselves fantastically for the purpose of parading our streets, or of eating sumptuous dinners, or of making pot-valiant speeches, — so long as they do not disturb the peace of well-disposed citizens, there is nothing to be said; but we cannot see why the state should assist them in their efforts to resemble harlequins or should remunerate them for their exertions at the festive board.
>
> . . . The riot which occurred in the city [in 1837], in Broad street, about ten years since, is often cited as an instance of the necessity of a volunteer militia, when it is an incontrovertible fact that the disturbance was quelled by the police . . . a full hour before the military made their appearance and claimed the glory of the achievement.[21]

But an organized police force was not sufficient for many middle-class citizens; the American political tradition still called on elites to demonstrate personal fortitude. The middle classes defended their volunteer companies against abolition even where organized police were in place. In Massachusetts, already heavily industrialized in the 1840s, and harboring a large, floating work force, the decline of the state militia system disturbed leading citizens, and they decried the pacifist voices that called for an end to the militia system.

Industrial disputes were inevitable, wrote a Whig editorialist from Worcester, and provisions for order were necessary. The Dorr Rebellion in Rhode Island was a case in point of the need for a ready militia. A recent strike of railroad workers was ominous as well.[22] This spokesman for the wealthy of Massachusetts defended the system of volunteer militias but readily accepted the demise of universal militia service.

The Decline of Universal Militias and the Rise of Volunteer Companies

Militia musters represented a serious imposition on the time and finances of citizens. Costs of equipment and uniforms, as well as time lost from productive work, were an unwelcome burden for many, and those who could not afford to pay a substitute fee resented this opportunity afforded to the wealthy to avoid compulsory musters.

Thus it was the persistence of the militia ethic rather than its demise that is striking. The actual usefulness of militias as keepers of order or as defenders against invasion proved to be marginal. Working people rebelled against militia service when it became an instrument of compulsion, with rules and leadership imposed by state government. The opponents of universal militia service objected to appointed officers, and exemptions for the well-to-do, but military service was not necessarily objectionable to them when they could choose their own group affiliations and their own leaders —even if those leaders were from an elite economic or political background.

In the 1820s and 1830s poor and middling folk in Philadelphia, New York, Albany, New Haven, and other cities showed blatant contempt for compulsory militia service. The notorious Colonel Pluck was a half-witted stable hand elevated to leadership of a Philadelphia militia battalion. Militia conscripts paraded him through the streets ridiculously mounted and uniformed, followed by militiamen likewise out of uniform and carrying cornstalks and broomsticks. This was a deliberate affront to the system of appointed officers and preferences granted to wealthy members of volunteer companies.

In the 1820s and 1830s Pennsylvania allowed paid deferments for those who could afford it, while laborers, mechanics, and artisans gave up their time and supplied their own weapons and uniforms. Those who could afford to, formed volunteer militia companies composed of their social equals, and it was out of the ranks of the latter that the smartly caparisoned regimental officers were chosen. Workingmen criticized the officers and the volunteer companies as unrepublican in their finery and because of the preferential political connections through which they obtained their commissions.[23]

But at the local, or company, level the social and political function of the militia had a strong appeal and the voluntarist impulse was alive and well, manifesting itself in political clubs and volunteer fire companies. Volunteer organization was not only for the elite; it allowed people at all social levels to assert group identity.[24] Fire companies became even more popular than militias in the 1830s and 1840s as egalitarian expressions of small-group democracy, combining solidarity and an exemplary heroism. Like the militias, fire companies were often socioeconomically mixed, encompassing merchants, industrialists, tradesmen, and artisans. But they manifested strongly egalitarian ideas and practices: a manly solidarity in the face of danger and arduous labor; social cohesion within a small group; and a willingness to use violence against groups they perceived as a danger to the community, such as immigrants or lawbreakers. Also, like the independent militias, the volunteer fire company was swept away by large-scale politics and economic rationalism in the decades before the Civil War.[25]

The historian Susan Davis has noted that militia organizations and their public rituals tended to enforce middle-class proprieties and culture at the expense of more spontaneous and democratic festivities and street life.[26] It is true, that even in heavily working-class or immigrant militias, as in urban fire companies, wealthy and powerful men tended to have a great deal of influence. By the 1840s militias had become self-selected clubs with elaborate military rituals and eminent respectability. Even ethnic militias drew patronage and leadership from the middle-class elements of their groups. But as universal militia service disappeared, other informal groups took on military characteristics, sometimes organized as political or neighborhood clubs. However, the militia could be in itself an important expression of working-class political and social goals, as in New York when radical Democrats and agrarians fought *for* the retention of a universal militia law.

Despite widespread discontent with the volunteer militia system and calls for its abolition from across the political spectrum, some saw the *inequalities* of a volunteer system as dangerous to republican principles; however, they were quite dedicated to the idea of a citizenry in arms, under reformed universal militia service. Spokesmen of artisan and workers' groups who had fought compulsory militia participation in the 1830s were seeing even graver dangers in the new system in the 1840s. They called not for an abolition of volunteer militias but for an extension of their benefits to all. In 1844 a New York City agrarian reform paper, the *Working Man's Advocate*, objected to the abolition of militia service, accusing elite New Yorkers of secret designs for "an *Armed* Police, and finally, a *Standing Army*."[27]

The *Advocate* rejected any notions of republican virtue in the existing system. The system subsidized wealthy volunteers from the pockets of the poor. A more authentic approximation of revolutionary principles would bring men of all classes under arms and offset the crushing weight of wealth.

> What we want is an *amendment* of the Militia System, on the following principles: 1. The arms and equipments to be furnished by the State, and to be in possession of the citizen. 2. All citizens to be enrolled, and all who turn out to drill to be paid $1.50 or $2 a day for their services. 3. All who do not turn out, to be fined in proportion to their property. . . . As the object of a Militia is the defence of property, it is clearly right that property should pay the expense.[28]

Despite pressures of the Working Men's Party on the Democratic Party of New York City and State, the militia system continued to subsidize volunteer companies and fine nonmembers. The state reorganized the militia in 1846, providing for a seventy-five-cent fine for those not enrolled in a volunteer company.[29]

Mike Walsh, a Working Men's spokesman and member of the New York Assembly, denounced the "miserable mock reforms," the result of which was "the abolishment of the present militia laws, without . . . any thing in their stead. This idea originated with the aristocracy, and it has been responded to by the very class for whose hopeless enslavement it is intended." Walsh further alleged that the militia bill was "nothing but a ruse to get the poorer portion of the community entirely out of the knowledge of fire arms and military discipline, so that in case of any civil disturbance, the rich, who compose the uniform companies, would have everything in their own hands." The only solution in Walsh's view was a system that paid a journeyman's wage to militiamen for their drilling and muster time and put weapons in their hands free of charge.[30]

Walsh seized upon a key issue for workers and others at the bottom of the economic pyramid, one that would create a cauldron of dissension during the Mexican War. During the war, as in peacetime, forming a volunteer company depended on the patronage of the politically or economically powerful. Workingmen were encouraged to enroll under this patronage, but demands for wages for soldiers went unheeded; instead, recruiters made hollow promises of plunder and glory.

Informal militias and their interconnections with other types of associations made for complex interactions of respectability and rowdiness. In New York unofficial militias were closely tied to political clubs and often to the urban underworld. It was more the principles of group solidarity and egalitarianism—within a select and limited group—than any dedication to strict military order that defined volunteers.

In Philadelphia, a Moyamensing Street gang, known as the "Killers," sent its own company to the Mexican War with the Pennsylvania Regiment.[31] The gang members were mustered under Company D of the First Regiment, known as the City Guard, under a Captain Hill, but referred to themselves by their gang name. The company's comportment was less than exemplary; at Pittsburgh the Killers burst into a theater and broke up a performance, and later triumphed in street battles with local gangs and police. "A few of the rowdies were arrested, but the main body, of about 50 men, moved off to their quarters."[32]

In New Orleans the Killers were not so successful in eluding arrest. After looting some stores and houses, most members of the company were imprisoned, though quickly released. The members of the company forced the resignation of their commanding officer, Captain Hill, by threatening to assassinate him.[33]

The structure of a military company, particularly one with the egalitarian principles celebrated by the voluntary militia, was not incompatible with street life, or with ravaging the citizens of rural Mexico, or New Orleans. Davis asserts that cultural changes obscured class warfare, and military discipline prevented democratic exchanges and class-specific organizations for the lower classes. But a variety of organizations incorporated military tactics, in a society that was increasingly being organized along lines of discipline and command.

The prestige and patronage of official volunteer militias was an enticement for men from all sorts of backgrounds. In the 1840s immigrant groups were quick to form volunteer militia companies, celebrating their right to bear arms and to display their active citizenship. One editor and patron of Irish militias in Boston estimated in 1850 that there were 10,000 Irishmen under arms in the United States; he strongly advocated the formation of more companies.[34] In Cincinnati and Baltimore, at the outbreak of the Mexican War, dozens of German companies paraded in uniform, and offered their services in greater numbers than could be accepted. The expense of volunteer drills, equipage, and celebrations was often defrayed by political patrons, who served as officers. Among ethnic groups, both natives and elites from their own nationality supported and encouraged volunteer companies.

As the compulsory militias fell into neglect, state governments passed legislation favoring the volunteer companies. In the 1840s some states, including Massachusetts and California, began to levy a tax on men who did not participate in a volunteer unit; Connecticut and Pennsylvania, among others, made direct payments to militiamen. Massachusetts did away with compulsory service in 1840, as did Maine, Ohio, Vermont, Connecticut, and New York within the next six years. New Jersey struck down imprisonment for nonpayment of the militia fine in 1844, as did Iowa in 1846, Michigan in 1850, and California in 1856. According to historian John Mahon, "despite costs, volunteer units proliferated. Three hundred of them sprang up in California between 1849 and 1856. Relative to population they were most numerous in the District of Columbia where one out of every twenty-nine persons was a member of a unit. Volunteer units virtually took the place of a police force there."[35]

Volunteer militias proliferated in urban areas and in newly expanding frontier regions. In these places masses of dislocated men competed for work or access to land. The discipline and camaraderie of military organization preserved for them a sense of an egalitarian, face-to-face society in situations where extremes of wealth and poverty and of economic and social domination were encroaching realities.

CHAPTER 3

Volunteer Excitement among the Masses

Cincinnati

The call for volunteers touched an elemental and proud American tradition. A Natchitoches, Louisiana, company set out for New Orleans wearing tricornered hats and playing on fifes. But the displays of patriotism among the volunteers were soon subsumed in the contentious politics of organizing regiments, deciding who should go, under what terms and under what officers. In Cincinnati these disputes quickly became a sore point. Camp Washington was the mustering point for the three Ohio regiments and was situated just outside the Ohio River city. Ohio was in the unique position of being a northern state with ready access to the theater of war—via river transportation—and so was among the first nonslave states, along with Illinois and Indiana, to send large numbers of volunteers into action.[1]

Ohio had a Whig governor and a Whig majority in its statehouse, as well as a strong nativist presence. Governor Bebb, despite his party affinity, quickly mobilized for war, coordinating and financing aspects of the war effort that Whigs in other states very plausibly asserted to be the responsibility of the federal government. The Democratic administration and War Department were laggard in providing funding, supplies, and transportation for the Ohio troops.

Governor Bebb understood the necessity of seizing control of wartime patronage in his own state; he went to the state's banks to secure temporary funding, against eventual federal reimbursements. (Eight months later the governor was still negotiating with the federal government for repayment of the mobilization costs, over $15,000.) Bebb appointed two officials, Culbertson and Mitchell, to organize the mustering of the regiments. Mitchell was elected colonel of the First Regiment, in a vote of the line, or company, officers. Company officers were elected by the private soldiers. Two Ohio regiments left in June 1846 and a third was mustered in April 1847.[2]

The Democrats complained about the governor's denunciations of Polk's conduct of the war and cast aspersion on his loyalty to the national cause. The Whig *Cincinnati Gazette* retorted sharply: "The Whig Governor is scouted by these worthies as a tory, because he performs, and does more than perform, his duty to carry on the war, and to supply the wants of the man volunteering to fill the ranks of the Army; while not a whisper of disapprobation is uttered against a Locofoco [Democratic] President and Secretary of War, for their total neglect of these essentials to an efficient volunteer force."[3]

The strength of nativist politics and the dog-in-the-manger stance of the Democrats produced a great deal of posturing over the role of immigrants in the state forces, and also over the class composition of the volunteer troops. The *American Citizen*, a Cincinnati nativist paper, became apoplectic over the droves of "foreigners" enlisting in the service. The "natives," however, had neither a hold on the patronage machine nor a base of supporters desirous of enlisting. A Democrat challenged them in print to "name one of [their] *political* friends that has 'volunteered' where we can name fifty of these awful foreigners, whose *voting* and *fighting* drive [them] into hysterics."[4] A Catholic resident of Cincinnati chided the nativists as shirkers, reporting that of the 850 men who volunteered in the initial call at least 450 were "adopted citizens." Furthermore, he said, "the Citizens' Guards, a *native* company, composed of counter hoppers and a sprinkling of young Lawyers and Doctors, organised themselves into a company for the express purpose of protecting our good citizens from the d——d Irish and Dutch in the time of peace; but when their services were likely to be needed on the Rio Grande, they dissolved, and are now lying low until peace is restored."[5]

The Democratic paper in Cincinnati, the *Daily Enquirer,* accused the governor of playing favorites with enlistments, that is, of having allowed German companies into the state's regiments—but only those which had demonstrated Whig sympathies. The *Enquirer* charged that those Germans associated with the Democracy of the state were excluded as not meeting the language requirement. The governor, to satisfy nativist elements, had issued an edict prohibiting non-English-speaking companies from enlisting. Several of the German companies were among the hundreds turned away when the volunteer quotas were filled.

The *Enquirer* also framed the enlistment question in the light of class politics, echoing the sentiments of the Catholic quoted earlier, that clerks and professionals were avoiding the call, while laborers and immigrants enlisted en masse. An editorialist contemplated the effects of a draft, which would truly create a citizens' army, drawn from all ranks of society. Under these conditions Congress might be forced to lay out sufficient funds for the troops and increase the miserly wage of seven dollars a month for private soldiers.[6]

Cincinnati's Catholic establishment reacted almost immediately to the declaration of war with public avowals of unqualified support, as did the national Catholic Church hierarchy. The *Catholic Telegraph* of Cincinnati urged each Catholic to "enter with all his heart into the conflict," and that he should do so even "if war should be proclaimed by the United States against the Sovereign Pontiff." The *Telegraph* urged those of the faith to gird themselves in the time of peril to "propagate feelings of true concord among all classes, and learn to submit with greater patience than ever to the taunts and opprobrious observations" made against Catholics.[7]

Clearly, in Ohio the political divisions over the war damaged the potential for harmonious relations among an army of white freemen. Large numbers of the volunteers were immigrants, with marginal status as citizens, their economic subservience in the civilian economy a negative asset in the eyes of natives. Yet immigrants were working to obtain rights equal to those of natives, forging political connections, and establishing their own professional and commercial elites. The German companies traveled with their own officers and clerks, and even a physician.[8] The formation of a volunteer company presupposed some level of private contribution, given the dire shortage of funds for uniforms and other necessary equipages for foreign travel.

For several weeks after reporting to camp the volunteers had to be put up in private quarters in the city, because the government had not yet provided tents.[9] Also, individuals and communities were responsible for taking care of families left behind. This required some level of organization. These immigrants, then, were not the rootless proletarians who supposedly made up the ranks of the regular army. At least in the first volunteer calls, response was overwhelming, and there was no need to dragoon paupers into the ranks.

Among the common soldiers, however, both immigrant and native, expectations of comradely treatment were soon disappointed. On the riverboat trip down the Ohio, the officers made periodic attempts to divest the troops of their liquor supplies, and on the Fourth of July disembarked the men in a wilderness clearing to dry out and to listen to patriotic speeches. Of the 800 men who embarked with the First Ohio Regiment, 56 deserted before reaching their first Mexican port of call. Nearly 200 more would desert or obtain discharges in the following year.[10]

The atmosphere in Cincinnati during recruiting drives was tumultuous, with demonstrations of support for the war challenged by protests against the war or against the way the recruiting was being conducted. Volunteers swarmed into Cincinnati, bivouacking where they could, while accommodations were being prepared for them at Camp Washington. Many swaggered about the town, drinking, swearing, and insulting various persons on the street. Cincinnatians did not necessarily sit still for this: one report had it that "the volunteers now here are in some quarters, subjected to indiscriminate abuse, by opponents of the Mexican war." A Whig correspondent protested, stressing that only the rowdy element should be singled out for punishment.[11]

In Ohio feelings ran high against the war. One antiwar partisan wrote scornfully of the mindless enthusiasm shown by the citizenry, with military parades, cannons booming from boats in the river, and even religious revival meetings held "by the priests of the God of war, in which excitement has been raised by song as well as speech."[12]

Nonetheless, when the first two Ohio regiments were filled in June 1846, 700 men were turned away from Camp Washington, their companies rejected as the state quota was filled. The rejected were angry and wasted no time in demonstrating their feelings. They tore an American flag to pieces and dragged it through the camp, and made other vocal and defiant demonstrations. Four or five frame buildings, occupied by African American families, were burned the night after the disbanding of the volunteer companies.[13]

One of the "rejected" left the city with a loaded musket and fixed bayonet for Camp Washington, intending to assassinate the commandant of the post, but the sentinels knocked him down as he was in the act of firing upon the crowd, and he was thrown into the guard tent.[14]

The disbanded companies' behavior presaged to no small extent the actions of their enlisted peers later on in Mexico, both including racial violence and contempt for the rule of American law, with their primary loyalty being to their companies. The contempt shown for appointed "political" officers, as opposed to their own elected officers, was to erupt more than once in assassination attempts.

Illinois and Indiana

Illinois had the largest volunteer quota, and highest enrollment statistics of any nonslave state.[15] Its access to the Ohio and Mississippi Rivers placed it geographically almost on the front lines of the war. Chicago, though, was a Yankee bastion in a state with strong southern and expansionist sympathies. Volunteer recruiters tried gamely to stir up enthusiasm in that city but met with contention and indifference. One such recruiting meeting in February 1847 was well stocked with members of the antislavery, antiexpansion Liberty Party and others with a strong antiwar political agenda.

The "war meeting" turned into a debate over the merits of the war. Interspersed with patriotic speeches of various "generals" and "colonels" were pointed questions and objections, as well as a great deal of general merriment. A Mr. De Wolf introduced a resolution "declaring that all war is sinful and anti-Christian," but it was voted down. DeWolf later objected to the "my country right or wrong" spirit, citing Davey Crockett's injunction, "'Be sure you're right, *then* go ahead.' His remarks were very well received, though it was some time before he was permitted to speak." A man by the name of G. S. Wells "made some very sensible remarks on the iniquity of the war, notwithstanding a wild buffalo of a fellow attempted to bellow him down."

According to the correspondent from the Liberty Party paper, the people attending the meeting "evidently saw through the 'sound and fury' of the speakers, and treated them accordingly . . . We understand that the recruits numbered some ten or eleven at the close of the meeting, and that to the music of drum, fife and triangle, they made the tour of the grog shops before retiring to rest. One of them showed his bravery by kicking a small boy who happened to stand in his way. By the time he gets to Mexico he may be prepared to kill women and children. So much for volunteering in Chicago."[16]

This meeting, it should be noted, was conducted at the time of the war's greatest unpopularity, when commitment of men and matériel had been large, and the war effort seemed to be going nowhere. Within a few months the news of General Taylor's victory at Buena Vista and Scott's landing at Veracruz would reach the United States. In the initial recruiting excitement in mid-1846 Chicago contributed three or four volunteer companies. The commentator of the Liberty Party paper noted bitterly that they were a disreputable lot, and the city was well rid of them.[17]

In downstate Illinois, recruiting was faring considerably better. In the smaller towns, men rallied to the patriotic speeches and the whiskey barrel. Samuel Chamberlain was a Yankee transplanted to the Midwest, caught up in the volunteer "enthusiasm" purely by chance and necessity: he would very soon grow deeply disillusioned with the volunteers. Chamberlain left the Illinois volunteer service and joined the U.S. Dragoons in Texas, fed up with the electioneering and lack of discipline in his volunteer regiment. His memoirs, written after distinguished service in the Civil War, reflect a heightened antislavery sensibility and the belated vindication of antislavery condemnations of the Mexican conflict. However self-serving, his memoirs convincingly reproduce the bombast and chicanery of the recruiting drive, with a keen ear for western dialect and syntax.

Chamberlain was living in Illinois in 1846, though a New Englander by birth and temperament. Chamberlain spent his teens and early twenties drifting from Massachusetts to New Orleans, Illinois, and other places. He claimed to be under an "indenture," for five years, to his own uncle on an Illinois farm. The Illinois boom had subsided considerably since the late 1830s and such arrangements were not uncommon as late as the 1850s. Drifters like Chamberlain and the families of poor farmers provided a surfeit of laborers and servants.[18] Chamberlain fled this captivity and was living in Alton, Illinois, when war broke out. The election for officers of the Alton Guards was held "in a ten-pin alley." While Chamberlain looked on incredulously, "a large red-faced man mounted the bar" and delivered an enthusiastic speech: "Fellow citizens! I am Peter Goff, the Butcher of Middletown! I am! I am the man that shot that sneaking, white livered Yankee abolitionist s—n of a b—h Lovejoy! I did![19] I want to be your Captain, I do; and I will serve the yellow bellied Mexicans the same. I will! I have treated you to fifty dollars worth of whiskey, I have and when elected Captain I will spend fifty more I will!"

Goff was elected nearly unanimously. Chamberlain entertained hopes of a lieutenancy in the company but ran out of money to buy drinks before his opponent did: "My money was all gone—but I made a spread eagle speech, with plenty of the 'Halls of Montezuma' and 'Golden Jesus's of Mexico,' but alas, the 'suckers' preferred whiskey present to Jesus's in the future."[20]

The men who went off with the Illinois volunteer regiments eventually made their own choices about the war and their own place in it. Like Chamberlain, many were eager to leave a frontier that was becoming crowded, a venue for low-wage agricultural work and tenancy.[21] The new frontiers that they would encounter in Texas, Mexico, and California were places of labor scarcity, high wages, and military subsidies from the government.

A correspondent to the New York *Weekly Tribune*, apparently an educated Whig, dismissed Indiana volunteers as "insensible to fear" and motivated by "a spirit of romance and adventure. . . . Many, nay most of them, part from their families and homes as they would to go to a corn shucking, flax-pulling or house-raising. They look upon it as a fine frolic, and mirth, jesting and profanity are the prominent evidences witnessed of the feelings which prompted them to enlist."

The correspondent bemoaned the fact that most of the volunteers were Whigs, caught up in the frenzy of a Democratic war. But the prevailing lack of nice manners and decorum fooled this easterner; small-town Hoosiers could be quite well informed about what they were getting into, and they engaged in frequent and detailed correspondence with friends and relatives in the war zones.[22]

In the town of Marion, Indiana, antiwar sentiment ran high. Still, en-listments were plentiful, and political patronage in the form of officer's commissions eagerly sought; those disappointed in getting commissions or clerkships often returned home without even going beyond the Indiana mustering point in Jeffersonville. As the war progressed, and bonuses and land bounties were offered to common soldiers, enthusiasm for enlisting increased. Eliza Dodd, of Marion, wrote to her husband John, a lieuten-ant in the Fourth Indiana Volunteers, in May 1847 and described the atmo-sphere in the town. "There is a very great change come over the spirit of things since you left. there is more bold and brave men here *now* than you ever saw. every man is a war man and honor and respect the volunteers. they are raising another company preparatory to the next call."[23]

In previous letters Eliza Dodd had mentioned to her husband the openly critical attitudes and comments of the townspeople toward the war, most cuttingly the remark of one woman that the volunteers deserved whatever misfortunes befell them. Her emphasis on the word "now" indicated her disgust with the opportunism of her fellow Hoosiers, for whom the entice-ments of land bounties and signing bonuses were attractive — notwithstand-ing that her own husband went off seeking a commission and reputation. Eliza Dodd noted that many of these same townspeople were of the opin-ion that the war was already over, which did not dampen their enthusiasm nor self-sacrifice one bit; in fact it made it keener. John Dodd recommended to friends back home not to enlist as common soldiers unless they were assured of the land bounty.[24] These mobile and enterprising westerners most likely knew where to take their land scrip to get maximum cash value for it, or may have exchanged it for land, although very few did.

New Orleans

Recruiting in New Orleans, as in Cincinnati, reflected political and social hierarchies and conflicts. In the former city, however, conflicts over the conduct of recruiting hinged on immediate commercial interests, not just political factionalism. There were significant sectors of the population opposed to the war, but their opposition was scattered and muted. The *Delta* and the *Picayune* vigorously expressed and coordinated war enthusiasm. But similar, if not worse, conditions prevailed for the ordinary volunteer, and, as in Cincinnati, soldiers took revenge in socially salient ways.

In May 1846 news of the first clashes along the Rio Grande, at Palo Alto and Resaca de la Palma, reached New Orleans. Taylor's small army was victorious but as yet outnumbered and besieged. The merchant community of the city took stock of its position as commercial entrepôt and staging area for the war with some trepidation, fearing disruption of trade and, possibly, privateering in the Gulf.

In May 1846 Isaac Charles, a clerk in a shipping firm and a recently transplanted Philadelphian, took a cynical and worldly air toward the war excitement: "We are in a great hubbub, and have been since last Saturday morning. The news of the attack of Gen. Taylor's army . . . was brought on that day and drums and fifes have been playing Yankee doodle and Hail Columbia, The Star Spangled Banner and other airs too tedious to mention all about the city ever since, for the laudable purpose of collecting volunteers."[25]

The attitude of Charles and others in New Orleans's business community lent credence to charges of commerce's profiteering on the war at no personal risk to themselves. But clearly certain sections of the commercial community were engaged in financing expansion, for example the banker Glendy Burke, who loaned the state $9,000 interest free to expedite volunteering.[26] Isaac Charles was an erudite and breezy fellow, who felt himself quite above the fray, his work for a shipping firm merely a stepping-stone, as he plied family and business contacts to advance his personal career.

Charles found New Orleans a disagreeable place; he was the archetypal lonely Yankee in the hospitable South. Charles expressed his disappointment with scorn for the popular classes and for the corrosive influences of popular culture on the more refined. He remarked in 1847 that the yellow fever epidemic of that year was not entirely to the ill since it carried off thousands from the dissolute "Irish and Dutch" population. These immigrants lived in "long ranges of one story frame houses crowded with the lower order of men, women and children, —a set of rumdrinking, fighting people" who "comported themselves in a miserable, filthy, loathsome manner."[27]

Justin Smith, in his massive 1919 study of the Mexican War, claimed that the old Southwest was alive with expansionist sentiment. The teeming mobile population of New Orleans, according to contemporary observers, smelled opportunity, and was unusually restless. The New Orleans *Tropic* observed in 1845: "There appears to be no limit to the insatiable lust of territorial acquisition which pervades the minds of many of our citizens."[28] In the best of economic times there were drifters and paupers abroad in the land, and 1846 was not the best of times. New Orleans was a magnet for this floating population, offering a diverse range of employment, from counting rooms to docks. It was a regular army and navy recruiting depot in peacetime, and a volunteer depot not only during the Mexican War but for filibustering campaigns and the wars of the Texas Republic. The army had its hangers-on, many of them ex-military men; a principal reason for joining the military in the first place was to secure lucrative employment in the private services that clustered around armies in camp or on the move.

A satirical piece, printed in the New Orleans *Delta* just before the Mexican hostilities purported to outline the career of a colorful scoundrel, drifting in and out of military service, the workhouse, and other disreputable pursuits. The *Delta's* reporter supposedly encountered "Billy White" loitering on a city wharf; Billy claimed to have joined the regular army, and been drummed out in the 1830s, at the time of the Patriot's War along the Canadian border. Billy said he had volunteered to put down the antirent wars in the Hudson Valley and had served in Dorr's Rebellion, though on which side it is unclear.

The character Billy White was a military camp follower, having been thrown out of General Taylor's encampment at Corpus Christi for, as he put it, "totin' off a keg of whiskey, to have it inspected." White was a thoroughpaced rogue, a caricature in the mind of a middle-class writer, and his absurdity was heightened by his grandiose pronouncements on affairs of state. He predicted a bull market for warriors such as himself, with war imminent between France and England. "Lewis Phillips is too old for Wictoria, and don't help her along for nothin'. There'll be a bust between 'em 'forelong."

And he pontificated, "England ain't paid her rent reg'larly in Oregon, and her old landlord, Kongress, has given her notice to quit—to move out bag and baggage. I wish I was the constable that had to serve the writ on her! I'd ketch her by the nape of the neck and I'd—but there's my walor agin risin' above bilin' heat!"[29]

Despite the obvious condescension in this portrait, there is a touch of admiration for a man who was powerless and friendless, yet resourceful and spirited, and whose world view was nationalistic and proud, if somewhat warped and self-serving. New Orleans had already seen waves of regulars and volunteers pouring through during the Texas wars and the recent mobilization of Taylor's army on the Mexican border, and had a coldly disparaging attitude toward such men. Billy White's noblest aspirations were a burlesque of the "laurels" and "honor" that more respectable citizen-soldiers would soon be seeking in Mexico. As an impecunious wastrel, he was unlikely to capitalize on the land, resources, and labor waiting to be seized from the republic to the south.

But there was a significant opportunist trading and investing class in New Orleans, for which the *Delta* was the mouthpiece, and for this class Billy White represented masses of available, energetic, and hungry men, sufficiently primed with expansionist propaganda. Although these men were a socially regrettable fact on the streets and quays of New Orleans, the direction of their energies to the Southwest would be excellent for trade and land speculation.

Part of the payment for service in prior military exploits had been implicit or explicit guarantees of land or plunder. In the Mexican War part of this wage was speculative: talk of "golden Jesuses" implied that looting was ready to hand in Mexico and would be winked at by officers. The recruits' own memoirs and letters suggest that they also believed that Mexico itself would be parceled out to its conquerors, through permanent American control.[30] In February 1847 the federal government passed the Bounty Land Bill, providing 150 to 300 acres of U.S. land to all those who served at least one year in Mexico. This was not, however, Mexican land, or even Texan land, but the republican notion of land for soldiers was in some way gratified by this proposal, largely in a symbolic way. For many recruits enlistment in the volunteer service provided a short-term opportunity for free room and board or for transportation to the frontier, and Texas and Mexico held the lure of jobs with the federal government and related enterprises, and legal or illicit plunder.

A few months later, volunteering was well underway, and the *Delta* printed another report of a patriot from the lower classes. This man was mate of a steamboat that operated out of the Crescent City. Upon departing for the volunteer service he apologetically made his leave.

> Now captain, I have been on board your boat for four years; I have had during that time $75 a month, paid regularly up, and my grub—devilish good grub at that—thrown in. But after all this, I am not worth the first red cent. Fact is, it all went from me in the shape of expenses for occasionally whaling fellows: now, I'm off to Texas this evening, where I can do all my fighting—all my beating on those rascally Mexicans free gratis for nothing.[31]

Again, the implication is that this caricature proletarian can only find his destiny in war and restless motion, and that his destructive impulses could be channeled by propaganda, on behalf of race or nationality. The *Delta*, alongside these fanciful vignettes, appealed to the educated and wealthy classes of New Orleans to volunteer, and issued an indignant call for a draft if superior men did not step forward. The presentation of social inferiors as patriots obviously was intended as a goad to the merchant community of the city, segments of which had strong Whig sympathies and were dubious about the economic advantages of expansion.[32]

But an actual fragment from the life of just such a drifter suggests that the choice between a squandered wage in the city or catch-as-catch-can wages on an embattled frontier was more complicated. Anthony Sinclair was a printer who made his way from New Jersey to New Orleans in search of work. He met with only sporadic employment, and the troublesome relatives he left behind were replaced by others who turned up in the South. In a letter to his niece back home, Sinclair complained acerbically about an uncle, Gilbert, who arrived in New Orleans with the Mississippi volunteers. Gilbert showed up at Anthony Sinclair's door with regrets at having enlisted. Sinclair and Gilbert went to the captain of the company but were unable to secure the uncle's discharge. That night the uncle "gave them the slip." Sinclair gave him money and clothing and helped him find work until he could make his way back to Natchez. Uncle Gilbert, however, seemed to have acquired a taste for the big city, since he returned within weeks, "engaged work, got on the spree a drunken frolick, now on repentance." Sinclair added disgustedly "I am now inclined to think he will do no good for himself or any other, I regrate he did not go to Texas."[33] Clearly, New Orleans in wartime offered increased opportunities for employment, as the main do-mestic mobilization and supply depot. Thousands of the soldiers passing through to Mexico never left with their companies.[34]

Before these volunteers came pouring into the city, from surrounding areas and states, it was feared that a draft would be necessary to fill Loui-siana's quota. The appeal of volunteering in New Orleans is indicated by the fact that a judge of the police court gave the sheriff orders to discharge disturbers of the peace from the parish prison if they were willing to "volun-teer for Texas." A local newspaper reported that a few men "availed them-selves of this conditional discharge."[35] In addition, the first Louisiana vol-unteer regiments, called together in New Orleans before the declaration of war, and before federal funds were forthcoming, experienced shocking rates of desertion. More than half of the men recruited by Captain Blanchard, a career military officer, deserted within a few days of the company's forma-tion.[36]

Very quickly, however, the pace of volunteering picked up as the system of private recruiting became established. Would-be officers in New Orleans, as in Cincinnati, had to lavish comforts and gifts upon recruits. Volunteer officers were out of pocket for lodgings, food, bedding, alcohol—and even musicians at the rate of five dollars a day for each player. The New Orleans *Daily Tropic* complained that this mode of operation discouraged capable offi-cers and encouraged those with ready cash. The paper encouraged the state or federal authorities to provide barracks for use of volunteer companies until they were mustered into the federal service. Barring this, the editori-alist suggested that "rich and liberal merchants" of the city could patronize worthy officers while they raised their companies.[37]

William Christy, a prominent New Orleans merchant and organizer of numerous filibustering expeditions against Mexico, presided over one of the first large "war meetings" in the city. At this meeting, existing volunteer mili-tia companies recruited under their own name but with only a skeleton of their prewar members actually signing on for the war. Several of the politi-cal and business leaders of the city, along with "mechanics" and "laborers" unenumerated came together in a public demonstration of support for the first volunteer call. This public meeting was one of several held through the course of the war to whip up volunteer enthusiasm; the same sort of affair had been held to drum up volunteers for the Texas revolution and subse-quent filibustering invasions of Mexico.[38]

As the war mobilization built steadily into early 1847, New Orleanians found less and less to celebrate regarding the patriotic rabble engaged in the national cause. Hotels were filled with officers and gentlemen volunteers, while the masses of volunteers from the various states bivouacked in the swamps of Camp Jackson, ironically the ground on which the battle of New Orleans had been won, a sacred place in the iconography of the citizen-warrior. Fever and hunger were rampant in this camp; officers who had exhausted their recruiting funds in their home states had nothing left to maintain their soldiers — their constituents — and government funds were sluggish in coming.

The privations of camp and the temptations of New Orleans prompted the desertions of "uncle Gilbert" and thousands of others from this wretched place. Soldiers complained bitterly that their officers, elected in a comradely spirit, now lodged in town while they were left to forage for dry bedding and food. Adding further to their bitterness, troops of the regular army were housed in the U.S. barracks in the city, a capacious and healthily situated structure.

The *Delta*, indignant on this score, conveniently neglected to mention that the barracks served as a prison for the regulars, who were kept under close guard. A thirty-dollar bounty on the heads of U.S. Army deserters meant that local police and citizens eagerly assisted in collaring errant regulars.[39] Disgruntled volunteers easily obtained discharges or deserted.

At the height of the mobilization, when thousands of soldiers were accumulating in New Orleans for the seaborne invasion of Veracruz, serious riots broke out in the city, with bands of soldiers attacking individuals and looting places of business. The "Killers" of Philadelphia (mentioned in chapter 2) were prominent in the disorders, but Louisiana troops and Mississippians also indulged in riotous behavior.

Even the New Orleans *Picayune*, bastion of expansionist sentiment, condemned the mass disorder fomented largely by volunteer companies. In February the paper broke its previous silence on this issue and lashed out at "the repetition of the most heinous offenses — murder, rapine, robbery and rape."[40] The editorialist singled out the First Pennsylvania Regiment as particularly culpable, and as having been dealt with leniently by the city authorities. Almost simultaneously the mayor and other leading citizens called on the governor to provide state forces to defend the city from the volunteers.

Eventually the Louisiana Legion, a local militia, was called in as a police force to put down rioting. It seems that few prosecutions were ever made for offenses, in which public houses were looted, assaults and rapes perpetrated, and individuals robbed. The responsible parties were able to depart before action was taken. In addition, the victimized generally belonged to the immigrant and ethnic portion of the population. Several French names are mentioned as victims of the volunteers' crimes. An affray with some German citizens also was mentioned in the papers.[41]

The war may have served some commercial and slave interests, but it did a great disservice to elite paternalism by opening a landslide of competitive racial and ethnic activism on the part of white workers and farmers. The idea of everyman as conqueror pressured volunteers from the lower and middling classes to look for a new social order which would extend to them the full privileges of herrenvolk, that is, personal dominance over "inferiors." Many volunteers, in the desperate conditions of the camps, turned their anger against the neglectful paternalists responsible for their conditions, and against their social inferiors, among whom the authorities had thrown them.

Alabama volunteers made an unprovoked attack on two slaves while they were awaiting departure for Mexico. The soldiers killed one and the other narrowly escaped death. The captain of the company defended his men at sword point and refused to give up the offenders.[42] The paternalism of southern slavocracy was thus briefly upset, with common soldiers, poor whites from Alabama, acting with defiant impunity toward the property of their social superiors. The particulars of this incident are obscure, but, as in the attacks on African Americans by disgruntled volunteers in Cincinnati, volunteer service seemed to release soldiers from existing social constraints. Blacks were servants and laborers in the North and slaves in the South: white yeomen and artisans, now in the service of a war of expansion, had been inflamed by the prospect of new wealth and power over Mexicans. The paternalistic system of the South meted out swift and harsh punishments to whites who destroyed slave property: however, the speeches and editorials of Mexican War promoters promised propertyless whites the opportunity to seize the lives and property of nonwhites.

One critical observer of the volunteer troops blasted them for their behavior in the United States, and ridiculed their irrational behavior at home and on the Rio Grande.

Soon after their enrollment, in the march through their own States [the volunteers] began by committing depredations upon farm yards and poultry roosts, swaggering about with bowie knives and repeating pistols, frightening by their *martial* bearing, old women and timid maidens, and then inspired with confidence by the impunity attending these little eccentricities, they bruised, mangled, shot and stabbed each other, cursed and reviled their officers, and in some instances mutinied against them, and attempted to take their lives. . . . On landing at Point Isabel and Brazos Island, three hundred . . . miles from the nearest of the enemy, some of these warriors, glowing with military ardor and love of country crowed like bantam cocks, shouted "show us the Mexican niggers," and in one instance a whole regiment brought to their Colonel two or three trembling Mexican laborers in the U.S. Quarter Master's employ, "and standing around them with fixed bayonets, proclaimed in triumph to their astounded chief the glorious capture of the savage foe."[43]

Obviously wars within wars were being fought here; martial spirit contained many contradictory impulses, and the genuine patriotism that prompted widespread volunteering was barely sufficient glue for fragmenting social arrangements.

CHAPTER 4

Forced to Volunteer
THE POLITICS OF COMPULSION

Mexican War regiments suffered devastating losses to desertion and sickness. Over the course of the war the recruiting to replenish depleted state regiments became more like regular army recruiting. The government established regional volunteer depots—often at U.S. barracks, such as Fort Monroe, Virginia; Fort Adams, Rhode Island; or New Orleans Barracks—and enlisted men as they became available for the various state regiments.[1]

At Fort Monroe, Virginia, the volunteer officer, James Kemper, "saw a member of Capt. Young's Company forced off to Richmond to be mustered into service, and to be *forced* to *volunteer*."[2] Young, of Norfolk, organized a Virginia volunteer company in February 1847.[3] Frederick Zeh, a German recruit to an elite regular army artillery company, witnessed a mass roundup of men to fill out the lower ranks of the unit. Recruiting had gone slowly in Philadelphia, and the company was only half full as it went south to Fort Monroe, Virginia. The company officers enlisted fifty Irish and German ditch diggers, who happened to be making repairs on the fort, signing them en masse to round out the company. What degree of compulsion was used here is not clear, but the transition from one form of underpaid, dangerous labor to another may not have required much coercion.[4] Zeh himself, a recent emigrant from Bavaria, joined the service not from love of country: he had been subjected to nativist abuse in Philadelphia when he tried to join a volunteer company. However, Zeh, an experienced bookdealer in Germany, was able to find only sporadic employment as a farm laborer.[5]

Evidence of compulsory recruitment recurs in fragmentary form in published and personal accounts of the war mobilization, but a balanced picture of the motivations behind, and reactions to, "volunteer" coercion emerges in the stories of the regiments raised in New York and Massachusetts.[6] Both cases show how politicians sought to extend the political patronage—and political manipulation—of their respective localities, through the medium of volunteer companies. The leaders of the single regiment from Massachusetts and the two from New York were intimately tied to the national Democratic leadership. To a greater degree than their western and southern counterparts, these leaders sought to deliver their patronage to Washington rather than to the volunteers themselves; these volunteers, they felt, were powerless men, delivered en bloc by political machines, or gathered from the ranks of the desperate. These "volunteers," however, proved less tractable than the politicians had hoped.

The Massachusetts Regiment

The resistance of Mexican War soldiers was sporadic, disorganized, and generally passive. But in a few instances, volunteers recruited from the working classes mounted significant protests, and their status as citizen-soldiers elevated them to a public platform, from which their class and political protests were clearly audible. The sole regiment of Massachusetts volunteers made dramatic demonstrations in the streets and halls of Boston. But generally they were confined like regulars, and the fruits of manifest destiny, even distinction on the battlefield, were beyond their reach. The national Democratic Party owed little to Massachusetts; a few Democrats in that state raised the regiment, and with little patronage to dispense, these men reined in the volunteers, dispensing arbitrary discipline with one hand and drunkenness and license with the other.

In December 1846 state legislator Caleb Cushing began raising the Massachusetts volunteer company in the face of a storm of political protest. About one-third of the regiment was Irish, arousing nativist and class resentments long brewing in the Bay State. Without state funding, with only the limited private funding of their commanders, the regiment left Boston in 1846, scorned by the middle and upper classes, and with turbulent internal divisions over wages, rights, and leadership. These internal disputes only grew more bitter in Mexico and reerupted when the regiment returned to Boston in 1848. The efforts of conservative Irish civic and religious leaders to win stature in the community—by sending working-class Irish off to fight—failed, and the nativist political front returned stronger than ever in the postwar years. The Irish, badly served by their own elites, soon lost their right to independent military organization in the state; however, they remained conscious of their group identity, and of the importance of military service, and continued to bargain for the patronage of the ruling political classes of Boston.

"No Strife Here as to Who Shall Go"

So tepid was the competition for commissions in the single state regiment that William Watts Hart Davis, a Pennsylvanian studying at Cambridge Law School, had no trouble in getting elected lieutenant in one of the companies. Davis observed the resistance to recruitment in Boston. Member of a wealthy and politically connected family of Bucks County, Pennsylvania, he at once enlisted in the Massachusetts Regiment as it moved sluggishly toward its quota. Davis wrote his father that there was "no strife here as to who shall go, they seem perfectly indifferent about the matter." He complained that volunteers were "slandered and vilified daily by various papers. Those who volunteer are denounced as murderers and robbers."[7]

At the core of the effort to create a state regiment were influential Massachusetts Democrats Robert Rantoul, Isaac H. Wright, John A. Bolles, Benjamin Butler, and, most critically, Caleb Cushing, who personally financed and led the regiment. This odd assortment of bedfellows had been bitter political enemies in the past. Even among the state's Democrats few were willing to stake their reputations on the war.[8] That is why an out-of-state Democrat like W. W. H. Davis could gain influence in the regiment, becoming Cushing's adjutant.

Cushing had served as a Whig representative to Congress in 1836 and spoke out against Texas annexation. But by 1845 his views on Texas had changed, and he supported President John Tyler in his bid to admit Texas. Rejected by the bulk of his own party, he drifted into the Democratic camp. He served Tyler as special commissioner to China in 1844 and negotiated the first treaty between the two countries.

Caleb Cushing's family had extensive international trading operations, and he became a dedicated economic nationalist, despite being nurtured in antiexpansionist New England. Cushing worked intimately with Polk and Secretary of the Navy George Bancroft—another Massachusetts man—and was promised a general's commission even before he had been elected colonel of the Massachusetts Regiment.[9]

Massachusetts governor George N. Briggs (a Whig) received an administration requisition for one regiment in December 1846, and despite much criticism from his party, he ordered it put into effect. The only influential Whig in the state who took part in the mobilization was Fletcher Webster, son of Senator Daniel Webster; Fletcher was a company commander and was to die in Mexico.

The dilatory governor and Whig-dominated legislature forced Cushing to act as patron of the company, initially supplying $5,000 for equipment and a month's wages for the troops. Despite, or maybe because of, his all-encompassing patronage, Cushing had trouble getting elected to the colonelcy of the regiment. In three polls of officers above the rank of sergeant, Isaac H. Wright won a plurality. On the fourth ballot Cushing was elected 20 to 19. Isaac Wright exhibited more of a military man's demeanor and common touch. Wright took the lead in organizing an Irish company and was effective in speaking to diverse constituencies. Cushing, however, was already negotiating with Polk for a U.S. Army commission, and eventually was appointed general of the brigade that encompassed the Massachusetts Regiment.[10]

Recruiting proceeded in fits and starts in December 1846 and January 1847, the companies beginning with an enthusiastic core of officers and slowly building their lower ranks. Competition came from regular army recruiters, in whose ranks Irish and other immigrants would face less of the nativism rife in the volunteer companies. But regular recruiting also went slowly in Massachusetts. The new regular infantry regiments authorized by Congress in early February 1847 filled up quickly almost everywhere in the nation but Boston. New Orleans was already recruiting a second regiment, when Boston had only 258 recruits. By October 1847 Boston had four recruiting offices, one for the regulars, one for the U.S. Marines, and two to replenish the state volunteer companies, and none of them fared too well.[11]

In late January, as departure was imminent, rumor had it that the regiment lacked 300 of its full complement of 700 men.[12] One enterprising company sent canvassers out of state to Nashua, New Hampshire, and set up a recruiting office. A Whig journalist reported an anecdote in which Lieutenant C. J. Emery exhorted the "green ones" of the Granite State to sign on:

> He had three or four around him, and was addressing them in something like this style: "Now," said he, "I don't want to force you to go; I want you to use your own judgment about it; we only appeal to the patriotism of the people; if you don't want to go, don't go; but"—and here he lowered his voice and gave a knowing look— "I tell you what it is, boys, if you've a mind to go, I guess we shall have a first-rate time!" One of the fellows straightened up, looked round, raised his right leg and planted it down again, with emphasis, and exclaimed, "I've made up my mind to go."

The journalist asked whether Massachusetts taxpayers should support New Hampshire recruits—eventually a moot question, as the Bay State did not fund its regiment at all.[13]

At the same time, other volunteer officers scoured the countryside for recruits who had already deserted. A lieutenant and a detachment of eleven men arrived in Waltham one Saturday looking for "a number of deserters" but went away empty-handed after searching several houses and one of the cotton mills, "it is said, in opposition to the wishes of the superintendent, and with some threats of violence in case of resistance." A Boston paper reported a rumor that "abolitionists" aided recruits in deserting, offering them money and free legal advice.[14]

Antiwar and antislavery forces waged a massive propaganda campaign against the regiment and the war, producing scathing critiques of the officers and volunteers that remain hallmarks of antiwar literature. James Russell Lowell's series of satires in the Boston *Courier* voiced the indignation of middle-class Whigs with the extent to which the Democrats had twisted patriotic rhetoric to serve nefarious ends of slavery extension and executive power. Lowell's "Birdofredom Sawin" represented a middle-class view of a lower-class man responding to Democratic propaganda. Like the New Orleans caricaturist who produced "Billy White" (see chapter 3), Lowell mixed condescension and admiration for the common man, but in the latter case the "wise fool" of rural New England used native common sense to deflate the war propaganda.

Afore I come away from hum I hed a strong persuasion
Thet Mexicans worn't human beans,—an ourang outang nation,
A sort o' folks a chap could kill an' never dream on't arter,
No more'n a feller'd dream o' pigs thet he hed hed to slarter;
I'd an idee thet they were built arter the darkie fashion all,
An' kickin' colored folks about, you know,'s a kind o' national;
But wen I jined I worn't so wise ez thet air queen o' Sheby,
Fer, come to look at 'em, they aint much diff'rent from wut we be,
An' here we air ascroungin' 'em out o' thir own dominions,
Ashelterin' 'em, ez Caleb sez, under our eagle's pinions,
Which means to take a feller up jest by the slack o' 's trowsis
An' walk him Spanish clean right out o' all his homes an' houses;
Wal, it doos seem a curus way, but then hooraw fer Jackson!
It must be right, fer Caleb sez it's reg'lar Anglosaxon.[15]

Antiwar Massachusetts citizens maintained a steady barrage of criticism against the volunteers, the Democratic administration, and the proslavery doughfaces in their own parties. They struggled to retain the mantle of patriotism as their critics accused them of disloyalty.

Abolitionist editor William L. Garrison lashed out at the motivation of the volunteers, asserting that they were of the lowest orders and therefore had enlisted for pay and not out of patriotism; this theme resonated in the Whig press. Elite militia companies, meanwhile, continued to meet and drill as if in peacetime. The Worcester Guards held their annual election in 1847, and the local Whig paper congratulated the company for "the zeal, with which, under many circumstances of discouragement, they have kept alive the old martial spirit."[16]

Caleb Cushing was steeped in the military traditions so dear to the old stock of Massachusetts, yet in spite of his powerful appeals to that tradition he could not win the support of the Massachusetts Legislature. On January 28 Cushing appeared in the House in his volunteer uniform to resign his seat and make a final appeal for a $20,000 grant to the regiment. He made an eloquent and stirring appeal, even in the opinion of some of his opponents, and the assembled were visibly moved. According to one observer, "Many members who have credit for stoical indifference were seen to wipe their eyes. The scene was dramatic, for the house was packed in every part, and in the pauses made by the speaker, it seemed as if all extra breathing were suppressed. When he concluded, there was an oppressive silence of some moments." Nevertheless, the House voted down the appropriation 191 to 47, and Cushing continued throughout his Mexican campaign to fund the regiment, eventually spending more than $12,000. He ultimately recovered less than $2,000 from the federal government.[17]

Donations trickled in from a few sympathetic individuals, notably from Abbot Lawrence, the textile manufacturer who sent Cushing a large consignment of shirts, socks, and handkerchiefs to be distributed among the privates. But criticism of the regiment continued wholesale. "Whigs, abolitionists, non-resistants, and deputations from the various factions of the day," according to a Democratic paper, were responsible for organizing a series of antiwar meetings that took place in early February.

The volunteers and their supporters had clearly had enough, and turned out en masse to disrupt the largest of the meetings, a principal speaker at which was the Reverend Theodore Parker. Several soldiers appeared at the turbulent meeting with bayonets on their belts and on at least two occasions drew them to menace those calling upon them to be silent.[18] Parker reveled in the controversy; as an abolitionist, he had faced larger mobs. In this dispute he could see that public opinion was overwhelmingly on his side:

> I think there is a good deal to excuse the volunteers. I blame them, for some of them know what they are about. Yet I pity them more, for most of them, I am told are low, ignorant men; some of them drunken and brutal. From the uproar they make here to-night, arms in their hands, I think what was told me is true! I say, I pity them. . . . I blame the captains and colonels, who will have least of the hardships, most of the pay, and all of the "glory. . . ."
>
> I say, I blame not so much the volunteers as the famous men who deceive the nation! (Cries of "Throw him over; kill him, kill him!" and a flourish of bayonets.) Throw him over! you will not throw him over. Kill him! I shall walk home unarmed and unattended, and not a man of you will hurt one hair of my head.[19]

Boston's middle-class Irish closed ranks in support of the volunteers. Businessmen, editors, and clergy formed a committee to organize and support the Irish company, under the sponsorship of Lieutenant Colonel Isaac Wright. The Irish in Boston had little in the way of an independent political organization, at least compared with organizations in New York or Philadelphia. The local Irish nationalist faction was led by John W. James, a native Protestant lawyer and supporter of "Young Ireland" nationalist activity. The Boston *Pilot* was the voice of Irish nationalism in Boston; on national and local issues, the paper was Democratic and proclerical. *Pilot* editor Patrick Donahoe was a firm booster of the Irish volunteer company; in his view it would silence the nativist criticisms of the Irish as disloyal citizens.

Throughout the war, the *Pilot* fought a running battle with nativists, in defense of loyal Irish participation in the war. The *Pilot* ran weekly reports of deserters from the army, broken down by nationality—taken from the *Police Gazette*—showing clearly that Irish soldiers deserted far less in proportion to their numbers than did other Americans.[20]

The *Pilot* optimistically proclaimed the death of nativism, as a result of Irish patriotism in the Mexican campaigns, but expressed disappointment at some of the conduct of the national Democratic Party. The *Pilot* replied angrily to suggestions in the Washington *Union*, the "official" administration paper, that the U.S. Army seize church property in Mexico. The *Pilot* acknowledged that the promoters of the war had for some time been dangling the gold of the church before volunteers, and it was nearing the status of an official pronouncement. Still the editors doubted whether the administration really supported this measure.[21]

Departure of the Regiment

The Catholic clergy, in the person of Bishop Fitzpatrick and the Reverend Nicholas O'Brien, editor of the diocesan paper, blessed the Irish company in a ceremony a few weeks before its departure. Their invocation scrupulously avoided political issues. At a mass one day before their departure, however, the Reverend Fitzsimmons, a South Boston pastor, gave his blessing but specifically refused to bless the soldiers' cause.[22] Catholics were divided over the war, and despite the position of the church leadership, they could not find a prowar clergyman even to bless the troops on embarkation. The clergy had moral objections to the war and also recognized the unequal treatment accorded to the Irish company.

Bishop Fitzpatrick steadfastly refused to comment on the war, except for one item in the diocesan *Observer* objecting to the proposal to seize the wealth of the Mexican church. He personally gave religious instruction to Captain Barry's Irish company at the cathedral. Reverend O'Brien ministered to the hundreds of Irish regulars passing through the forts in Boston Harbor, saying mass in the barracks and troop transports.[23]

A leader of the conservative Catholics, Orestes A. Brownson, defected from the position of the church on the war and left the editorship of the *Catholic Observer* to edit his own *Review* in New York. As the men of the Irish company became deeply disaffected with their treatment, the subject drew only silence from the voice of the Catholic middle class, the *Pilot*.

On February 11, 1847, eight companies, including the Irish Company B, marched to the docks to embark for Mexico. The latter company arrived at the transport and refused to board, in protest over not receiving an advance on their pay as promised. They also objected to confinement in barracks and not having an opportunity to say good-bye to their loved ones. The company marched back to their barracks in Pitt Street and refused to move until their demands were satisfied. Colonel Cushing followed them with a detachment from the other companies armed with muskets and surrounded the barracks. He brought with him manacles to take the unarmed Irishmen by force if necessary. The standoff continued through the afternoon, and Cushing and a deputation of officers negotiated a "compromise" with the Irishmen.

According to a Whig paper, the Irish company was given "rum and false promises of money" by the noted temperance lecturer Caleb Cushing. At any rate the recalcitrant soldiers were allowed to meet with their families in Pitt Street, which was packed to the rooftops with the curious. Individual soldiers attempted to escape, and a few succeeded, although one man was stopped by a severe cutlass wound to the head.[24]

An armed escort marched the Irish company down to the transport vessel to the hisses and insults of the crowd. The troop ships were hauled out into the stream, to await departure and to prevent desertions. A few men attempted to desert from the ships, one of whom was successful. The regiment, by the time it reached Mexico, was approximately one-third Irish in composition, as observers testified, and as the roster of returning soldiers in 1848 shows.[25] The soldiers aiming muskets at Company B might very well have included a few Irishmen among them, although Cushing would have carefully picked this detail to include men likely to deal harshly with the strikers.

The Charlestown company would have been particularly unsympathetic to the Irish. The Charlestown men marched to the embarkation point with 200 of their friends and supporters from that nativist redoubt. The Charlestowners were not confined to barracks or kept from their families, at least not all of them. Clearly, some recruits were brought along with trickery and coercion and were expected to desert, and as such were locked up, deprived of weapons and visitors: some recruits were more "Irish" than others, and the Irish company was the most distrusted of all.

As the recruits languished on the transports for several days, the strike of the Irish in Pitt Street must have touched feelings of guilt or sympathy in those remaining behind. The "Weighers and Gaugers and Measurers" gave seventy dollars expressly for the Irish volunteers a few days after the company was led on shipboard under armed guard.[26]

The Irish company, however, was not to be the only source of rebellion and resistance to arbitrary power, nor was it to be the most troublesome of the companies. As correspondence and newspaper reports from Mexico showed, the regiment was plagued with disciplinary problems, officerial misconduct, and another company strike. The dialogue between soldiers and the home front was quite lively, and soldier-correspondents had a wide choice of political journals in which to make their opinions known, from the conservative *Pilot*, to the subversive *Chronotype* and *Liberator*.

The Massachusetts Regiment found few allies at home: the antiwar elements were determined to expose them as base hirelings; the organizers of the regiment closely circumscribed the rights of the common soldier. Nativist and Irish soldiers found themselves in the same predicament, and still did not forbear from fighting among themselves. In New York City, workingmen's advocates tried to bring egalitarian principles to the volunteer regiments. Though largely unsuccessful, their efforts were but part of a larger movement for an armed and organized working class.

New York City

In New York City, Mike Walsh and his Bowery Democrats attempted to create a popular base for manifest destiny. This would have involved a meaningful expansion of the constituency of racist democracy, putting the urban masses in the field of colonial expansion, and giving them a share in the exploitation of land and people. The politicians of New York's Tammany Hall, a tightly organized patronage machine, raised the main volunteer force for the invasion of California. Colonel Stevenson, a veteran Tammany politician was chosen to lead the Seventh New York Regiment, filling it with "volunteers" from the streets of New York. These same politicians maintained a firm grip on the recruiting of the First New York Regiment, which fought with General Scott from Veracruz to Mexico City.

Radical Democrats and Working Men's Party activists agitated for a volunteer army built on consent, one in which working people would participate fully as citizen-volunteers and claim fair wages, land, and booty. The chief proponent of this plan, labor reformer and independent politician Mike Walsh, embodied the contradictions and impossible complexities of a racist populism. Walsh advocated real equality for the waged (white) population of New York, even as it was losing ground to manufacturing capital. His aggressive pairing of economic democracy and full political rights was a radical program, the apotheosis of Jacksonianism, in a time and place at which Jacksonian democracy was sinking into self-parody. Walsh toyed with and then abandoned agrarian antislavery politics, attempting instead to link his dynamic popular politics to the engine of expansionism and racism. This pairing of a populist white man's democracy and aggressive colonialism seemed to ape the high-flown rhetoric of the editors and propagandists of the time. But to attempt to put it into practice, as Walsh did, revealed severe contradictions; self-governing citizen-soldiers might have turned Mexico into the democratic paradise envisioned in the rhetoric of manifest destiny—if they were able to shed the racist element of their program. Walsh's racism was his admission ticket to national politics, but it eventually doomed his democratic program.

The Political Clubs

New York, like other American cities, had its own "war meeting" in May 1846, at which patriotic speeches were made and volunteers solicited. News reports that circulated around the country emphasized the patriotic enthusiasm of the great gathering.

A prominent political gang in New York, the Spartan Band, had already organized a volunteer company, and its leader, Mike Walsh, disparaged the meeting as an orchestrated affair, from which dissenting speakers were forcibly barred by cordons of police. Wealthy political insiders occupied the platform, Walsh said, while the people were left only "the privilege of braying a response like so many jackasses, to whatever their lordships on the stand might feel disposed to utter."[27] Walsh and his political allies held their own war meeting under the aegis of the "Working Men," in previous decades an independent political party, but at the time a loose agglomeration of radical Democrats and agrarian reformers. In its own meeting at about this time the Working Men forthrightly criticized the organizers of the war meeting.

> We have great reason to believe that these difficulties [the war] have been brought about by Texas scrip and Texas landholders, and other speculators on the products of the people; seeing, as they do, that Texas has little public lands, with which to satisfy them; and that if this "disputed territory" could not become, by some means the property of Texas, they might not be able to live in such luxurious idleness on the products of the workingmen.[28]

The Working Men called on the government to resolve the dispute with its sister republic of Mexico, but if resolution was impossible, then "all landless men, who may volunteer . . . are deserving of fifty dollars per month." They offered a denunciation of the Senate for setting the pay of volunteers at a mere eight dollars a month.[29]

The presence of powerful and dynamic volunteer political organizations in New York ought to have boded well for the formation of volunteer military companies; the political gangs already had their own consensual hierarchy and close ties to militia and fire companies. However, the preeminence of New York as a center for expansionist merchant capital and a power center for the Democratic Party did not bode well for the formation of democratic armies. Democratic leaders in Washington and in Tammany Hall worked together closely to squelch meaningful participatory democracy within the regiments; political power brokers appointed officers based on their political reliability, and recruiters selected privates on the basis of their perceived docility.

The position of the gangs at the center of the controversy over recruiting is not surprising given their political preeminence in the antebellum period. The decline of direct patronage of wealthy merchants in Jacksonian politics left an organizational void in New York. The political "machinery" of the post–Civil War years was as yet in its infancy. Politicians relied on networks of smaller organizations for support—fire companies, militias, and gangs. The fire companies were the most widespread and popular outlets for proving one's manliness and leadership ability, and membership was obligatory for those wishing to enter politics. But the fire companies were fiercely independent and tended to shift their partisan allegiances.[30] Higher in the political order were the gangs, which served as informal militia, poll watchers, and distributors of patronage. They served to connect disparate ethnic groups through a welter of interconnecting social functions.

The political scientist Amy Bridges notes that the gangs lived up to their image of toughness, but were not necessarily disreputable or criminal bands. "Gang members were not laborers, but butchers, carpenters, or mechanics of various sorts; one well-known leader was a printer for the *Sun*. Headquartered at a saloon or liquor-grocery, gangs had distinctive dress and names, fashioning clothing styles that became their hallmark."[31]

Mike Walsh

The most adept practitioner of gang politics, Mike Walsh formed his Spartan Band in 1840, using the Custom House patronage of the Tyler administration as operating capital. Although the Spartans were largely Irish in composition, Walsh was too astute a politician to be hemmed in by ethnic limitations. President John Tyler planned to establish a base of power in New York and he sought the assistance of Walsh, who, in 1845, was Washington correspondent of the New York *Aurora*. Walsh used his patronage to build his political movement, largely aimed at disrupting Tammany politics as usual, on behalf of a labor constituency.

His Spartans specialized in turning party meetings into melees, or in turning the agenda against the leadership—essentially inventing the tactics of the political gang, which would be widely imitated by Isaiah Rynders and others. Walsh's dogged advocacy of the working class and his outrageously defiant rhetoric won him friends among natives and immigrants. An Irish immigrant himself—and never naturalized—he proudly called himself one of the Bowery b'hoys, and was a close friend of nativist gang leader Tom Hyer.[32]

From 1842 to 1846, Mike Walsh spoke and acted tirelessly on behalf of working-class causes. His newspaper, the *Subterranean*, excoriated self-serving politicians and advocated a class-conscious politics. The backing of a powerful gang imparted an unusual candor to Walsh's journalism in an age when outspoken editors faced horsewhipping or worse. Walsh proclaimed to his constituents that "Demagogues tell you that you are freemen. They lie—you are slaves, and none are better aware of the fact than the heathenish dogs who call you freemen. No man devoid of all other means of support but that which his labor affords him can be a freeman, under the present state of society. He must be a humble slave of capital, created by the labor of the poor men who have toiled, suffered and died before him."[33]

During the early 1840s, Walsh was a spokesman for George Henry Evans's National Reform Association (NRA), which advocated free distribution of the public lands. As the annexation of Texas loomed larger on the political horizon, friction developed between Walsh and the NRA, which was composed of middle-class intellectuals, small masters, and dispossessed artisans. Walsh disavowed any sympathy with antislavery objections to annexation and advocated unqualified support for Texas annexation, falling in line behind his patron Tyler. Walsh, viewing abolitionism as an affectation of capitalists and particularly of the hated British, was already shaping his own proletarian vision of manifest destiny. At a public meeting he declared,

> It has been alleged as a reason why Texas should not be annexed, that we have too much territory already. Such an argument may hold good where a government is compelled to maintain its right to territory by force; but here, under our free government, where every man's voice can be heard, the whole continent, or the whole world, would not be sufficient. I go for the re-annexation of Texas, even if it should involve us in a war with Mexico, or with England, or with the whole world![34]

The agrarians of the NRA, however, maintained the democracy of the small landholder as their first principle. Under no circumstances would it accept the annexation of Texas as it was, completely engrossed by the claims of speculators.[35] Walsh brushed aside this issue and antislavery. He looked to his upstart Democrats to gain control over the party without the interference of middle-class reformers, reflecting his limited perspective on a distant issue. But at the time of the Mexican War he was still confident that his Bowery radicalism could be successful on the frontier.

Walsh had thrown himself into the cause of the NRA; in an uncharacteristic move he even took the temperance pledge. But by 1845 he broke with the reformers, looking more and more to his street-level organizing, using popular pressure and Democratic Party patronage to bring his issues to the fore. Mike Walsh worked even harder at forcing Tammany to recognize his political faction; his crusades on behalf of labor and a political storm over his imprisonment on a libel charge brought him to a high state of visibility; the Democracy was forced to recognize his influence with working-class voters. Fresh from prison on Blackwell's Island Walsh was nominated and elected to the New York State Assembly.[36] As he entered the legislature in early 1847, Walsh was already deeply embroiled in controversy over the volunteer regiments, and he would continue his fight on the statehouse floor.

The California Expedition

In May 1846 the War Department called upon the governor of New York to provide seven regiments, about 5,500 men as volunteers in Mexico. Governor Silas Wright specified that the regiments be formed under state militia laws, providing for election of officers. The regiments were to be formed immediately but not mustered into the U.S. service until needed, whereupon they would serve for twelve months or the duration of the war, according to their preference. Secretary of War Marcy informed Wright that no funds would be forthcoming for the raising of regiments. Wright's proclamation and general orders appeared in the New York City papers on May 29 and 30, and recruiting got underway speedily across the state.[37]

Prominent militia and U.S. Army officers appointed themselves as officers of regiments and began to recruit. A Colonel Thomas, commandant of cadets at West Point, formed a company in New York City, selecting his own officers from state militia companies.[38]

Other regiments drew leaders from the ranks of the working people. The Oregon Guards, formed some months before, was "a body of hard working young men . . . not a portion of the State militia—its officers are only commissioned, as all officers should be by the voice of their comrades" It was intimately connected with Walsh's Spartan Band, and its captain, Fowler, was secretary of the "Spartan Association." The company formed in response to the threat of war with Great Britain over Oregon and anticipated thrashing that haughty nation. In a meeting in late May 1846, the guards declared that Mexico was a feeble enemy, hardly worthy of their manly attention. But believing that Britain was plotting with Mexico against the United States, they offered their services as volunteers.[39]

Walsh's friends soon dealt a comeuppance to the presumptuous Gibbs McNeil, a volunteer officer selected by the politicians to raise New York volunteers. "General" McNeil went to the Alabama House, a Bowery tavern and redoubt of the Oregon Guards, soliciting the Oregons as a company in *his* regiment. After abusing McNeil as a "base-born, false-hearted dog, and a craven dunghill," the guards emptied a pitcher of water and two pounds of flour over his head, and sent him on his way pursued by a barman with a paddle.[40]

Eventually Walsh's allies organized into a brigade (two regiments, or about 1,500 men) under the command of a "General" George A. Rice, a popular figure on the Bowery and frequenter of the race tracks and taverns, but their organization was ignored by city and state politicians.

In May 1846 President Polk, Secretary of War Marcy, and General Scott met to organize an expedition to seize and occupy California, employing as their main infantry force a regiment of New York volunteers. William Marcy quickly secured authorization to commission a political crony from New York, Jonathan D. Stevenson, as commander of the expedition, which would sail around the Horn to San Francisco.

On June 26, 1846, Marcy sent Stevenson a letter officially detailing the mission of the regiment and instructions for recruiting. The regiment was expected to form the nucleus for permanent U.S. colonization of Upper California, and as such should be composed of

suitable persons, I mean persons of good habits, as far as practicable of various pursuits and such as would be likely to desire to remain at the end of the war either in Oregon or any territory in that region of the globe which may then be part of the United States. . . . The condition of the acceptance in this case must be a tender of services during the war and it must be explicitly understood that they may be discharged without a claim for returning home, wherever they may be serving at the termination of the war provided it is in the then territory of the United States or may be taken to the nearest or most convenient territory belonging to the United States and then discharged.

The men must be apprised expressly that their term of service is for the war and that they are to be employed on a distant service.[41]

Governor Wright, informed of this plan, objected at first, due to its violation of state militia laws, but soon acceded. Recruiting for the seven regiments was not going too well, and he secured promises that individual companies from the already formed, but not completed, regiments would be eligible for the California regiment.[42]

Mike Walsh expressed outrage at this plan. Stevenson had immediately begun recruiting operations, largely in New York City, and promised 350 acres of land to any man joining the regiment. He neglected to specify that recruits would not be provided with transportation home at the end of the war. Several newspapers published Marcy's letter to Stevenson, and the recruiting was embroiled in controversy from the start.

Walsh began raising a company, the officers to be elected upon completion of recruiting. Stevenson was well known to Walsh, and the latter presented himself and his regiment as ready and willing to join the California expedition. Stevenson, aware of Walsh's political muscle, "jumped at the offer, and appeared mightily pleased with the idea, until I informed him that we were going to elect our own officers, and make an equal division of all we received or made, and wanted to know our duties and our rights previous to departing, so that there would be no grumbling or dissatisfaction after our arrival in California."[43]

Stevenson received this information coldly but told Walsh to go ahead and organize the company. But when the Bowery company reported for mustering at the arsenal, Stevenson denied having made them any offer of service. He claimed that the regiment was full up, obviously a deception, as the regiment would be plagued with shortages and desertions for months, and would indeed leave short-handed.[44]

Colonel Stevenson, a seasoned political hack with a lucrative position in the Custom House, appointed his son adjutant of the regiment and tried to get other positions for relatives. Stevenson and his son obtained a monopoly on uniform sales and extracted inflated prices from the volunteers.[45]

Several of the companies from around the state that had been promised places in the regiment were sent home when they would not comply with Stevenson's wishes. Walsh claimed that Stevenson held commissions up for the highest bidders. One company captain, Francis J. Lippitt, a lawyer, and longtime militia officer, was appointed to his commission on the recommendation of a general of militia and immediately set to work recruiting his company from the "rough" element of New York City. Most of the companies had a core of "respectable" officers and volunteers, comprising doctors, lawyers, clerks, skilled artisans, and even a few "gentlemen."[46]

Walsh, in the *Subterranean*, detailed the corrupt patronage behind Stevenson's commission and acknowledged the impossibility of forming a democratic military force under this martinet. "Had he ever went to California with us, we would either have hanged him, or made him behave himself." Walsh was rueful at this missed opportunity: "In regard to the grant of land, while I knew the idea of our government offering land which they did not even claim, to be an absurdity and imposition, I would not give a fig for the sanction of every government on earth to unoccupied land, as I would take it if I had the physical force to do so, and I would be satisfied with a moderate quantity."

Dozens of unhappy recruits deserted the volunteer encampment on Governor's Island in the weeks before the regiment's departure. Most were dissatisfied with Stevenson's arbitrary discipline and the lies of recruiters. Stevenson responded by bringing in "replacements," last-minute recruits who were an assortment of drunks, ne'er-do-wells and downright criminals, "decoyed into the expedition by every species of fraud and misrepresentation."[47] Seventeen men were picked up in one sheriff's sweep of the Island, for warrants outstanding. Lippitt's Company F, by the time of its departure, contained thirty-one out of seventy-seven men who had replaced others who had deserted, been discharged, or arrested.

The *Herald*, chief promoter of the regiment, published several articles praising the manifest destiny fulfilled by its mission and reported the companies fully staffed with "strong, able-bodied mechanics generally in the prime of life, and already somewhat schooled in the discipline of the service."[48]

Walsh used all his political connections to press for Stevenson's prosecution for malfeasance. The *Subterranean* blasted the character of the regiment and its officers. Walsh claimed his exposés were responsible for the high desertion rate, with "droves" of volunteers coming to his office to thank him for opening their eyes.[49]

Walsh's journalistic crusade led to a warrant for Stevenson's arrest — for the uniform swindle — in late September. Colonel Stevenson was racing to depart, pursued by the local law and under pressure from the administration. He managed to bribe and otherwise stall the sheriffs until the day of his departure. A sheriff tried to arrest him on shipboard but was rebuffed. One hundred Metropolitan Police were called out, but the ships had already set sail. A sheriff's deputy commandeered a steamer and pursued Stevenson's ships as far as Sandy Hook. As the pursuers bore down upon Stevenson, he ordered a sentry to fire upon the pilot of the steamer; seeing a gun pointed at him the pilot veered off course and the California expedition went on its glorious way. Ten days out of New York there was talk of mutiny on board all three ships, and these rebellious impulses were kept down only with the harshest of discipline.

The California Regiment would achieve fame and notoriety in the West; a few of the soldiers found opportunities in California, but still more found the land engrossed by speculators, and wages in the gold mines were used up quickly. The deep class divisions and imperious rule of the regiment would surface again. A few years after the war, officers and soldiers of the regiment were armed against each other in a struggle for property and rights in the new state.

The First Regiment [50]

Mike Walsh lost the first phase of his battle for a democratic New York regiment, and the second stage degenerated into a parody of the first, with a remarkably similar parade of Custom House rogues making a mockery of the idea of the citizen-soldier. The coercion of "volunteers" continued, much as in Massachusetts, and the First New York Regiment returned as it left, hungry and ragged, but, unlike the Massachusetts companies, having played an important role in the crucial battles for the Valley of Mexico. The largely Irish and German forces of the First New York stormed up the precipitous slopes of Chapultepec Castle spilling a great deal of their own blood. They left a formidable legacy of pride to the immigrant militias of New York, which remained strong through the antebellum years.

In early November 1846 the War Department called upon New York for yet another regiment, which was to proceed to Veracruz with General Scott. Influential Democrats in Washington and Albany appointed the officers, once again ignoring the state's militia law. Cronies of William Marcy from the New York Custom House secured three field appointments: Colonel Ward B. Burnett, Lieutenant Colonel Charles Baxter, and Major J. C. Burnham. The officers selected ten places of rendezvous in the city and issued handbills and newspaper advertisements for "'able-bodied recruits willing to live or die in defence of our common country' *promising* three months extra pay, or three months advance, and six months clothing."[51] By mid-December 800 recruits signed on and marched off to Fort Hamilton in Brooklyn, to drill and await transport.[52]

Walsh, serving his first term in the New York State legislature, spoke out angrily as the $10,000 appropriation for the "First New York Regiment" was siphoned off by profiteers. His protests had little effect, however.

Like the California Regiment, the First New York Regiment started with a core of middle-class professionals, gentlemen, soldiers, and respectable tradesmen, which was gradually alienated by the high-handedness of the officers. The ranks were once again filled out with the unfit, the coerced, and the conned. The officers retrieved men rejected by the U.S. surgeon at Fort Hamilton and reintroduced them into the ranks. Corporal Lombard, of the First New York Regiment, described an amazingly diverse body of men, including nonwhites, embarking on this adventure for white Anglo-Saxon supremacy:

> The New York Regiment consisted of about eight hundred rank and file, three hundred Americans, the balance Dutch, Irish, French, English, Poles, Swedes, Chinese, Indians, &c. . . . For officers we had barbers, tailors, sportsmen, bar-tenders, politicians, and a *few* gentlemen. . . .
>
> The privates were generally smart active men, with the exception of about two hundred totally unfit for service, or scarcely anything else. Thus was our regiment composed of rejected boys, men who were diseased and broken down, some lame and blind in one eye, others, were sixty-year old *boys*—with many *beautiful* subjects, selected especially "by order" of the commander-in-chief of the First New York Regiment, bound for Mexico, among which were *gentlemen* from the Tombs, ragamuffins from Blackwell's Island, Alms House, and a sprinkling of "Five Pointers"; and a more rascally, *lousy* set was never thrown among decent men.[53]

The wretched conditions at Fort Hamilton, along with the lack of promised funds, left the volunteers with little to do but drink doctored whiskey at a few taverns in the vicinity. The usual profiteers frequented these places, and the men sold most of their meager clothing and kit in exchange for drink. An observer described the volunteers, crawling with lice, drinking "the most villainous poisoned liquor" in "the bar-room of Col. Church," promiscuously mixing with "negroes."[54]

79

In early January, as the date of departure approached, grumbling among the New Yorkers took a more organized form. A deputation of noncommissioned officers met to discuss the issue of a promised three months' advance of pay. Word of their meeting reached Colonel Burnett, and their leader, a Sergeant O'Reilly, was arrested and discharged from the service. A committee of privates actually approached the colonel, asking about relief for their families. He immediately had the entire committee arrested.[55]

The very next day, five of the ten companies, those thought to contain the most troublesome men, were marched on board ship to await departure: "The men raved and swore they were 'cheated,' . . . and that they never would go aboard with a '*whole skin*' on." There were cries of "'traitors in the camp!' no 'money!' no 'extra pay,' no chance of bidding 'FAREWELL' to families and friends! but *drove* on board-a-ship like *slaves*!" Of the men who swore revenge on this occasion, most did not live to return and carry it out. Only about one in five of the original recruits survived the sickness and combat in Mexico.[56]

On January 9, the last of the New York companies boarded ship, and the regiment set sail for Mexico. The officers successfully controlled the men and prevented any mutiny, confining them on the ship at all ports of call.[57]

Through 1847, recruiters in New York worked to supplement the volunteer and regular regiments in Mexico. They resorted to intensified coercion to fill troop transports. According to Walsh,

> It has long been customary, even in times of profound peace, for our judges to suspend sentence upon convicted offenders on condition that they should enlist in the army or navy. Since the present root-beer war in Mexico has been in operation, poor fellows have been purposely arrested for the recruiting sergeant, against whom no one pretended to bring any charge but poverty and large numbers of them have been unceremoniously handed over to Uncle Sam by the magistrates, as fitting food for Mexican powder.

Walsh cited the case of one man whom a local magistrate sentenced to enlist in the army for stealing two old jackets. "This certainly was not as bad as has been the conduct of the magistrates in picking up men whose poverty-made helplessness rendered them utterly incapable of resisting the outrage, and forcing them to join the army."[58]

In May Mike Walsh reported that he had received more than fifty letters from friends in Veracruz with the New York Regiment. One correspondent wrote that all hands in the regiment and the army were reading the *Subterranean*, which was sent to them by friends, and that Walsh was sorely missed, that his presence in Mexico would cut the imperious officers down to size. The soldier concluded: "By the way what good will conquering the Mexicans, and annexing their country be to poor people unless a fair share of your doctrines take root here." Walsh declared he would gladly go, but not for seven dollars a month, or even twenty, because such a paltry amount would not keep a family in New York or provide one with pocket change in Mexico. Walsh had abandoned any idea of the Mexican War as amenable to the struggle of workers for democracy and land, and focused his efforts on the rights of soldiers. He continued to do so in the state legislature and during his one term in Congress in the 1850s.[59]

The ideal of volunteer companies organized for and by themselves had been lost in the streets and in the chambers of power in New York. The coalition that Walsh dreamed of between northern workers and elite expansionists, in actuality, was played out in a brutal military hierarchy, intensifying rather than mollifying class conflict.

Had Walsh's plans for the volunteers come to fruition and an organized, self-governing white artisan and laboring class been placed in Mexico, American workers and Mexican peasants might have found they had much in common. The issue of class exploitation was even clearer in Mexico than in New York, and, as will be seen in the following chapters, American soldiers and Mexican rancheros, or smallholders, had a great, though largely unrealized, affinity, while American officers and large landowners, or hacendados, had much in common. Mexican and North American smallholders, armed and united against the large hacendados and the Texas land speculators might have made manifest destiny the universal revolutionizing force it was originally proclaimed. As it was, manifest destiny bogged down hopelessly in the resistance of Mexican peasants, and in the ruthless insubordination and disaffection of the American troops.

CHAPTER 5

Discipline and Desertion in Mexico

The political project of volunteering influenced the conduct of American armies in Mexico before they set foot on foreign soil. The military command attempted to create categories of service, with differing standards of obedience, but promises of freedom were infectious and had an unsettling effect on the U.S. Army as well as on the volunteer forces. This chapter discusses the conflict of discipline and democracy within the volunteer forces and concludes with a discussion of desertion among the soldiers of the regular army, showing how the most confined of soldiers also struck out on their own for recognition as heroes and citizens.

The Volunteers in Mexico: "To Dwell Together in This Place"

The Mexican War represented a temporary experiment in racial governance in a new and confusing environment. Using what experience they had in governing or coercing Indians and African Americans, the political and military implementers of expansion created a structure of class and racial rule in which white Anglos were a distinct minority.[1] This minority, to the extent that it was successful in geographically extending American society, had to encompass a reasonable facsimile of American political, social, and economic life, and to maintain and enforce existing distinctions among whites.

In Mexico conventional racial and class hierarchies burst into pieces as discipline and freedom clashed. Ethnic and social distinctions became crystallized in rank, and became clear points of contention. On the other hand, the acceptable channels of opportunity in civil society—wage work, farming and small entrepreneurship—were distorted and hyperbolized into conquest, military honor, loot, and land. These were the wages that politicians promised and some volunteers sought. The promise of Texas-sized personal wealth and individual license had an infectious and uninhibiting effect that made the project of conquest unpredictable and tenuous.

In the narrative "histories" of the most articulate volunteers there are profound and troubled silences concerning the ad hoc and self-serving practices in this war for empire. Mexican War diarists and correspondents invoked "honor" and democratic fellowship to cover or mitigate the crimes of their fellows, recreating the disjunction between propaganda and action that mirrored the larger reality of American society.

Campaigns

The majority of the volunteers in Mexico followed the campaigns along the Rio Grande south to Monterrey and Saltillo, and garrisoned those places for the duration of the war. After January 1847 they also marched with General Scott along the route from Veracruz to Mexico City and were later dispersed along this route. The regulars were far better suited for taking the lead in pitched battles and assaulting fortified positions, and their discipline made them, far more than volunteers, suitable for garrisoning cities. The usefulness of the volunteers, in a military sense, came in their value in intimidating and policing the civilian population in occupied areas.

Approximately 59,000 volunteers served in this war as against 31,000 regular army soldiers.[2] In mid- to late 1846 large numbers of volunteers arrived by sea at the mouth of the Rio Grande and overland from San Antonio, Texas. They concentrated at Matamoros, Camargo, and, after October 1846, Monterrey and Saltillo. The supply train of the army in the north had its main terminal at Brazos Santiago, at the mouth of the Rio Grande. From there men and materiel went upriver to Camargo. Camargo became a large supply depot sending supply trains across the deserts to the south. At Brazos Island and Matamoros thousands of sutlers, teamsters, and other camp followers established temporary, but sizable, American cities.

In January 1847 General Scott established a new point of concentration of troops, on Lobos Island just off Veracruz, Mexico's major Gulf port, in preparation for the invasion of that city. Between March and September of that year Scott and an army that averaged about 10,000 effective troops forged a corridor of uneasy control from Veracruz to Mexico City with large garrisons at Puebla and Jalapa.

The northern front, under Zachary Taylor, presented the most consistently undisciplined and ad hoc version of military life, comprising every gradation of regular and irregular service. In addition to the U.S. Army and state volunteer regiments, there were Texas "ranger" companies — former

TABLE I   *Aggregate Numbers of U.S. Forces in the Mexican War,*
with Casualty Figures

FORCE	AGGREGATE NUMBERS	DEATHS IN BATTLE AND DIED OF WOUNDS		ORDINARY DEATHS	TOTAL DEATHS
		OFFICERS	MEN		
Regular Army					
Old establishment	15,736	63	729	2,623	3,554
New regiments	11,186	10	133	2,091	2,264
Aggregate of regulars	26,922	73	862	4,714	5,818
Volunteers	73,532 *	47	567	6,272	7,088
Aggregate of regulars and volunteers	100,454	120	1,429	10,986	12,896

FORCE	AVERAGE LENGTH OF SERVICE DURING WAR (IN MONTHS)	RESIGNATIONS	DESERTIONS
Regular Army			
Old establishment	26	37	2,247
New regiments	15	92	602
Aggregate of regulars		129	2,849
Volunteers	10	327	3,876
Aggregate of regulars and volunteers		456	6,725

Sources: U.S. House of Representatives, House Executive Document No. 24,
31st Cong., 1st sess., 6; and Justin Smith, *War with Mexico*, 1:512.

* *The aggregate number of volunteers who actually served was only 58,812, with several regiments formed but not called into service.*

militia units responsible for policing the Mexican population in Texas—and hordes of camp followers, who sometimes took on fighting roles.

The northern front provided a logistical challenge in moving men and matériel up the winding and shallow Rio Grande and across vast deserts. In addition to formidable physical barriers American troops faced rampant disease and a steady guerrilla offensive upon their army and supply lines. Guerrillas captured or assassinated stragglers and the sick during long marches of several days. Supply trains made inviting targets for guerrillas; teamsters and quartermasters' men could suddenly be forced into the role of infantry soldiers when their wagons were waylaid on remote stretches of road.

Under dangerous and sickly conditions, spending long stretches of time in camp or on the march, volunteers often had little opportunity for glory or battlefield distinction. Many volunteers' actions eerily reflected the political promises of the war and sought recompense for their hardships and sacrifices. Small groups of men banded together to decide how they would collect their rewards, and from whom. The war policy of the nation was often enacted in decisions of small groups of soldiers in a chilling evocation of the Jacksonian spirit.

The Negotiation of "Wages"

The sermon of Reverend R. A. Stewart, captain of the Louisiana Volunteers, resounded in the popular press in June 1846, striking notes both resonant and dissonant in the hearts and minds of Americans. His speech has been much noted by historians, as a ringing endorsement of manifest destiny: but the internal contradictions of Mexican War politics lie buried within his text.[3] The first Louisiana volunteer detachments arrived on the Rio Grande in May 1846 and encamped near Matamoros, the site of General Taylor's recent victory over General Ampudia. On Sunday, June 1, Stewart, "a fighting clergyman," regaled his volunteer company with the vision of earthly and heavenly rewards of which they could expect to avail themselves. The captain was a Methodist clergyman and a sugar planter of Iberville Parish. His first sermon south of the Rio Grande enjoined the volunteers against committing depredations upon the innocent.

At this early stage the volunteers had already established a reputation for wanton cruelty. Stewart admonished the soldiers to "oppress not the stranger, the fatherless, and the widow, and shed not innocent blood in this place, neither walk after other gods to your hurt." Promised in exchange for their good behavior was the bounty of the land they were entering: "'Then I will cause you to dwell together in this place, in the land I gave to your fathers forever and ever.' Jer. vii, 6–7." According to a newspaper correspondent, "the Rev. speaker showed most plainly and beautifully that it was the order of Providence that the Anglo Saxon race was not only to take possession of the whole North American continent but to influence and modify the character of the world."[4]

The contradictory nature of Stewart's advice is apparent: in order "to dwell together in this place," the volunteers would have had to uproot or subjugate large populations and obliterate their social and economic systems. This was not consistent with decorous moral behavior, but the message was implicit that good behavior and the will of Providence would somehow liberate the land for white American citizens.

As a representative of the slave-owning class, Stewart was treading on dangerous ground. In the slave South poor and middling whites were under close legal controls regarding depredations upon slave property. An elite southerner, Stewart was understandably nervous about unleashing unregulated racial violence.

As a clergyman Stewart was well positioned to lend moral absolution for the collision of acquisitive volunteers with the Mexican people. The fact remains that American soldiers in northeastern and central Mexico did not inherit the land, by whatever means. Volunteers interpreted the rhetoric of manifest destiny in many ways, and collected their "wage" or "reward" in whatever ways they could justify.

The very nature of volunteer service was ad hoc and entailed a great deal of ambiguity about terms of enlistment and payment, about rank and its perquisites and selection of leaders. Even after officers were selected and volunteers reached Mexico, questions remained about the basic conditions of service.

The Fourth Indiana Regiment's recruits enlisted in May 1847 but were unsure of whether they had enlisted for six or twelve months; they had initially been told they were signing on for six, but Congress in February 1847 passed a law prohibiting enlistments for less than twelve months. It was not until the Indianans had been mustered into service and transported to the main camp at Jeffersonville that they were even certain of their wages. The soldiers in camp discussed rumors that Congress had passed a law granting ten dollars a month to privates. When the men found out that their wages were only seven dollars a month, there was much complaining in the camp and talk of desertion.[5]

This uncertainty was essential to the process of volunteering despite all the consternation it caused. Volunteers wanted to see themselves as negotiating every step of the process, rather than contracting for a fixed wage and term. They asserted their right to withdraw their services when the terms of agreement were not satisfactory.

The soldiers' land bounty, passed by Congress in early 1847, was typical of this sort of open-ended arrangement. The law allocated 100 acres of federal land to privates with one year of service, but gave them the option of choosing $100 in Treasury scrip.[6] The land bounty was characteristic of the way the government hedged the promises of manifest destiny. The Bounty Land Bill offered land to soldiers from the vast public domain, not including Texas, the public domain of which was exclusively in the hands of that state.

Only a small percentage of soldiers actually redeemed their land claims, so that in effect the bounty was a cash wage but one nominally subject to independent choice by the individual. Soldiers could negotiate the sale of their land bounties after returning to the states. The land warrants were worth more than $100 if sold in the right place to the right bidder. Speculators bilked inebriated or indebted soldiers of their warrants for as little as $20.[7]

This sense of negotiation and self-interest followed to some degree the materialistic goals of manifest destiny, and these goals were paramount over idealistic concerns. American political writers invoked classical and revolutionary images of soldiers "rewarded with land," ennobling what might otherwise be seen as mercenary conquest, and attempting to clothe the naked contradictions between republican ideology and acquisitive individualism, or acquisitive nationalism.[8]

John Dodd, a lieutenant of the Fourth Indiana Volunteers sent some practical advice to a friend back home:

> Tell John Hall, for me, to stay at home. . . . I don't want to see any of my friends here as privates, particularly married men. An officer can get along quite comfortably, but a private, unless he be hardy, healthy and strong, must suffer. . . . If, however a treaty of peace should be pending and Wallace can get his men mustered into the service and in Mexico before it is consummated, then it will do, for he will get the land and get to see the southern country in a pleasant season of the year. But they must get into Mexico before they are entitled to the land [bounty].

With a year or less of service, the land bounty plus bonuses and back pay could amount to a tidy sum, even after deducting sutler's credits, loans from officers, and other charges. The returning Massachusetts soldiers averaged $150 to $250 in severance pay after cashing in their land bounties.[9]

The Negotiation of Discipline

Volunteer life involved a great deal of give-and-take and negotiation of discipline. Officers tried to respect enlisted men's sense of themselves as citizens and social equals. Risks to the health and safety of the camp were often overlooked for the sake of avoiding disputes; volunteers threw away clothes and equipment critical for survival in a harsh environment. The commanders of the American army in Mexico as a rule kept volunteers encamped away from the cities, trying to restrict their opportunities for conflict with residents. Volunteers, however, asserted their freedom of movement and took frequent liberties with the pass system and other measures regulating their presence in camp.

An Arkansas sergeant, John Palmer, provides a striking example of this freedom. He was originally from Kentucky and had numerous friends and acquaintances in the Kentucky volunteers, who were encamped several miles away. In the days leading up to the battle of Buena Vista, when Santa Anna and an army of 20,000 were known to be lurking in the vicinity of the American army (of 4,000 men) Palmer frequently absented himself overnight to visit his friends. Although he was placed under arrest for being absent without leave, he continued to visit the Kentucky camp without repercussions. Palmer was discharged from the service some five months later without ever being tried for his defalcations. Nor was he ever penalized for being asleep on guard, although as sergeant of the guard he and his command were caught sleeping by an officer in the tense days before Buena Vista.[10]

Images of swashbuckling and plunder drew eager throngs to recruiting centers, but much of the routine of the volunteer consisted of tedious camp life, with infrequent excitement occasioned by skirmishes with guerrillas or the visit of a paymaster. John Palmer's Arkansas company spent much of its time in camp outside Saltillo building a fortification. The very real threat of attack and an unusually conscientious and well-liked captain made this endeavor possible. At other times and places it was impossible to get volunteers to perform labor.

The Missouri volunteers that accompanied General Kearny in his invasion of New Mexico preferred time in the guardhouse to work on fortifications. One of their officers noted that "great complaint is made that the volunteers will scarcely work; daily labor was not embraced in their conceptions of war; it goes some way to prove that democracy and discipline—of the military sort—are not entirely congenial."[11] It took a much more powerful formation of national ideals—that is, the intense commitment to the survival of the nation that existed, for example, in the American Civil War—to get men to accept even temporary restriction of their rights.

Within the volunteer regiments the terms of service were worked out on a daily basis as well, with food, drill, training, obedience, and discipline very much in the realm of negotiation. The kind of politicking that served to elect officers often continued in camp, and it was a standing joke in the regular army that the only way a volunteer officer could get his men to obey an order was to make a particularly stirring stump speech, so that the discipline of a volunteer regiment was commensurate with the eloquence of its colonel.[12] This was an exaggeration, but it accurately reflected the give-and-take of volunteer discipline.

The obsession with democracy in camp life led to severe casualties due to lax enforcement of maintenance of health, provisioning, and shelter and indiscriminate and careless use of firearms. General Winfield Scott observed of the volunteers that they neglected basic camp routine, including trenching, stacking of arms, and the securing of dry bedding. Scott claimed that the volunteers "lose or waste their clothing, lie down wet or on wet ground—fatal to health, and in a short time of life leave the arms and ammunition exposed to rain and dews; hence both are generally useless and soon lost."[13] Sickness took a devastating toll upon volunteers, their vulnerability to tropical diseases enhanced by the lack of cleanliness and regular habits in camp. Apparently personal standing and equality were more important than health.

The sort of pride and individualism that caused men to disregard health and safety comes through clearly in statements of volunteers. Volunteers consciously emulated the romantic image of the Texas volunteers, particularly the Rangers: fiercely independent, organized in small bands, protecting their own territory against savage Mexicans and Indians. Texan cavalry units played important roles in the Mexican War as scouts and in counterguerrilla warfare action.

An Ohio officer, more an admirer of discipline than of bravado, offered a keen analysis of the appeal of the romanticized Texans to volunteers. A Texas soldier told the Ohioan that he was thoroughly sick of the arbitrary behavior of officers. "'Why' said he 'in our Texas war, an officer was no better than a private. . . but here if we speak to one these d——d regulars who has a strap on his shirt or one of our own officers familiarly or pretend to dispute his word or differ with him we are treated like dogs. Bucked, bucked sir, and I assure you Texans will not be bucked.'"

The Ohioan registered some grudging admiration for the independent spirit of the Texan but remarked grimly that the foregoing statement was "a pretty good account of the feelings of Volunteers of all classes—it appears hard for them to be able to come under the army regulations—which they have sworn to do."[14]

General Zachary Taylor, an astute leader of volunteer soldiers, was aware of their yearnings for independence and distinction and knew how to balance military necessity with political considerations. An Ohio private angrily importuned upon him, inquiring why regular army soldiers had been sent ahead on the road to Monterrey, while the volunteers languished in camp. "The Gen. very pleasantly told him he sent the regulars to open the path because they were inured to hardships, fighting was their *trade*, they knew nothing else—and assured the boys that before they returned they should have enough of it."[15]

The selection of officers by popular mandate exacerbated indiscipline and led to excessive casualties in battles, and on marches. Despite these very tangible inducements to discipline and military order, volunteers resisted vehemently and violently the loss of caste that apparently came with acknowledging privileges of rank. Many of the field officers had regular army experience and military academy training and sought to abide by the professional ethics and standards they knew to be effective. But they either modified their professional standards or literally came to blows with their men.

Colonel Robert T. Paine of the North Carolina Regiment engendered the animosity of his volunteer troops by insisting on rigid adherence to military procedure, and also because he was selected by a Whig legislature rather than elected. From their very first mustering in North Carolina the troops seethed with resentment over the political maneuverings that had placed such officers above them. At least two companies, from Rowan and Mecklenburg Counties disbanded and sent back all funds to the Whig legislature, stating that they objected to the preamble to the legislature's funding bill, which "asserted the historical fact that the war was brought on by the President's order to march our forces from Corpus Christi to the Rio Grande."[16]

A Whig editorialist objected that these finicky soldiers were "unsafe" and that regular soldiers would be preferable. Among such volunteers, the "officers must be all to their own taste, and they must be especially careful to adapt their phrases to the political creed of these sensitive gentlemen!"[17]

The *Tarborough Press*, the *Wilmington Journal*, and other Democratic sheets attacked Colonel Paine, accusing him of "a want of judgment, tyranny and cruelty," according to Paine's own testimony. Paine imposed daily drills, and also enforced punishments for men who were asleep on watch. In addition,

Colonel Paine, before receiving his commission, had been a Whig member of the North Carolina legislature and, it was complained, endorsed the resolution condemning the war. A private in the regiment passed around a letter from a friend back home that urged the soldiers to shoot the colonel, and a subsequent full-scale mutiny in the company nearly fulfilled this request.[18]

In the months after the battle of Buena Vista the encampment of General Wool's division outside of Saltillo boiled with political contentiousness, gambling, and insubordination. Paine countered with tightened discipline over his battalion, and with a menacing, though largely symbolic, step: the erection of a wooden horse in front of the North Carolina regimental headquarters. This implement of corporal punishment was widely used in the regular army: an errant recruit was seated and tied upon the narrow wooden rail of the "horse," for hours at a time, sometimes at intervals over several days, suffering excruciating pain and humiliation. The volunteers viewed this threat of corporal punishment as a gross affront.

Before it was ever employed, about 100 soldiers from the neighboring Virginia regiment led a mob of soldiers in dismantling the hated symbol of authority. The North Carolina volunteers disobeyed orders to arrest the rioting soldiers. Colonel Paine and a few loyal officers personally rounded up mutinous soldiers in a series of riotous incidents. In one of these Paine, using his sidearm, fatally shot a soldier. During several turbulent days soldiers from the Virginia, Mississippi, and North Carolina regiments threw stones at the colonel's tent.

Some of Paine's junior officers were less than assiduous in punishing these incidents: a subsequent court of inquiry cashiered two officers for disobeying Paine. The inquiry revealed that the captains of the North Carolina companies were engaged in election campaigns and were hesitant to take punitive action. One captain was observed playing cards with his men while on duty. The process of electioneering contributed to the general disorder, as the men were plied with liquor.

Paine was indeed a stormy commander, not only discharging his pistol at volunteers but also threatening them at sword point. In another incident he threatened a disobedient teamster. The teamster rounded up twenty of his fellow drivers and tried to make a stand. Paine single-handedly faced down the rebellious group.[19]

Private soldiers in volunteer regiments could muster not only the popular will of the camp but, through communication with the community upon which they were drawn, exert the censure of public opinion against officers who were too strict or unfair. An Indiana volunteer captain, Stanislaus Lasselle, complained that unfavorable reports had been written up about him in his hometown newspaper, and he suspected it was because he attempted to maintain a modicum of discipline in the company. He claimed to be the only captain in his regiment to require daily drill, and the only one of his peers to reside in camp; the other captains lodged in town, in Matamoros or Point Isabel.

Lasselle believed his fellow officers were avoiding the responsibility of their offices and disregarding the morale of the men, who were falling prey to disease and boredom.[20] Many volunteer officers, such as Lasselle, were West Point–trained and tried to adhere to a traditional military routine and discipline. But they met with resistance and threats, and the inevitable reproaches in the press back home.

Volunteer officers, for their part, also used the press to advantage, passing on accounts of battles that portrayed themselves and their regiments in heroic situations, often with scant regard for the facts. After the battle of Monterrey a regular army officer reflected on newspaper accounts of the fighting that "a Baltimore Captain it is well known ran in battle and yet the papers have it that he killed five men in a personal encounter. Another [volunteer officer] they say, with thirty men stormed a twelve pound Battery. There was no twelve pound Battery in Monterey, and this man, or rather hero was not in battle at all!" There were twice as many volunteer as regular officers engaged in the battle of Monterrey; of these four volunteer and thirteen regular officers were killed.[21]

Battles, in formal histories and popular accounts, were where history was produced. Leaders of American communities and ambitious citizens jumped at the chance to make and chronicle that history. American war correspondence was born in the Mexican War era and offered a chance to write history as it happened. The correspondents at this early juncture were overwhelmingly the soldiers themselves, whose letters home were regularly printed in local and national papers.

There is little in this correspondence that a twenty-first-century reader would recognize as journalism. The format of the personal letter is readily apparent, as is the stiff formality of the heroic narrative. Correspondents exaggerated the role of individuals, or individual regiments, stressing innate qualities of courage and chivalry, rather than adept strategy or fortuitous circumstances. Accounts of battles touted the merits of one regiment over another, or one officer over another. There was little direct appeal to a shared national consciousness.[22]

To their credit, many volunteers, officers included, fought bravely and well; volunteers absorbed severe casualties at all the major battles of the Mexican War; but the underlying logic of the volunteer system did not have as its goal disciplined and effective troops. More important were group identity and cohesion, and attaining distinction back home. This guiding mentality, whatever its effect in combat situations had a deleterious, and often disastrous effect on camp life and basic survival in a hostile and unhealthy environment.

Immigrant Volunteers in Mexico

Despite criticisms leveled against the regulars as foreign hirelings, the volunteer regiments from most states had large contingents of immigrant soldiers, particularly those from the northern United States. The officers of the Massachusetts Regiment took upon themselves the role of violent enforcers of nativist hegemony. During the latter half of 1847 a steady stream of articles appeared in Massachusetts newspapers describing the dictatorial conduct of the officers. Soldiers described incidents in which officers Cushing, Abbott, and Wright inflicted severe corporal punishment on soldiers for offenses ranging from liquor selling to "fast riding" in the streets of Matamoros. The officers, except Cushing, were said to be constantly drunk, well fed, and temperamental, whereas the men were ragged and starving, the officers selling the men's rations. The volunteers respected Cushing as sober and above the fray of the petty crimes of his subordinate officers, but he reportedly took a hand in whipping a Massachusetts volunteer and also a teamster for selling liquor to soldiers.[23]

Cushing's enemies made great political capital off these incidents and eagerly sought the reports of soldiers and others on the scene. Cushing's sympathetic biographer reports of one these scenes, "Cushing took the law into his own hands and had the fellow [the teamster] soundly horsewhipped, even administering some of the blows with his good right arm. He made no attempt to be tactful, but he was always scrupulously just."[24]

The news from the Massachusetts volunteers remained steadily negative through their eighteen months of service; a noncommissioned officer, a member of the Sons of Temperance, was the regular correspondent of the *Chronotype*, and he graphically described the drunkenness of the company

officers, and their brutal treatment of the men — ironically, the most frequently punished crime was drunkenness. The Irish company was a particular target for punishment, and according to the temperance man,

> The officers including Major Abbott and the lot kept so beastly drunk
> that the citizens of Matamoras petitioned Col. Davenport, the com-
> mander of the post, to have the regiment moved out of the city. Where-
> upon the Col. orders Major Abbott to move out within 24 hours, to
> which he added a threat that if he did not, he, Col. Davenport, would call
> the regulars up from Palo Alto and force him out. . . . This Regiment,
> when it arrived in Matamoras, was very much liked, but went away de-
> spised by all. The cause of all this was too much stripping men to their
> bare backs and whipping them most unmercifully, shaving their heads
> &c. These men belonged to Company B [the Irish company]. What their
> names are I don't know.[25]

The First Ohio Regiment was, according to one member, about one-third
Catholic, with "seventy or eighty gallant Irishmen." These latter were proof
against Mexicans trying to procure their desertions and even helped to arrest such procurers. On the other hand, this "Irish Co." was often "quarrelsome, riotous and insubordinate. The officers were obliged to use force and
blows to put down the disturbances, and a number of blackened eyes and
broken heads were the result."[26]

When the regiment left Cincinnati, the steamer left a portion of the men
still on shore drunk and brawling. A guard had to be placed over those
men who managed to get on board the ship, and their canteens forcibly
emptied.[27]

There was a German company as well in the First Ohio, and its choral
renditions of native songs filled the camp on the Rio Grande and mingled
with the "banjo and bones" of popular minstrel tunes.[28] The "Dayton German Co." kept quite to itself, and even had its own physician, who was
trusted more than the company's commissioned surgeon, Ephraim K.
Chamberlin. Chamberlin noted, perhaps manifesting some professional jealousy, that the German company had a precipitously high death rate.

Chamberlin had more than a professional mistrust of the Germans, actually having come to blows with them. In one of the numerous brawls that
erupted on the long journey to Mexico, Colonel Mitchell, the commander
of the First Ohio, confronted an "insolent" German soldier who had refused
to obey an order. The soldier "collared and choked the Col." at which point

Chamberlin intervened and beat the soldier with his cane. This brought a tense moment in which "Muskets, German muskets were turned on the Col.'s rescuer." Colonel Mitchell, however, seized the moment, "got hold of a musket" and wielding it as a bludgeon, "laid out the dutch right and left."[29]

Another ethnic riot among volunteers in Mexico turned deadly and was widely publicized in newspapers across the United States. The Georgia Regiment had an "Irish" company, the Jasper Greens, many of whom were American-born Scotch-Irish, and had existed for some time as a respected Savannah militia company.

The other Georgia companies goaded the Greens with relentless nativist insults and provocations to violence, until a full-scale riot broke out between the Greens and the Kenesaw Rangers company. Some of the Rangers challenged a "young Scotchman" to a fight, and when he declined they threw a claret bottle at his head, and called him a "d——d Irish son of a B—ch." On this occasion and others, Captain McMahon restrained his men from retaliating. The riot took place near the Rio Grande depot town of Camargo. This well publicized melee ended with serious injury to Captain McMahon, to the colonel of the Illinois Regiment—who personally intervened in the riot—and one death.[30]

The violence between native and "foreign" volunteers persisted in many of the regiments, and, as in the case of the Georgia company, the relative respectability, and even nativity, of the ethnic company in question did not seem to make much difference, as long as they identified themselves in ethnic terms. The Jasper Greens were one of the best-uniformed and best-drilled companies in the volunteer service, and, ironically, Colonel Baker, before he came to blows with the company, had publicly praised its discipline and spirit.

The volunteer service offered an extension of the provisional citizenship of new immigrants. A group of immigrants who had a community populous and wealthy enough to sponsor a company was grudgingly welcomed in the volunteer regiments and frequently publicly criticized for the sort of misbehavior that characterized the volunteers in general.

African Americans

African Americans formed a significant element of the American presence in Mexico, though how many and exactly what their role was remain obscure. This group performed labor in the American camps and, moreover, bore the burden of southern racial codes transplanted into a nation that had abolished slavery. Southern volunteers, in particular, set themselves up as vigilantes, dispensing their own judgments on African Americans, or on the Mexicans who violated American social mores about dealing with blacks. This was the only American war in which African Americans were not mobilized as combatants, which in itself speaks for the extreme sensitivity of race as an issue in this conflict.[31]

Isolated accounts exist of black soldiers, fighting in irregular units. An 1853 obituary of "Thomas Savoy, *alias* Black Tom, *alias* the Special Citizen of Bexar County," related the history of this veteran of the Texas and Mexican wars. Savoy made his way to Texas during the 1836 revolution with a company of Mississippi volunteers, apparently a free black and a barber. He quickly demonstrated his skill as a soldier and accompanied Texas troops on subsequent forays against Mexico.

In the Mexican War he fought with the Texas volunteers at Monterey and Buena Vista. Savoy returned to Texas with a company of Kentucky volunteers and spent his remaining years living "like a lord" and pursuing Indians on the frontier.[32]

With the exception of an occasional "Black Tom," a camp follower who showed extraordinary mettle in combat, most African American participants in the war accompanied the army as servants and laborers. Many slaves had escaped to Mexico prior to the war, that nation having abolished slavery in 1829, and in some cases were requisitioned as translators and guides for the army. The supposed benevolent conditions enjoyed by blacks in Mexico were certainly exaggerated, particularly by Texans with an interest in slavery. This heightened the sense of racial war in that former province of Mexico. Refugee slaves encountered on Mexican soil were stolen property in the Texans' view and, as such, created justifications for reprisals against Mexicans.

William Gardner's servant, Moses, was more typical of African Americans serving the invading army. Moses was the slave of a North Carolina volunteer officer; he escaped in occupied Mexico City and was only able to remain at large a few weeks. Moses found out that Mexico offered a hard living for its own people and starvation for many. He returned to his master and slavery. Gardner remarked that the slave "certainly looked both hungry and seedy when he returned" from his several week escape from bondage.[33]

If an escaped slave could claim the sanctuary of a political or military figure, he might be able to find a secure position, in effect claiming political asylum, like other American deserters. But no guaranteed status came with such asylum.

A Texan claimed to have seen several runaway slaves among the Mexican soldiers that marched out of Monterrey under truce—along with several members of the San Patricio Battalion, American deserters who fought with the Mexicans. Some American blacks found places and, perhaps, commissions in the Mexican military, although the racial language of white Americans from this period is wildly, often deliberately, imprecise.

The racial justice of the slave South was put under great stress in Mexico, and its finer legal distinctions were sometimes unenforceable there. Soldiers thus engaged in vigilantism to reinforce racial dominance.

In 1847 a black man, servant to a volunteer officer, was tried and hung by a military commission for the killing of a Mexican. The day following the hanging two Mexicans were found, one dead, and one nearly so, the victims of retaliation by undiscovered volunteers. Unlike the slave South, an individual would not be compensated by the state for the execution of his "property." The loss of this slave for the killing of a Mexican was particularly galling to a southerner's sense of justice.[34]

The violence that Americans directed toward their slaves was easily diverted upon Mexicans, and any progress that the latter country had made toward racial tolerance became an incitement to American soldiers to reinforce their native standards.

Camp Followers

Another element of the American contingent in Mexico comprised civilian camp followers. The quasi-military nature of the volunteer forces and the short terms of their enlistment made them barely distinguishable from civilians, but the presence of an opportunistic commercial and laboring contingent had a marked effect on the character of the war effort. Many of these were classic army followers: prostitutes, gamblers, and liquor sellers; others were Texans looking for plunder and excitement. In the months before the war, camp followers assembled at Kinney's ranch, near Corpus Christi. From there they moved forward with the occupation of Matamoros and turned that border town into a veritable hell of gambling, drinking, and violence. The principal streets were quickly transformed, the storefronts occupied entirely by American shopkeepers and grog sellers. "Several actresses and bawds were among the live cargo from the U.S." commented one observer.[35] In June 1846, only one month into the occupation, Americans were responsible for at least twenty murders in the city, along with other crimes of every description. The city excited the disgust and horror of even hardened military men, with frequent unfavorable comment upon the promiscuous inter-mingling of races and nationalities. A volunteer officer observed that:

> About the principle corners loiter groups of men of all colours and coun-tries are collected cursing, swearing fighting, gambling and presenting a most barbarous sight. . . . Murder rapine and vice of all manner of form prevails and predominates here. . . .
>
> It is a conquered city much the receptacle of all the dregs of the United States. As it now stands, it is a disgrace to our country; for our own citi-zens are much worse than the Mexicans who are mixed up with them. Oh vice! how hideous are thy features![36]

This promiscuity and confusion of morality, race, and nationality is em-blematic of the problems that the United States faced in prosecuting the Mexican War. The careful American social policies of racial segregation were unsustainable in locales like Matamoros or Mexico City, through which sol-diers passed. The principles and rationales of segregation only became more inflexible in the face of this, at least as held by officers and other prominent Americans. The good fellowship of white American males in small towns and working-class districts of the cities was being extended to all manner of unacceptable Mexicans and American immigrants, and the standard of com-munity values was very difficult to apply in a teeming depot like Matamoros.

Teamsters made up another huge contingent; most of the wagoners were hired in the United States but some hundreds were Mexicans. They re-ceived twenty-five dollars a month and a ration and a half a day—quite substantial compared with the private soldier's seven dollars a month. The teamsters were employed by the quartermaster, but were not considered part of the army, and therefore their subjection to military justice was ill-defined, and improvised over the course of the war. "The soldiers consid-ered themselves several grades above the Quartermaster's men and looked down with contempt upon the plebeian mule drivers. They never associated together, except when each expected to be benefited by the operation." A few of the drivers were, in fact, discharged soldiers and were more or less respected and thus able to obtain lucrative positions within the quarter-master's department or as sutlers or tradesmen. Surgeon Chamberlin, of the First Ohio Volunteers, noted that upon the discharge of the regiment many soldiers remained to work in the quartermaster's department, "where the Mechanics can get much better wages than in the United States." Some men also joined a Texas Ranger company that was forming.[37]

Wagon drivers profiteered at the expense of soldiers and incurred the soldiers' hatred. On long marches, sick soldiers were offered or refused places in the wagons at the discretion of the drivers. Stragglers often fell into the hands of guerrillas and were killed. Water was a vital commodity on the march, and teamsters were known to exercise a monopoly over it, in one case selling it at twelve and a half cents a cup when they were under orders to distribute it free.[38]

Employees and camp followers took full advantage of their ambiguous status under military law, and their seeming immunity from Mexican courts, to prey upon Mexicans and sometimes American soldiers. Periodic crackdowns by generals Taylor and Scott alleviated but did not solve the problem. A regular officer complained of widespread, vicious despoliations of small towns on the route from Mier to Saltillo. These crimes

> were principally committed by some of the quartermaster's men, who, until they were taught to the contrary by the strong arm of power, did not consider themselves as being amenable to martial or any other law; and by desperate adventurers, called by the army "outsiders," who followed the army for plunder, and frequently organized themselves into bands to carry on their depredations, not being very particular as to whether they robbed Mexicans or their own countrymen. They emphatically "made war on their own hook."[39]

At the battle of Buena Vista, Arkansas Colonel Yell's corpse was plundered almost as soon as he fell. A soldier wrote that there was "a set of army swindlers," camp followers, preying upon the men. During the same battle, while the sentries were otherwise engaged, they took 300 overcoats and about 1,000 blankets from the wagons. This soldier reported that he was sleeping on the ground without a blanket as a result.[40]

Camp followers had more freedom to engage in systematic robbery, but volunteer soldiers also took a hand in the rape and pillage of Mexican civilians, often without much prospect or expectation of material gain.

Volunteers and Desertion

A fundamental privilege of the volunteer, was the right to abrogate his oath of service if he felt the terms of that service did not live up to promised standards. Regular army deserters went about with a bounty on their heads, payable to anyone willing and able to turn them in, and they also wore the immediately recognizable blue uniform with its brass buttons. Volunteers in most cases could desert with impunity, particularly before they left the United States. Soldiers simply decided they disliked the soldier's life and absconded, at some point along the journey to Mexico. Once in Mexico, desertions were less frequent, but volunteers could obtain discharges relatively easily. Nonetheless, volunteer desertions lagged only slightly behind those in the regular service. The volunteers moved about with surprising freedom and could choose from a range of options, even in Mexico.

The Massachusetts Regiment, under the inflexible General Caleb Cushing, not only experienced desertions at Matamoros, but in one instance deserters corresponded freely with soldiers remaining in the regiment, and this information made its way to newspapers back home. Two deserters, fed up with the abysmal conditions in the Massachusetts Regiment made a difficult trek across the wastes of the Nueces River country to Galveston. "After reaching Galveston, they found Yankees in such demand that they easily obtained employment, one as a *school-master*, at $60 per month, and the other as a manual laborer, at $45."[41] The choice of wages over the marginal honor attendant upon remaining with their comrades was quite clear, and the information on which to base such a decision readily available for most recruits. The Massachusetts papers circulated this report with little comment, and on the face of the report the deserters were portrayed as having made a sound and sensible choice.

The Massachusetts volunteers experienced some of the most arbitrary and cruel discipline in the service, with corporal punishment and humiliation equivalent with that of regular soldiers. However, their status as citizen-soldiers was of great value to them and gave them a range of freedoms unavailable to the despised regulars. The volunteers prided themselves on their unorthodox and unmilitary appearance. As citizen-soldiers they had great freedom of movement; little attention was paid to enforcement of passes, and volunteers could fraternize or travel for days away from their regiments. The blue uniform was, ironically, as the symbol of the United States, virtually a prison suit; military personnel and civilians, including Mexicans, took a keen interest in errant regular soldiers, largely because of the bounty that could be collected for turning them in.

Colonel Cushing provoked another "strike" in the Massachusetts Regiment when he ordered the volunteers to replace their, by now ragged, gray uniforms with standard U.S. issue blue uniforms. The blue tunics with brass buttons were the only clothing available for their long trek inland from Veracruz. This protest went to the heart of the volunteers' fundamental right of freedom of movement and desertion. A single company—not the Irish company—refused to don the garb of the regular army despite the threat of imprisonment. Cushing detached an armed guard and had sixty-five men locked up in the Castle of San Juan de Ulúoa, marching on without them into the interior.[42]

Local officials and concerned citizens in the United States wrote the adjutant general's office inquiring as to the proper procedure in apprehending and punishing volunteer deserters, who had often drawn clothing, rations, and pay prior to decamping. The standard procedure with regular army deserters was detention at the nearest U.S. Army depot and a reward of thirty dollars paid to the apprehender. A resident of Cincinnati claimed there were several members of the Fourth Ohio at large in the city, but civic and military officials were unsure of their authority and had as yet taken no action against them. The adjutant general's office referred the matter to Secretary of War William Marcy, who decided that no action could legally be taken against volunteer deserters.[43]

If punishment was forthcoming for individual deserters, it was often meted out in personal confrontation or in community sanction. An Indiana lieutenant wrote his wife concerning two brothers who deserted while the regiment was still at the muster in Jeffersonville. He instructed her to have his business partner call in a considerable debt that one of the deserters owed him.[44] Men deserted from riverboats and trains but most often from encampments in New Orleans.

The Second Pennsylvania Regiment, while in New Orleans, lost fifty-nine men to desertion, from ten companies, or about 6 percent of its strength. Several others had deserted at the mustering point in Pittsburgh. Many recruits expressed shock and indignation at their billeting conditions and, at the same time, at the inequality of conditions, as officers and well-heeled volunteers checked into hotels or took private cabins on steamers. The conditions in the holds of steamboats were so oppressive that they made stops only when necessary, and then with heavy guards posted, to prevent mass desertions or raids on neighboring taverns.[45] In the interest of preserving good order, some of the more disciplined companies, made up of the relatively well-off members of private militia companies, helped keep order while in transit.[46]

The Regular Army in Mexico: Deserters

The Mexican War produced new categories of regulars, irregulars, and camp followers in the U.S. Army; desertion offered men the chance to change their station in the U.S. service or to leave it entirely, for the ranks of the enemy. The most restricted category within the military, the old regiments of the regular army, was most subject to desertion, even though it levied the most severe penalties on deserters and offered civilians cash incentives to capture absconding regulars. The most famous deserters of this war were the soldiers of the San Patricio Battalion; this group was made up entirely of regular army men, a powerful argument for their having been driven into the arms of the Mexicans by the excessive discipline of that branch of service. Mexican authorities claimed that Catholic soldiers joined their ranks, as a matter of conscience, not wishing to fight on the side of Protestant bigots. Catholics, it has been seen, were numerous in the ranks of the volunteers, but volunteers were not driven to such desperate measures; discharges from service were easily obtained and desertion, although nearly as common as in the regular service, rarely punished.

The letters that a Louisiana and a Massachusetts regular wrote to hometown newspapers reveal the coercive environment prevailing in the regular army and show the restlessness that often led to desertion. The young man from Louisiana was swept up in the midwar recruiting drive and joined the regular army with the understanding that he would serve under the famous Texas Ranger Samuel Walker, who had been commissioned as a captain in a U.S. cavalry company. The recruit wrote his brother that he expected to be "dashing through the country on horseback as a free Ranger," but soon found himself assigned as a replacement in an infantry company, which had taken heavy casualties at the battle of Cerro Gordo.[47] He was slightly wounded in the severe fighting around Mexico City but did not feel to any degree glorified by his experience. It seemed that real battlefield distinction had to be witnessed and shared by worthy companions, of the estate of citizen and gentleman. The Louisiana recruit lamented that he was "disgusted with the low base villains, among whom I have been thrown. We are worse off than slaves; confined within narrow walls; very few liberties allowed us. . . . There is a great deal to be seen in this city and much to please the fancy of any free man; but as a soldier I can appreciate nothing."[48]

Another recruit in one of the new regular army regiments, from Boston, found some degree of comradeship in the regular army. This doughty

Yankee expressed pride in his service, apparently feeling that his fellow recruits were his equals, and the trials inflicted by a hostile land and their own
officers were nobly and manfully borne. In a letter published in the *Liberator*,
this soldier denounced the harsh punishments inflicted: "One of our Boston recruits was gagged with a bayonet, his teeth broke and loosened, and
his mouth cut severely." However, the Boston recruit held fast to an outlook
that valued personal survival in the face of injustice and hardship; any day in
which he escaped the lash and infectious disease was a triumph and a vindication of his own work ethic and discipline. He also expressed admiration
for veteran soldiers, those whose opportunism and experience gave them a
certain degree of respect within this degrading system. "The best soldiers
I have met with in the U.S. Army are deserters from the British. They all
damn this service and would give a years pay to be back again under the
Union Jack."[49]

This Bostonian, unlike the recruit from rural Louisiana, was more com-
fortable with the sundry ethnic and social groups among which he found
himself in the regular army. For him doubtful origins did not preclude man-
hood or fulfillment of duty. Aristocratic, cruel behavior was the source of the
troubled state of the army, not individual recruits. He did not find discipline,
in and of itself, degrading or unmanning, except perhaps to those who administered it. The Boston recruit respected the British veterans who had developed courage and initiative under both British and American discipline,
and had already deserted one service where conditions were intolerable.

The army's semiofficial discountenancing of Catholics was one of many
grievances soldiers bore, and it was no doubt a factor in desertions. A letter to the New Orleans *Delta* reported secondhand the account of an English physician who met two "sons of Erin," army deserters, headed for the
Mexican army stronghold of San Luis Potosí. The doctor inquired of them
why they had deserted, and "the man with the musket told him that he had
fought too much against his religion already, and that he wouldn't fight for
the United States again until she 'got into a war with England,' when he
'would go for a volunteer.' The other one had thrown away his musket, and
would never pick up another one whilst he lived." Both men had obtained
passports from Mexican military authorities, and were looking to get to a
port where they could get a ship "to the old country," or "get employment in
the country."[50]

Desertion to the enemy became attractive for hundreds of regular army
soldiers, despite the problems of blending into the alien culture and caste so-

ciety of Mexico. For those in the regular army the attitudes of Americans resident in the Southwest and of the volunteer soldiers and their own officers were equal or greater in strangeness and harshness to them.

A French missionary priest, Emmanuel Domenech, observed military life along the Rio Grande in the years following the Mexican War. He noted a deep-seated contempt on the part of the officers for the Irish and Catholics serving under them. He remarked that he had seen soldiers "suspended from the branches of trees for drunkenness. Sometimes too they tie their arms and legs, and fling them repeatedly into a river, and then drag them to the bank with a cord." Another soldier, deathly ill, was kept in chains on his sickbed, for some recent offense. "He died in his chains; and perhaps in consequence of being kept chained." The surgeon and commanding officer responsible faced a court-martial but their fellow officers found them not guilty. The tribunal, according to the Abbé Domenech, was "quite as intelligent in matters of caste and religion as the accused."

Domenech admitted these atrocities were isolated incidents and added that most of the officers were accomplished and intelligent. "Still these cruelties serve to nurture a bitter animosity in the hearts of the Irish soldiers, and to teach them that the liberty, equality, and fraternity of the United States are either hollow phrases, or applied ironically to European novices."[51]

The distinctive crime of the Mexican War, however, was desertion to the enemy, a crime of a different order of magnitude, and one that suggested forces of attraction—on the part of the enemy—as well as the negative factors that drove recruits away from the U.S. Army. Contemporary commentators and subsequent historians have noted the affinity that Irish and German troops had with the Catholic society of Mexico. Indeed, the programmatic strategy of the Mexican government to induce desertions focused on the issue of religious persecution.

The Mexicans issued broadsides and leaflets by the thousands harping upon this theme. Priests and European nationals acted as clandestine agents enticing U.S. soldiers. They offered money, land bounties, and officers' commissions as inducements. The Mexican government authorized these recruiters to disburse funds and safe-conduct passes as well as to make promises of land and commissions. Mexican guerrillas shadowed the U.S. Army, and captured soldiers who took unauthorized leave or fell out of the ranks. The guerrillas subjected these men to intense coercion to join the Mexican ranks—threatening them with physical harm and death if they failed to comply.[52]

CATHOLICS, Irish, Frenchmen, and Germans of the Invading army!

The american nation makes a most unjust war to the mexicans, and has taken all of you as an instrument of their iniquity. You must not fight against a religious people, nor should you be seen in the ranks of those who proclaim *slavery of mankind* as a constitutive principle. The religious man, he who possesses greatness of mind, must always fight for liberty and liberty is not on the side of those who establish differences in mankind, making an unhappy and innocent people, earn the bread of slavery. Liberty is not on the part of those who desire to be the lords of the world, robbing properties and territories which do not belong to them and shedding so much blood in order to accomplish their views, views in open war with the principles of our holy religion. The mexican people raises every where in order to wage an insurrectionary war, and that american army however illegal it may become, shall find here a grave. The mexican people wishes not to shed the blood of those who profess their own religion, and I, in the name of the inhabitants of the state of Vera Cruz, invite you to abandon those ranks to which you must not belong. I have given the necessary orders, so that, should you abandon them, you may be respected in all the towns and places of the states where you happen to go, and all requisite assistance shall be given to all, till brought before me. Many of your former companions fight now content in our ranks. After this war is over, the magnanimous and generous mexican nation will duly appreciate the services rendered, and you shall remain with us, cultivating our fertile lands. Catholic Irish, French and German!! Long live Liberty!! Long live our holy Religion!!

Huatusco june 6, 1847.

Juan Soto.

Governor of the free and sovereign State of Vera Cruz.

ORIZAVA.—IMPRENTA DE LA CAJA DE AHORROS.

CATÓLICOS, irlandeses, franceses y alemanes del ejército invasor.

La nación americana hace á la mexicana la guerra mas injusta y á vosotros os ha cogido para instrumentos de su iniquidad. Vosotros no debeis pelear contra un pueblo religioso ni se os debe ver en las filas de los que proclaman la esclavitud de la especie humana como un principio constitutivo. El hombre religioso, el que posee nobleza de alma debe pelear siempre por la libertad y la libertad no está del lado de aquellos que establecen diferencias en la especie humana haciendo mendigar á una raza desgraciada el pan de la esclavitud. La libertad no está del lado de aquellos que ambicionan ser los señores del mundo robando propiedades y territorios que no les pertenecen, y derramando tanta sangre para conseguir sus miras que pugnan con los principios de nuestra santa religión. El pueblo mexicano se alza ya por todas partes para hacer una guerra de insurrección y este ejército americano aunque se aumente hasta donde se quiera encontrará su sepulcro. El pueblo mexicano no quiere derramar la sangre de aquellos que tienen su misma religión y yo en nombre de los habitantes del estado de Veracruz os escito á que abandoneis esas filas á las que no debeis pertenecer. He dado las órdenes correspondientes para que si las abandonais se os respete en los pueblos del estado por donde paseis y se os den los auxilios necesarios para ser conducidos á mi presencia. Muchos de vuestos compañeros pelean ya muy contentos en nuestras filas. Despues de concluida la guerra, la magnánima y generosa nacion mexicana apreciará debidamente los servicios que se le presten y os quedareis entre nosotros cultivando nuestras feraces campiñas. Católicos irlandeses, franceses y alemanes viva la libertad, viva nuestra santa religion.

Huatusco junio 6 de 1847.

Juan Soto.

Gobernador del estado libre y soberano de Veracruz.

A handbill distributed among American soldiers during the war to encourage desertion to the enemy.

Courtesy of the Beinecke Rare Book and Manuscript Library, Yale University, New Haven, Conn.

Most of the enticements held out to the deserters were as illusory as the advance pay and bonuses held out by U.S. volunteer recruiters. Even those who were given officers' commissions were ill-fed and clothed; some officers made do without uniforms or even shoes.[53] It was clear that a great many deserters could not make their way in Mexican society and experienced it as alien and hostile, despite certain inducements held out to them. The estate of common labor in Mexico was that of peonage or of tightly knit indigenous communities. Even artisanal labor involved close legal and physical confinement. The court-martial records were full of cases of men who managed to stay away from their regiments for several months, living on handouts from Mexican officials, or from resident foreigners. Others performed manual labor of one sort or another, but most tended to drift back to the vicinity of the American army, where they were recognized as deserters and turned in for the thirty dollars bounty.

The San Patricio Battalion, which numbered from 200 to 500 men during the war years, was the organized body of American deserters within the Mexican army. These soldiers fought capably and bravely on the Mexican side, particularly at the battle of Monterrey, and in the final battles outside Mexico City. They provided expertise and daring with artillery, a U.S. tactic that had devastated Mexican defenders. In the battles around Mexico City the San Patricios offered formidable resistance to their former comrades.

The battle at Churubusco, outside the capital, was a bloody U.S. assault on a fortified Mexican position. The defenders mowed down waves of U.S. infantry before the walls were breached with artillery. Mexican soldiers in the convent of Churubusco ran up the white flag three times, each time the San Patricios tore it down and continued fighting. About fifty of the San Patricios were tried and hung following their capture at Churubusco in August 1847. After a mass court-marital, the army quickly staged a public execution of thirty-five of the San Patricios. General William S. Harney ordered them dropped from the gallows just as the American flag was raised over the Castle of Chapultepec, during one of the last battles for Mexico City.[54]

The motivations of San Patricio deserters remain somewhat elusive. Individual deserters offered desultory explanations in their own defense, before hostile courts-martial; others remained completely silent as to their motivations. They were of American, German, Irish, or British birth; not a few were career soldiers who simply saw an opportunity for advancement in their own line of work.

Accounts in the U.S. press always referred to San Patricio deserters as Irish. Accounts by those on the scene declare this to be a false characterization of that body of men. The foremost historian of the San Patricio Battalion, Robert R. Miller, looked at a sample of 103 known members of the battalion and found only two-fifths (40) to be Irish-born. The United States contributed 22 members and Germany 14. There was an overwhelming need for the popular press and many Americans to characterize unworthy behavior in some essentialist way, and the Irish were an opportune scapegoat. Even to this day, historians characterize the San Patricios as "Irish." In the days after the battle of Monterrey, desertions occurred at an alarming rate. A U.S. Army officer, noted that desertions were confined largely to English and Germans, and that the "sons of Erin can not be seduced."[55]

John Reilly, major and commanding officer of the San Patricios, was an Irishman by birth, but in his defense before a U.S. Army court-martial identified himself primarily as a British subject, serving in the U.S. Army though not an American citizen. General Arista, of the Mexican army, reportedly told Reilly, that, as a stateless person, he could be shot as a spy unless he agreed to serve in the Mexican forces. This type of coercion was widely reported, though it may have been exaggerated by those on trial for their lives. Another British subject claimed that his enlistment in the U.S. military was invalid, considering that he was a deserter from the British service, and that he had a preexisting pledge to that nation.[56]

However, fealty to national origins or citizenship was but one consideration in the choices of the roving international proletariat that fed the ranks of the regular army. Wages and fair treatment were equal if not superior motivators. These men crossed oceans and continents in search of work and respect, shifting from laborer to seaman, operative, soldier, or navvy, as economic conditions dictated. This comes across powerfully in the statement of a British merchant seaman, in the early 1850s, who deserted to an American ship. Like many British soldiers, this sailor found Quebec a convenient depot for escaping contractual obligations by switching national affiliation. "The living [on British ships] is so bad that men won't put up with it. . . . Nothing will check desertion in the English Service but better wages, better treatment, and better food. The discipline is much the same on board the American as on board the English ships. An English seaman is very little thought of in his own country, but he's well thought of in America. He's a man there."[57]

Several merchant seamen interviewed by a British journalist vowed they would never go to war against the United States, or even that they would fight for America against Britain: "I'll not fight for a country that starves and cheats you. I'll never fight for short weights and stinting in everything, not I."[58] The American merchant marine may have offered a decent living, but Irishmen and Englishmen who deserted the British military in the Mexican War era found precisely "short weights and stinting" in the U.S. Army, as well as disregard for their basic dignity. They sought better conditions wherever available and became serial deserters. But aside from those actually serving with the enemy forces, a small percentage of American deserters were able to remain at large in Mexico, receiving some support from the enemy but avoiding service in their army.

Out of a total of 26,922 enlisted, 2,849 regular army soldiers deserted during the war. Not all of these deserted in Mexico, but enough of these and of volunteer deserters — 3,900 out of 59,000 — were abroad in the land. More compelling than treason were simply opportunism and self-preservation, the very substance of manifest destiny, which wartime propaganda had served to intertwine with patriotic service.[59]

Judging by a sampling of the court-martial records of this period, a more common offense than desertion to the enemy was desertion from a regular unit to an American volunteer regiment. Also not uncommon was desertion from one regular unit to another. In the former case a soldier could hope to negotiate better treatment, and respect, and in the latter case to at least receive an additional signing bonus. A few were among the considerable number of peacetime deserters who left their companies in the United States and later were caught up in the volunteering spirit. Private Philip Smith said in his defense that "when I deserted [from Jefferson Barracks, Missouri] there was no work to do, and as soon as I heard of war, I was one of the first to volunteer." Smith was apprehended in July 1846, only two months into the war.

A William Elliot deserted the regular service in Fort Hamilton, New York, and was apprehended in the First New York Regiment, in Puebla, Mexico. He claimed that "As soon as I heard there was fighting out here in Mexico I joined up."[60] Another regular army private deserted on a march from Brazos Santiago to Matamoras and turned up several months later serving in a volunteer regiment.[61]

The wartime memoirs of William W. Carpenter, a Kentucky volunteer, provide compelling insight into the activities of regular army deserters in Mexico. Mexican cavalrymen captured Carpenter while he was guarding a supply train near Cerralvo, on the Rio Grande. From late 1846 until September 1847 Carpenter was imprisoned in various locales. By the latter date he was in Queretaro, the city to which the Mexican Congress had fled after the fall of the capital. There he made contact with some remnants of the San Patricio company, about fifty men, he claimed, who were at that time serving as a body guard for a general.

Carpenter observed the San Patricio deserters immediately after the heavy losses outside Mexico City; many of these became involved in the fighting among rival Mexican political factions. There was a great deal of civil and military strife over whether to accept a peace treaty: this dispute dragged on until April 1848. The San Patricios were said to be among the peace party, as continued fighting would put them in peril of execution by the Americans.[62]

Carpenter escaped from his captivity and traveled on foot across Mexico, posing as a member of the San Patricio company. He tramped across 2,500 miles of enemy territory, to San Blas, a Pacific port. At major towns along the way he encountered hundreds of American deserters, calling themselves San Patricios, and using that status to obtain lodging, employment, and handouts of cash. American army deserters were fleeing to the west to escape the advancing American troops, and they were afforded a great deal of support from both the government and people according to Carpenter. Each Mexican military garrison was under instructions to aid American deserters on their way west.

Much of the population was incensed by reports of the U.S. Army's atrocities against civilians: the peasant and laboring classes of Mexico were highly conscious of the progress of the war and also quite exercised on behalf of the national cause. Carpenter, traveling on his own, was alternately hailed as a valued ally and threatened as a potential spy. Carpenter's treatment by ordinary townspeople improved dramatically once he assumed the character of a San Patricio. While still a prisoner of war, he contracted a fever in a small town near San Luis Potosí. Some wealthy citizens and the local priest nursed him for several months and befriended him. The "lower classes" of the town, though, abused and threatened the foreign soldier and made at least one attempt on his life. By 1848 the "lower classes" were the only ones still presenting resistance to the North American invaders. Guerrilla warfare against U.S. soldiers and supply trains continued after the central government stopped raising and funding armies, and relied heavily on peasant support. The wealthy classes mixed freely with a variety of foreigners in their midst. Away from the combat areas even American merchants were permitted to do business during the war, although suffering threats and harassment from the local people.

With the help of an American manufacturer, at Salamanca, Carpenter obtained a passport, which entitled him to assistance from alcaldes and military commanders along the way. At Guadalajara he found several "Irishmen," former San Patricios. These men were living wretchedly on handouts and their wits. One of them opened a military academy where he taught "the sword dance," among other things, and apparently was doing a steady business.[63] Mexican tradition valued the military profession as one of the few worthy of a gentleman, and in this regard a soldier might earn more respect, if not financial reward, than in the U.S. service.

Others of the company obtained work at an arsenal making gunstocks. Carpenter was befriended by the Spanish vice-consul; this gentleman offered Carpenter work on his hacienda, but the fugitive was less than enthusiastic. Carpenter observed "that Mexican rancheros were on a level below American slaves," and that he as an American could not perform this sort of labor.[64] Carpenter had knowledge of harness making and applied in the harness and coach building shops of Guadalajara. A Frenchman accepted Carpenter's terms of twenty dollars a month wages, but demanded a six-month contract, unacceptable to the American.

Carpenter moved on when rumors arose that the San Patricios were to be mustered back into service. In a town further west, he appealed to an American businessman, securing his trust by showing him his Oddfellows' card, which he had carefully preserved through all his adventures. The American community of the town rallied around him and gave him money and clothing for the road.[65] In this respect William Carpenter, in the guise of a San Patricio, had a marked advantage over regular army deserters. He was a volunteer of modest but solid origins in an American community. A simple item like an Oddfellows' card was an entrée into that sort of community and its values.

It is apparent that Carpenter's skills as a workman were not enough in a setting where contract labor was the norm, and for an average regular army deserter the types of labor arrangements available in Mexico were far worse than what was available in the United States, and perhaps even worse than contractual service in the U.S. Army. Carpenter finally made his way to San Blas and an American ship in June 1848.[66]

By August 1848 the San Patricios had entirely dispersed, with a small remnant serving in other units. It was remarked that many went west to Guadalupe, and others took to the highways.[67] Amid this general dispersion Carpenter made his own escape. In the aftermath of the peace treaty, many of the deserters were at large, notably on the streets of Mexico City; Americans resident there complained that they made nuisances of themselves as drunkards and beggars.

Despite the inauspicious conditions that San Patricio soldiers encountered in Mexican society, they were for a time lionized by that same society, and their bravery and heroism lauded. Wealthy Mexicans rose to their defense during their trials by the American military; the first families of Mexico City visited them in prison.[68] In a very real sense they had become the "volunteers" of Mexico, valued for their ideals, for their manly and independent choice, and not despised as laborers under contract—this, ironically, in a society that Americans said despised labor. In fact, those who escaped capture by the Americans availed themselves of the privilege of a second desertion, fleeing the crumbling Mexican military cause.

Even in this act they were accorded honor and the thanks of the nation. Like American volunteers, they were not compelled to serve out a contracted term. They had served with honor, shown courage in the field—or merely deserted the infamous invader—and accordingly had proved themselves men and patriots. San Patricio deserters valued the freedom to negotiate honorably the terms of their service. This was a fundamental value of the American volunteer system, and in forming the San Patricio Battalion, American deserters formed their own "volunteer" company, and whatever its ephemerality or precariousness, it came with the familiar honors, rewards, and trappings.

 Atrocity THE WAGE OF MANIFEST DESTINY

The Dirty War

Volunteers committed and repeated the same sort of atrocities as the regulars with the same sorts of justifications, ruling out explanations of these crimes as compulsive or random. The propaganda surrounding the war effort was nakedly opportunistic and expressly promised plunder as the right of the volunteer. The failure of expectations of substantial material gain—in fact, the impoverishment of most Mexican War soldiers—may have raised expectations to the point of a collective consensual justification of plunder and rapine. There were enough contradictory strains in the rhetoric of the war and different interpretations of that rhetoric by soldiers that it is impossible to classify reactions to it neatly.

It is clear that among the despised regular soldiers the characteristic crimes were desertion, desertion to the enemy, and some degree of foraging upon civilians. There was, of course, more restraint placed upon regulars, but in the environment of wartime Mexico, that restraint should not be overemphasized. Regulars were quite willing to choose escape from confining and degrading servitude, rather than seek psychological recompense in meaningless violence. They justified their crimes with reference to oppressive officers and were willing to reject the norms and prejudices of a nationalism and racism to which they were but marginally attached.

Volunteers, on the other hand, often acted with the approval and understanding of their peers. Their proclivity for racist, religious, or nationalist rationales for their crimes took up the language of manifest destiny, suffusing their criminal activity with the heroism and comradeship implicit in that cause. The small-scale community, then, the town-centered peer group, and a less disciplined, more democratic structure of work and living fostered racist violence, perhaps compensating for diminished expectations, but almost certainly offering a link with a broader group of soldiers, particularly with that idealized group, the Texas volunteers.

Volunteers' crimes against Mexicans were not committed under pressures of regimentation, or severe discipline, or the dictates of large anonymous institutions; rather, atrocity was a social phenomenon developing in tandem with the volunteer process, which brought together men and communities ostensibly in celebration of republican principles, and acquisitive nationalism.

It is revealing that the Texas ideal was not entirely rooted in a place or restricted to the inhabitants of that place. One of the most celebrated of the Ranger companies was that of Captain Samuel Walker, who raised his company mainly in Baltimore.[1] It was possible to manufacture volunteer units, creating communities that had no local basis, drawing upon a national population. A charismatic leader like Walker and the popular identification with the Texan cause were powerful enough to create volunteer communities. A national war press made this group identity accessible to tens of thousands of American men.

Widespread volunteering for the war brought together white men from diverse social and economic strata in service of territorial expansion and brought them into contact with a troubled but undeniably sovereign and nationalistic neighboring republic. The considerable resistance of ordinary Mexicans, their ability to confound expectations of servility and easy conquest, paradoxically, did nothing to decrease pronouncements of Mexicans' inherent unfitness to inhabit their own land.[2]

It was common for more articulate soldiers, those who wrote about their experiences, to deplore the random commission of atrocities and yet, at the same time, to express admiration for the Texans, with perhaps some reservations about their excesses. The massacres perpetrated by the Rangers were "not justifiable" according to Luther Giddings, an Ohio volunteer. The "reprisal" killings outside of Monterrey of twenty-four Mexican men "forms one of the darkest passages in the history of the campaign."[3] This massacre was largely perpetrated by Gray's Texas cavalry, which Giddings acknowledged to be a bold and effective fighting force. Giddings denied that any of his own regiment had any part in any retaliation killings whatsoever.

But diarists and correspondents who proclaimed detachment from criminal activity often uttered the most damning racial and national denunciations of Mexicans, as if to blame the Mexicans for causing the depravity of American volunteers. The Mexicans' want of energy and prowess, Giddings said, condemned them to the lot of "vagrant herdsmen shepherds while others would reap the wealth of their land."[4]

YOUNG TEXAS IN REPOSE.

An antislavery view of Texas, ca. 1845. This cartoon portrays a Texas society situated, literally, upon the back of slavery. Courtesy of the Beinecke Rare Book and Manuscript Library, Yale University, New Haven, Conn.

It was extremely rare for an individual volunteer to break ranks with his fellows and unashamedly declare that his comrades were out-and-out murderers. Even to admit this to oneself without rationalizations was virtually impossible for a volunteer, so fused was he with the group identity. There were, of course, regulars and civilians who indignantly noted the wanton violence of the volunteers, but the sheer volume of heroic accounts in the popular press overwhelmed these notes of protest. Regular officers and soldiers, for example, bitterly denounced the crimes of the volunteers.

One of the few newspapers that solicited their commentary was the *Mercury* of Charleston, South Carolina, which published the dispatches of Lieutenant Daniel Harvey Hill and other regulars. The *Mercury* published the letter of a regular private to his father, which read in part: "The majority of the Volunteers sent here, are a disgrace to the nation; think of one of them shooting a woman while washing on the bank of the river—merely to *test* his rifle; another tore forcibly from a Mexican woman the rings from her ears. Their officers take no notice of these outrages, and the offenders escape. If these things are sent to the papers, they are afraid to publish, and so it happens."[5]

There was a very vocal antiwar press, and they published many accounts of unprovoked depredations upon the Mexican people, but the closed mouths and closed ranks of the volunteers made it difficult to achieve corroboration of these stories. Also, Whig political papers had large constituencies in the army, which they were not eager to offend.

If the Mexican War was a step forward for U.S. "nationalism,"[6] it was in the achievement of state-sponsored murder through a loose confederation of communities and irregular companies. A vigorous national press and popular culture aided in the manufacture of these groups, out of individuals from diverse backgrounds.

Bowery B'hoys and Sports
The ad hoc communities that were Mexican War volunteer companies had a powerful influence over individual behavior This phenomenon was certainly familiar to those from small-town backgrounds, but urban cultures of sociability provided a strong normative social environment for workers and others on the margins of city life, and were themselves important communities in the 1840s. Urban life created a much broader swath of shared language and values, transcending locality. It idealized violent and entrepreneurial models of society and was more suited to a mass military structure

than the more idiosyncratic values of the small town. The popularity of the minstrel show, with its jocular racism, the sociability of the music hall, the barroom, and the prize ring were all recreated in Mexico and provided a common basis of community.

The language of the streets came through poignantly in the last words of a condemned soldier, about to be hung under sentence of a military court. A regular army dragoon ascended the scaffold outside Mexico City in January 1848 for "the killing of an inoffensive Mexican." A soldier witnessing the event commented that "the miserable wretch was intoxicated and of course incapable of appreciating the awful condition into which he was plunged, and to show his recklessness he called out and said tell old Scott he was going home, that he was one of the b'hoys."[7]

It is possible to dismiss this individual as purely pathological in his violence, but this fatal evocation of solidarity suggests deeper roots of his criminality. He thumbed his nose at General Scott, an embodiment of national identity, yet he called on his fellows to validate his life and death, invoking the widespread idiom of street culture. This individual met his doom essentially for following the norms of his peer group, and those norms clashed with a rule of law that was imposed harshly and sporadically—only when the officer class had the means and desire to enforce it upon individuals who viewed that law as alien. If colonization and racial dominance were goals of the U.S. occupation, then the U.S. government needed an obedient, law-abiding white caste to police the boundaries of herrenvolk democracy. When regulars and immigrants claimed to be part of the ruling group of citizens—one of the b'hoys—they broke a crucial link in the chain of control.

Another figure with obvious Bowery antecedents comes to light in connection with racial brutality in the war. Chris Lilly was a lieutenant in a Louisiana cavalry unit and served on the staff of General Joseph Lane, the commander of a special antiguerrilla regiment. Lilly was a New York prizefighter and protégé of prominent gamblers, including Moses Chanfrau—that is until he killed the boxer McCoy in an illegal bare-knuckle contest and found it expedient to disappear from the New York area. In 1846 Lilly was one of the "fancy" in New Orleans, involved in gambling and "sporting" life. An Indiana volunteer posted to Lane's brigade noted that Lilly's superior, Captain Lewis, of Louisiana, was commonly styled "the Count" and that the men in the company rode only the finest mounts, brought directly from the States. The Indianan noted the "Count"'s chivalric nature, and that he

Lewis Cass, Democratic presidential candidate, in the role of Bowery B'hoy. This political cartoon skeptically regards the presidential election of 1848 as a back alley brawl. Even Zachary Taylor, with a reputation as the unassuming friend of the common soldier, is no match for the "b'hoy," a cultural hero celebrated on the popular stage. Note how Cass's words echo those of the defiant soldier on the gallows in chapter 6.

"abhorred mean acts." In the characteristic ambivalent manner of volunteer chroniclers, he noted that he never "entertained a good opinion of Lilly": on the other hand his "bravery cannot be questioned."[8]

Daniel Harvey Hill, the censorious regular officer, observed that Lilly off-handedly murdered a Mexican man, in a display of bravado. Hill tended to admire the Texas Ranger companies, who were brutally effective against the guerrillas. The Rangers asked few questions when retaliating against Mexicans, and Hill was not sentimental about Mexican lives lost. Lieutenant Hill, however, deplored Lilly's random violence as an act of self-gratification that might cause unnecessary reprisals against U.S. soldiers. Despite his frequent criticisms of the government's conduct of the war, Hill saw himself as a professional, loyal to the national cause, whatever elite interests might be controlling that cause. Chris Lilly moved easily from the world of urban sport, to dashing cavalryman, to filibuster, to political boss in San Francisco after the war. He was killed by Guatemalan authorities while running supplies to William Walker's filibusters in 1857.[9]

Lilly's presence in Mexico evoked a complex interweaving of old fashioned notions of chivalry and honor with newer phenomena of print culture, street life, and popular entertainment. The boldly theatrical elements of manifest destiny had their actors, and for these players Mexico provided a flamboyant setting. Aristocratic trappings were adopted by gentlemen and urban sportsmen alike, and in envisioning themselves in the roles of conquers these individuals lived out, for a brief time, the fantasy of playing aristocrat in a foreign land, surrounded by subjects. As a northerner in a southern regiment, Lilly was extraordinarily adept at playing the game of competitive racism. He had not the deference to "betters" that might have inhibited southern white yeomen.

Scorched Earth: Official and Unofficial Policy
In the aftermath of the Mexican War a regular officer commented on what he felt to be an unprovoked reign of terror in northern Mexico.

We have often heard of deeds of extreme cruelty perpetrated by [Mexicans] on the Rio Grande; but it remains to be seen how far they were acts of retaliation, provoked, (but not justified) by the outrages they have endured. From Saltillo to Mier, with the exception of the large towns, all is a desert, and there is scarcely a solitary house (if there be one) inhabited. The smiling villages which welcomed our troops on their upward march are now black and smouldering ruins, the gardens and orange groves destroyed, and the inhabitants, who administered to their necessities, have sought refuge in the mountains. The march of Attila was not more withering and destructive.[10]

In order to place some limits on terror, or at least to funnel it toward genuine antiguerrilla activity, the American command was determined to garrison volunteers away from Mexican towns. The regular troops were stationed in the towns, and Mexican citizens quickly learned to differentiate between the two branches of the service, the volunteers, reputed to be thoroughly savage, and the regulars, of a more gentlemanly demeanor. Official accounts and histories of the war have portrayed the relative magnanimity of the Americans as an occupying force. Generals Scott and Taylor insisted that all food and supplies needed by the troops be paid for in cash and in voluntary and negotiated sales. In the case of confiscated or stolen goods the army honored claims of aggrieved Mexicans and frequently made good on those claims. The precarious position of a relatively small invading force made it advisable to pursue this course. Goods that might have otherwise been secreted or destroyed by local populations were offered up for sale to the Americans in return for premium prices. In fact, ordinary Mexicans viewed some of the policies of the American occupiers with favor, particularly the suspension of onerous taxes and internal tariffs. In the occupied regions the alcabala, an excise tax on trade goods, was abolished. This tax was levied on goods sold in the public markets; it was especially hard on the indigenous peoples and other rural people who traded in the towns.[11]

The official American military policy toward civilians was quite lenient, with respect to the voluntary payment for supplies. The superior wealth of the American forces meant that they brought at least some of their own food, clothing, and weapons. The Mexican forces levied contributions of food, clothing, and recruits upon their own population; this had also been common practice in the interminable civil and regional wars of the young republic. Some but certainly not all of these contributions were voluntary.

The loose disciplinary structure of the American army made enforcement of a compensation and reparations policy rather difficult. The volunteers' presence in the countryside acted to discourage claims upon the quartermaster: a very real threat of retaliation was ever present. Beneath the official war of campaigns and strategy simmered guerrilla conflicts, reprisal and counterreprisal. The Texas Ranger companies, in particular, were notorious for establishing a reign of terror upon the countryside and elicited unfavorable comment from even some volunteer soldiers. Some of the Texans had deep-seated grudges against Mexicans, remnants of years of guerrilla warfare with the Mexican government, and Hispanic and Indian peoples living in Texas.

The Rangers were attached to each army division as scouts and were allowed a large degree of freedom in their movements. In battle and in occupation duties, the actions of the Texas volunteers were closely coordinated with the actions of the regular army. Regular officers were deeply suspicious of the discipline and fighting ability of most of the volunteers, but the Texans were relied on as scouts and as light cavalry in major engagements. Their utility to the army meant that no questions were asked when they went on rampages against civilians.

After the fiercely contested battle for the city of Monterrey in October 1846, General Worth briefly discontinued military patrols in the city, and a massive bloodletting was soon underway. One regular officer estimated that at least one hundred inhabitants were murdered, other outrages committed, and the thatched huts of the peasants burned (the other buildings in the city being fireproof). Apparently the crime spree was the responsibility of the Texas cavalry under Colonel Hays while the remaining volunteers were quartered outside the city.[12]

An ambush on a U.S. wagon train outside Cerralvo, north of Monterrey, left a dozen teamsters dead and 40 of 120 wagons missing or destroyed. This occurred in March 1847 after the battle of Buena Vista. A body of Texas Rangers detached itself from the main force, ostensibly to seek out forage, but actually looking for revenge. "Mustang" Grey, the notorious Texan colonel, and his men sought revenge upon "the first Mexicans they encountered," according to Ohio volunteer Luther Giddings: "The departure of the Rangers therefore, seemed to bode evil to the neighboring rancheros; for human vengeance, —especially Texan vengeance of the *Gray species*—armed with power is seldom over nice in the exercise of it."[13] It was soon learned that a village near the American camp was attacked and twenty-four men put to death.

According to Samuel Chamberlain this infamous incident was part of a larger campaign of reprisal "unleashed" by General Taylor upon the people of Nuevo Leon and Tamaulipas. In addition, a "tax" was assessed on the population to pay for goods lost from the wagon train. Taylor collected more than $1 million from Mexicans in Nuevo Leon in recompense. "The people

Lieutenant Abner Doubleday, First U.S. Artillery Regiment, with unidentified Mexicans. This daguerreotype reflects the immersion of occupying U.S. soldiers in the Mexican population. Relations between soldiers and civilians were often casual and cordial. Doubleday's motley garb is typical of the hard-pressed and individualistic volunteers. Courtesy of the Beinecke Rare Book and Manuscript Library, Yale University, New Haven, Conn.

of these states had a hard time during the summer of 1847, plundered by both sides, their lives often taken and their wives and daughters outraged and carried off." [14]

General Taylor responded to the protests of aggrieved Mexicans with denial of complicity in or prior knowledge of the massacre. He claimed to have investigated the matter rigorously but said he was unable to identify the culprits. Witnesses to the massacre failed to come forward, "being afraid that they might incur a similar fate." [15]

In early 1847 the outrages occurring north of the Sierra Madre excited protests from even staunchly promilitary commentators. George W. Kendall, correspondent and editor of the New Orleans *Picayune*, excoriated the cowardly, unmanly behavior of the Indiana and Ohio troops. Common sol-

diers committed rape and pillage throughout Nueva Leon, while the democratically elected officers looked the other way. Ever the diplomatic friend of
the volunteer, General Taylor uncharacteristically lost his temper and said
to an Ohio company of volunteers, "You are all a G-d d——d set of thieves
and cowards; you never came here to fight, but to rob and plunder, and will
run at the first sight of the enemy."[16]

George W. Kendall commented on the behavior of the garrison near
Punta Aguda; it had committed offenses "that *negroes* in a state of insurrec-
tion would hardly be guilty of."[17] Kendall, like many prominent New Orleanians, had significant personal and business interest in the Texan and
Mexican wars and was not one to make pious pronouncements on behalf
of Mexicans or anyone else in the way of American expansion. He had participated in the 1842 Texas military expedition against New Mexico and
had been imprisoned by the Mexican authorities. A carefully coordinated
strategy of robbery and reprisal was not outside his experience as a Texas
partisan. In the Texas experience, however, these raids were coordinated by
organized bands, led by respected and seasoned officers. With such a background, he must have considered the wholesale and unplanned foraging in
the north of Mexico not only brutal but ineffective or downright counterproductive.

Kendall was limited in the ways in which he could make criticisms of
other racists—by equating the offenders with the race whom they were attacking, or with another subject race. The accused had violated the code of
honor, in which violence was dispensed in hierarchical, albeit rudimentarily
organized ways. Captain John S. Ford, a Texas cavalryman under Colonel
Jack Hays, gave insight into this code in his memoirs, in which he admitted
to wholesale massacres to avenge one murdered ranger; he cast aspersion,
however, upon petty theft by an individual ranger.[18]

Whatever violence and looting were acknowledged, among the volunteers
or in the press, were usually justified as reprisal for the attacks on American
stragglers and small patrols. One Ohio volunteer commented that he found
it "understandable, but not justified," that many soldiers sought retaliations
for assaults and murders made upon their ranks by civilians and guerrillas.
It was more honorable in his view to seek blood upon the battlefield.

But an insider, in one of the regiments most noted for attacks on civilians, took a different view. Sergeant John Palmer of the Arkansas Regiment
wrote the following in his diary: "A portion of our Regiment are assuming to

act as *Guerrillas,* and have been killing, I fear *innocent,* Mexicans as they meet them, and then come into camp and report that the Mexicans tried to lariate them. This has led to reprisal and recrimination until it is dangerous to be out alone."

Sergeant Palmer took for granted his freedom to move about alone in occupied country, demonstrating the relative friendliness of Coahuilans toward Americans early in the occupation. Toward the end of December 1846 Palmer noted that a soldier had been badly wounded by Mexicans while on guard, and he feared that the Arkansans would perpetrate a severe retaliation.[19] In February 1847 affairs between the volunteers and Mexican civilians deteriorated. After further outrages by American soldiers, Mexicans murdered an Arkansas cavalryman, Archibald Colquitt. In the view of Samuel Chamberlain, the regular army dragoon, the murder of Colquitt was in itself a reprisal for a raid upon the Agua Nueva rancho on Christmas Day 1846. This "rancho" was a village, comprising the dwellings of several small ranchers. Chamberlain characterized this incident as an orgy of rape and robbery by the volunteers.

The revenge for Colquitt's death was swift and brutal. Men from the Arkansas cavalry companies of captains Danly and Hunter rode out to where the inhabitants of Agua Nueva had taken refuge from the impending clash of the Taylor and Santa Anna's armies—the battle of Buena Vista, as it turned out. There the Arkansans claimed to have found personal items belonging to Colquitt. By the time other Americans intervened twenty-five to thirty Mexican men, civilians, were dead, while their families stood by in horror. General Taylor vowed to hang the responsible parties, but after a court of inquiry failed to identify specific culprits, the general ordered the two companies back to the mouth of the Rio Grande. Archibald Yell, colonel of Arkansas volunteers, protested to Taylor, threatening to withdraw the entire regiment. Consequently, Danly and Hunter's men remained and participated in the battle of Buena Vista. In April, only two months before their enlistments were to expire, they were finally sent downriver to await shipment home.[20]

In addition to political complications, General Taylor found major legal obstacles to prosecuting criminal acts by soldiers and others. The existing articles of war made no provision for punishment of crimes of soldiers against civilians, and Congress was loath to authorize any punitive action against the volunteers. American military law stated that crimes against civilians be turned over to civil courts—either American or foreign—and in

Mexico, American soldiers could easily intimidate or buy off the courts. American military governors shipped offenders to New Orleans for trial, at which place they were generally able to obtain their release under habeas corpus. Regulars, however, continued to be punished according to the strict standards of the U.S. Army. D. H. Hill, the judge advocate of a military commission near Chalco, tried a number of soldiers for stealing from the Mexicans. He considered the sentences to be quite severe, typically thirty lashes with a rawhide, and commented, "It seems inconsistent and cruel that regular soldiers the veterans of so many fights should be punished so severely for foraging upon the enemy . . . when the volunteers commit far worse acts in times of tranquility with perfect impunity."[21]

In a war in which the United States never lost a battle, the much vaunted magnanimity of the victors was belied by the hidden dirty war. As the Mexican War stretched into 1847, and a quick victory was clearly out of reach, the difficult advance on the city of Mexico got underway. General Winfield Scott was determined to eradicate the problems with discipline that had plagued Taylor in the northern campaigns. He deemed many of the volunteer regiments unsuitable for an efficient force, operating in the heart of enemy territory. General Scott took aside the Ohio volunteer general Samuel Curtis and lectured him on the "abominations" committed by his troops. Scott left this general and the Third Ohio on the Rio Grande, despite a previous promise to bring them along to Veracruz.

General Scott made genuine attempts to impose better order and had some success. A particular problem was with civilians and discharged soldiers attached to the American army; they were beholden to no one for their behavior. Military law gave no jurisdiction over civilians, and the Mexican civil courts were intimidated by the American presence. Scott issued Field Order 20 in February 1847, which established military courts to try all Americans for crimes against Mexicans. He was prompted to this measure by egregious behavior from the very outset of the campaign, when troops rioted immediately after the taking of Veracruz. Soldiers and sailors together went into a hamlet, Boca Rio, broke into a liquor store, robbed and raped their way through the settlement, and partially burned it. Public whippings and a hanging followed and served to somewhat deter subsequent pillaging.[22]

Scott desired a controlled campaign, with any irregular attacks to be focused tightly on actual guerrilla activity and its support networks. In many areas, however, hostility to the invaders was so great and random depredations by soldiers so pervasive that almost any Mexican acquired the intentions if not the capabilities of a guerrilla. Scott, like Taylor, levied a "tax" on Mexican towns and cities when his men were picked off by guerrillas, and during 1847 extracted $300 from localities for each soldier killed in their vicinity.[23]

The entrance of American troops into the Mexican capital on September 14, 1847, after some of the bloodiest fighting of the war was attended with bitter irregular skirmishes and looting. Scott brought up his crack anti-guerrilla forces from Puebla, composed of several companies of Texas cavalry, and they made forays into the city before the entry of the army, burning, looting, and killing. Santa Anna publicly promised the citizens of Mexico City that he would defend the capital street by street, but on the night of September 13 he and his army retreated quietly northward.

The citizenry were left to defend themselves, and did so fiercely for two days, in hastily formed bands, and with some militia units possessing limited resources of artillery and muskets. The entry into the city went quietly in the early morning hours, the army occupying the central square and the Alameda. But by midday a bloody street fight broke out in part of the city. Lieutenant D. H. Hill claimed that American casualties that day were a little less than 200 killed and wounded and the Mexican loss significantly greater, "as we repeatedly fired on the Mob with grape and cannister."

The American troops adopted the practice of rifling every house from which a shot came and killing every armed Mexican found on the street. "This stern course . . . corrupted our men most fearfully. Many of them were perfectly frantic with the lust of blood and plunder. In order to sack rich houses many soldiers pretended that they heard firing from them."[24]

The Americans occupied and administered Mexico City for the next eight months, waiting for the negotiation of peace. There were no more staged battles, and the remainder of the action was guerrilla and counter-guerrilla fighting. But the undisciplined, and officially discountenanced war between soldier and civilian continued.

In early 1848 Mexicans murdered a Texas cavalryman known by his comrades as "Cutthroat" in the capital; the following night Texans perpetrated a massacre; random shooting persisted in the quarter where the murder took place for at least two hours. The next morning the city morgue reported eighty bodies unclaimed by friends or relatives. It was reported that regular army patrols heard the shooting and joined in the massacre.

General Scott later summoned Colonel Hays, and inquired:

"Colonel, is it so that your men have killed six Mexicans in the city?"

"Yes, general, the Mexicans piled rocks on a house and began stoning my men, and they used arms in self-defense."

The general said it was right, and the matter ended.

Depredations ranged from drunken assaults, rapes, and horse thievery to carefully planned and massive robberies. Of the latter there was one widely publicized incident involving what seemed to be a burglary ring, which included several officers and a handful of enlisted men. Their bungled robbery of a merchant house in Mexico City left three dead and several wounded. Four of the bank robbers were sentenced to be hung by the military authorities.[25] The convicted were three lieutenants of the Pennsylvania and Massachusetts volunteers; a fourth was a French Canadian. The treaty of peace was signed a few days before the scheduled hanging, and the death sentences revoked.[26]

Violence and the Catholic Church

Given the strongly anti-Catholic rhetoric embedded in manifest destiny, and in American political debates of the 1840s, it is not surprising that churches were particular targets of both calculated and spontaneous raids by Americans. Even the "soft" side of manifest destiny, which allowed for ameliorative reform of the Mexican people, called for the annihilation of the church as the chief corrupting element in the society. In the press back home and within the army, the church was fair game for attacks. It represented wealth and inordinate social power, the remnant of a colonial system. Attacking churches was more in line with the underlying legitimizations of the war than stripping peasants' fields. Soldiers clamored for democracy in the ranks of the army, and if they believed that they were bringing democracy to Mexico, then churches should be stripped of their ostentation, just as their own officers needed to be brought in accord with republican principles.

General Scott and his field officers realized the potential for a powerful backlash, by the Mexican people, against religious persecution and desecration; they sincerely tried to implement policies of respect for religion. Scott courted the Mexican clergy, soliciting and attaining their goodwill. The church hierarchy, in fact, saw more danger to its extensive property from its own nation's liberals than from the U.S. Army, despite the rampages of individual soldiers. As the Cincinnati *Catholic Telegraph* phrased it: "The altars of our holy faith have been profaned, and the hope of plunder, loudly proclaimed by many, will doubtless be gratified, notwithstanding the warnings of Generals, and of those who regard the honor of their country. . . . No power of the sword can subdue the reason and conscience of a Catholic people."[27]

With the sweeping success of the U.S. armies in Mexico, the sense of mission and license grew in the minds of the latter-day conquerors: they brought political and religious liberation and would surely be rewarded with gold and land. This bounty could be mined or looted. This unleashing of greed upon potential victims, variously categorized as political, racial, or religious enemies, had unpredictable implications, and would ultimately feed upon American society itself.

American Catholics played an important role in the fighting, and just as at home in the United States, they stood by and watched Protestants attack their churches, while the constituted authorities responded to these attacks in ambiguous ways.

As the Roman Catholic chaplain of the American army, Father John McElroy, celebrated mass in a church at Matamoros, he aroused the cupidity of two onlookers, which was remarked on with disgust by the Catholic volunteer Stanislaus Lasselle. "Last Sunday while the priest was taking sacrament in a gold chalice, I saw one volunteer wink to another as much as to say that that was not quite a little 'Jesus' but the next thing to it. The chalice was of solid gold and must be worth at least one thousand dollars."[28]

Others were more specific in identifying the Catholic Church as the main enemy and obstacle to freeing up the hoarded wealth of Mexico. For some Protestants the church was the master spirit of the racial miscegenation, political corruption, and economic and social backwardness of Mexico. One volunteer officer wrote to his cousin, a Protestant minister:

> I wish I had the power to strip their churches . . . to bring off this treasure hoard of gold silver and jewels, and to put the greasy priests, monks, friars and other officials at work on the public highways as a preliminary step to mending their ways. . . . It is perfectly certain that this war is a divine dispensation intended to purify and punish this misguided nation. . . . Most of our officers concur with me that nothing but a divine ruler and commander could have brought us safely through so much peril against awful odds.[29]

Even an American Catholic could conceive of the war as a righteous chastisement of the Mexicans and their church: "I cannot help but think,

128

that God has fought upon our side, to chastise them for their sins." Julius Garesché, a Catholic regular army officer, attributed the fallen state of Mexico to lax morality and corruption within the Church. He believed that "with such a holy and zealous band in their place, as is our Catholic priesthood of the United States, I feel quite sure that all could be amended here; for the people are mild and amiable in their disposition, docile and easily led and born with an instinctive reverence for religion."[30]

But Garesché also believed, in common with many Protestants, that chastisement was also due to the United States, and that racial destiny was vainglory and folly. Far from lifting Americans to new heights, the experience of war had corrupted those who had gone to Mexico:

> What I allude to is the great and almost universal moral debasement into which our people have fallen out here [in Mexico]. . . . Is it not to be feared that, on our return, transplanted . . . with us will be the seeds of these vices and disseminated throughout the whole length and breadth of all the land, meeting with toleration and perhaps even finding favour in many eyes, from the prestige of military glory, so dear to our countrymen which will surround them—is it not to be feared that they may strike deep roots in our soil, and spread, and bring forth baleful fruit in the course of the next ten or twenty years![31]

From his vantage point of Camargo, on the Rio Grande, Garesché watched the volunteers dispersing to and from the occupied areas and was disgusted with their abuse of the local population. He observed destiny in the course of events, but it was a malign and immoral destiny. Garesché, with his strong Catholic outlook, was quite willing to attribute responsibility to individual Americans, rather than credit some overweening—and not particularly Christian—manifest destiny. But he was inclined to attribute an essential evil to Mexicans and their institutions.

About Mexican women, Garesché commented that, despite having become "reconciled to their dark complexions," he found it "impossible to entertain any respect for their morality."[32] As a member of a persecuted group in American society, Garesché was disappointingly quick to condemn others; but his logic defended his religious affiliation to some extent. The church was reformable, with American Catholic oversight; only then could the difficult job of reforming Mexicans' morality begin. Garesché's own entanglement in the language of racial destiny left him unable to speak out strongly against the stripping of churches by his comrades. He had imbibed the program of cultural and racial superiority, and had dutifully gone to fight for it. He could find fault with some of the methods of conquest but not the master plan.

Other soldiers were much less philosophical about attacking an easy and appealing mark. A member of the notorious "Killers" of the First Pennsylvania Regiment, and apparently a Catholic, robbed a priest of a gold crucifix and watch. The soldier, John (Pat) O'Brien, was arrested and defended successfully by regimental officers in a military tribunal. Private Oswandel, of the same regiment, said O'Brien arranged for his comrades to swear to his alibi. Oswandel commented skeptically that O'Brien "was lying in his camp sick, (in a pig's eye,) for during the trial, Capt. Small had the stolen watch in his pocket as his fee to defend Pat O'Brien. A good and heavy swearing company, D, [the Killers]. Pat and his friends are in high glee over his acquittal. He can sin again and ask the priest to forgive his sins."[33]

O'Brien was one of a handful of Irish-surnamed individuals in this company formed out of a notorious Philadelphia gang, known for nativist violence. He had obviously made the grade as "one of the b'hoys" and observed the codes of gang behavior. In Mexico this behavior was almost indistinguishable from the code of the volunteer, including especial hostility against priests. The connivance of the officers in a matter involving an attack on a priest is interesting, particularly considering that one month previously two of the members of Company D were prosecuted for robbery and attempted rape upon a Mexican woman. One of the offenders was hanged.[34]

The complicity and direct culpability of company officers in attacks on churches was widespread. Churches were an easy target and, as such, allowed officers to give their men access to plunder, shelter, and "glorious" triumphs over the enemy.

The prior of a Mexico City convent wrote a letter describing the typical sorts of abuses that he encountered as American troops quartered on the premises and foraged in the vicinity. He spoke of the rapacious stripping of his church, which included desecration of sacristies and altars, "raising the stones that cover the sepluchres, breaking to pieces the chairs, and tearing the cushions of confessionals in search of money or valuable articles."

> All of this I have proved in presence of a commissioner from the governor of the district and of several chiefs of the troops who have seen the images stripped and the coffers, the drawers and the pantries where we keep the sacred ornaments . . . entirely empty. . . .

Today when we were singing a solemn mass in the chapel of the Rosary, they threw in two four-pound balls.[35]

The misuse of artillery and ammunition in such a reckless escapade indicates the complicity or indifference of officers to crimes against churches.

Near Saltillo, in the north, Texas Rangers tore the crucifix down from a church altar and dragged it through the street. With their horses they trampled the venerable parish priest. The residents of the town, enraged, counterattacked, but the Rangers inflicted severe casualties upon the townspeople, "sparing neither age or sex in their terrible fury."[36]

The Fourth Indiana officers bullied their way into a monastery in the city of Puebla. They secured their lodgings by choking the "head monk" and threatening others with Bowie knives and pistols. When the priests continued to ring the monastery bells for the Angelus, the Indianans cut the bell ropes to dispense with this annoyance.[37]

Also in the occupied city of Puebla, American soldiers showed *respect* for Catholic priests; this raised a storm of nativist protest in the United States. The press published several exaggerated accounts of the incident, the chief feature of which was that American volunteers were ordered to kneel in formation as a procession of the host made its way through the main square of the city. The order to kneel was apparently given by Colonel Childs, military governor of the city, and a stickler for discipline. Accounts of the procession invariably mentioned that Childs bore the character of a martinet and that he had volunteers' heads shaved for petty crimes against Mexican civilians, marching them through the streets in public humiliation.[38]

This inexorable coupling of Catholic obeisance and military discipline shows the fervor with which volunteers hated the personally demeaning regimen of work and servility imposed by officers like Childs. They despised his imperious attitude and his treatment of them as inferiors.[39] They perceived this same entrenched caste privilege in the ritual of the Catholic Church and lashed out in that direction, the church being more accessible than the officer class.

Curiously enough, the volunteers came to regard Childs as a hero. A Mexican army under Santa Anna besieged Puebla for a month, while the main body of Scott's army was fighting in the Valley of Mexico. Childs defiantly held out against overwhelmingly superior numbers, and his discipline paid off in a difficult military situation. The Massachusetts volunteers feted Childs at their homecoming celebration for his leadership during the siege.[40]

American soldiers saw in Mexican institutions and society a corrupted reflection of themselves and their own institutions. Only occasionally did they admit the distinctiveness and tenacity of Mexican society. Mexico was indeed top-heavy with an entrenched, quarrelsome, and failing elite, which Americans recognized, but they reserved most of their scorn for the "inferior" mixed-race common people.

Actually, the most promising segments of Mexican society, for democracy and productivity, were buried in the provinces, and in the mixed-race lower classes. This was something that Americans had a great deal of trouble acknowledging, and which was equally threatening to Mexican elites, to the extent that they surrendered the war effort against the United States rather than cede control over the peasant masses.

Mexican Resistance

North American observers and participants in the Mexican War scorned and derided many aspects of the Mexican war effort. Formal military resistance collapsed within little over a year of the commencement of fighting. North Americans occasionally expressed admiration for the Mexican soldier, and even some of his officers, and wondered how well the U.S. invaders would have fared had the enemy been better organized and equipped.

But blanket condemnations or praise obscured the diverse political and class elements in Mexico, a few of which were energetically engaged in fighting the invader, but many more of which were fighting each other. The very survival of Mexico as a sovereign nation in the wake of the 1846–48 war was stark testimony that resistance continued from some important sectors of the population even after the central government was unable or unwilling to put armies in the field against the enemy. The continuation of guerrilla warfare in 1847 and 1848, along with guerrilla pressure on collaborationist Mexicans seriously hampered U.S. efforts to establish a permanent occupation. Popular resistance made the scale of the occupation project huge, putting to the test the political will of the United States, and ultimately forcing the occupation back to the northern territories.

The historiography of Mexico's war against the United States has focused overwhelmingly on the internecine struggles among political elites. The rift between liberal and conservative politicians and generals would continue to intensify in the 1850s and 1860s, during turbulent years of constitutional reforms, civil war, and French occupation. Divisions among Mexican elites sapped efforts to resist the U.S. invaders. The presidency changed hands two times during the short war; Santa Anna, the leading organizer of military resistance. was often at odds with the executive and congress. The squabbling politicians propelled Mexico headlong into a destructive, unwinnable war. In the years leading up to 1846, rival politicians and generals vied to outdo one another with anti-American posturing, which played well with the Mexican public. Absent from the elite political dialogue was any substantial advocacy of social and economic reforms. Military posturing over Texas precluded any serious negotiations with the United States and led Mexico into a war it had little chance of winning.[41]

Questions of mass participation in the war and, indeed, of social history in the pre-Reforma Mexican republic have remained obscure.[42] Recent histories of peasant revolts in nineteenth-century Mexico have disinterred some of the popular experience; even those lower- and middle-class elements most committed to resisting the invasion were simultaneously fighting against or alongside the elites in battles over politics and land. But class divisions and class warfare were even more destructive to the war effort than intraelite squabbling.

The most ardent patriots, whatever their social backgrounds, called for a temporary suspension of internal struggles until the invader could be driven out. The social portrait of Mexican resistance during the 1846–48 war prefigured the civil struggles to come over reform, the dismantling of colonial institutions and laws, and the rights of mixed-race and indigenous peoples.

When Santa Anna abandoned Mexico City to the ravages of the Texas Rangers, and the rest of the U.S. Army, it was the poor and middling people of the city that held off a well-equipped army for two days. An eyewitness noted that a priest on horseback, followed by a few men, called upon the patriotism of citizens to fight in the streets. He attracted a large spontaneous force to fight with him. One of the militia units that pinned down General Worth's division with artillery fire, the same witness reported, was led and composed of the city's physicians. General Scott pointedly declared the defenders of Mexico City to be "leperos," that is, vagabonds, supplemented by prisoners released from the local jails.[43] Scott shrewdly catered to the elite clergy and property owners, by echoing their opinion of these middle-class elements.

While some of these low-level clerics and professionals would become the backbone of the radical wing of Mexican liberalism, during the Reforma movement of the 1850s some of the conservative bureaucrats and clergy manifested strong national consciousness. Both conservative and liberal politicians, however, seemed willing to cede power to the invader rather than allow their political enemies to gain the upper hand.

The liberals advocated economic modernization, following the model of the United States, along with suppression of the political power of the church and the strengthening of secular institutions. The conservative faction in Mexico supported the church and wanted to ally the nation politically and economically with one of the stronger Catholic nations of Europe, perhaps even reestablishing a monarchy. Liberals fell into disfavor in the years immediately after the war, because it was the United States that had ravaged Mexico. Furthermore, despite middle-class resistance to the invaders in Mexico, a group of *puro* liberals led by Miguel Lerdo de Tejado secured election to Mexico City's *ayuntamiento*, or city council, during the American occupation with the support of U.S. authorities. They cooperated with the U.S. occupiers and took advantage of the situation to launch a program of radical political, social, and economic reforms. While other individuals, including conservatives, found reasons to work with the enemy, the collaboration of the liberal *ayuntamiento* earned them the label of traitors. Liberal politicians, despite their progressive views, were still a strongly elite group, unwilling or unable to reach across class and racial lines.[44]

Ultimately, it was guerrilla warfare, not the resistance of Mexican armies, that sapped the morale and resilience of the invaders. This form of resistance called largely on the rural, mixed-race people, and it was the most worrying aspect of the war, both for the U.S. military hierarchy and the Mexican upper classes. Sporadic peasant uprisings tore through rural Mexico during the early years of the republic, continuing during the 1846–48 invasion. The upper classes, liberal and conservative, were terrified at the prospect of arming the peasantry: "caste war" was a phrase that caused instinctive revulsion and fear among elites. Landowners and speculators covetous of village lands invoked this fear in order to continue armed suppression of peasant revolts during the invasion.

Peasants in the Huasteca region of Veracruz and Tamaulipas provinces had been battling seizures of their traditional lands through the 1840s. A new hacienda elite, fortified with foreign capital, had replaced the older owners; backed with political connections, they sought to expand their holdings and establish commercial plantations. The obvious arena for expansion was onto village lands, which were held by tradition, under incomplete or insufficiently documented titles. Hacendados seized entire villages in the region, making residents pay rents on their own lands.

Peasant revolts focused on not just land but also on citizenship rights and mainly on the onerous taxes imposed by church and civil authorities. In mid- and late 1847 peasants across Huasteca burned haciendas and regional archives and killed a prominent judge. By the time of the U.S. invasion, state National Guard units, in Huasteca and across Mexico, had stopped supporting the hacendados in their wars against the peasants, not wishing to involve themselves in a war of private interests, and not in any case able to recruit men who would suppress their own people.[45]

The besieged governor of Veracruz, driven from his capital by the North Americans and without revenues, called on the central government for assistance in collecting taxes and reestablishing the National Guard. He clearly stated his two main objectives: to finance the war effort through taxes imposed upon the peasantry, and simultaneously to repress those peasants' efforts to retain control over their land. Military action against the Yankees was secondary.

The Veracruz region was a critical point in the U.S. supply train and presented the foremost opportunity for guerrilla attacks on the invaders' resources. As mentioned, the central government was reluctant to organize or supply funds for an all-out guerrilla war. Local officials and priests formed informal guerrilla units that relied on contributions. It was, in fact the peasant rebels in Veracruz who made the strongest organized appeal for continued resistance in the face of the occupation.

In January 1848 peasant leader Juan Nepomuceno Llorente issued the Plan de Tantoyuca, calling nationally for an alliance of the agrarian rebels. In Veracruz this meant the establishment of local governments sympathetic to peasant rights and the war effort, which would be authorized to collect levies according to the means of individuals to pay. The plan called for a national suspension of rents on all hacienda lands. It also called for a suspension of internal taxes and tariffs, except those directly supporting the war effort.[46] The Plan of Tantoyuca circulated nationally and generated much interest in other areas under revolt. It presaged twentieth-century liberation movements in Cuba and China in combining resistance to invasion with universal land reform.

Coming from the most intensively occupied and contested region of the nation, it infused a patriotic, nationalistic spirit into what had been a local class conflict. The state government, such as it was, remained committed to suppressing the peasant revolt, and remnants of the militia pursued Llorente and his forces. The American invaders typically characterized the guerrillas as vagabonds and highwaymen, and no doubt some were, but it is clear that many were struggling for the same kind of citizenship and property rights as were the U.S. volunteers.[47]

The rural population of Mexico fought with mixed success against peonage and usurpation of its lands in the fifty years after Independence, and it was not until the Revolution of 1910 that smallholders' rights were given legal weight. Peonage was more severe and widespread in the North where indigenous villages were fewer, and haciendas larger.[48] This was the condition of servitude that many American volunteers witnessed, and which led them to observe that peonage was identical to slavery. For even the most oppressed of peons, the struggles for village rights and citizenship generated strong nationalistic currents, in a nation that had abolished slavery and declared racial equality. The declaration of citizenship rights by government and rebels, however neglected in practice, gave peons a status far above that of slaves in the United States, one for which they were willing to fight.

Juan Alvarez was the leader of the peasant movement in the region south of Mexico City. (In 1849 this region was reorganized as the state of Guerrero.) He was also a national political figure, who would in 1855, as leader of the Revolution of Ayutla, become president of the republic for a brief time. Alvarez had fought and was badly wounded in the War of Independence, and throughout the 1830s and 1840s continued to fight for rights of state and local government, tax relief, and land rights for peasants. The peasant movement in Guerrero reached new heights of scope and intensity in 1847.[49]

Nonetheless, Alvarez voluntarily refrained from attacks on landowners and called for cooperation with the war effort. He went as far as to disown his subordinate officers who led attacks on haciendas at this time. Alvarez's forebodings about pushing the hacendados into the arms of the invader came true during an 1848 peasant revolt in Cuernavaca. Hacienda personnel and U.S. troops stationed in the area acted together to defend haciendas from attacks.[50]

During the war the federal government reached out to leaders like Alvarez by revoking the extreme centralism of the past ten years and restoring some autonomy to local and state governments. As General Scott advanced on central Mexico, Alvarez raised 3,000 men drawn at least partly from the ranks of his peasant rebels and marched to Mexico City. The government would not, however, provide money for his army, and it was supported with donations from local supporters in Guerrero.

Alvarez urged the government to organize guerrilla resistance and again faced the opposition of elite Mexicans afraid of arming potential enemies. Santa Anna's strategy of formal battlefield confrontations was chosen instead. The historian Peter Guardino observes that guerrilla activity had mixed results, never completely cutting the U.S. supply trains. Santa Anna's military strategy was an outright failure. An all-out guerrilla war might have done more damage to Mexican society than the invasion itself. Nevertheless, he points out, during the French invasion of the 1860s a guerrilla war succeeded in repelling a foreign enemy that controlled every major city.[51]

The landed elite, by and large, welcomed the U.S. troops as friendly to the interests of propertied classes everywhere. This class had provided much of the financial support for the government's war against Texas rebels and, like most Mexicans, was disturbed by the harsh, blanket racism of the invaders. But the class affinity of landowners and American officers quickly became apparent, as these groups fraternized, and landowners profited from U.S. requisitions of food supplies.[52] As in New Orleans, in Mexico only large merchants and growers could cope with the demands of the army. Peasants and villages, meanwhile, were subject to the foraging and depredations of North American soldiers and irregulars.

CHAPTER 7

Dreams of Conquest and the Limits of the White Man's Democracy

Dreams of Personal Conquest

North Americans failed to establish social and military dominance in the areas of Mexico from which they withdrew in 1848. Sociologist Theodore Allen has pointed out that military, or at least paramilitary, rule is necessary to enforce herrenvolk—equality among a master race—where the subject race is a majority.[1] Even in the relatively lightly populated areas of California and New Mexico, military action was needed alongside paternalism. Anglo commercial elites married or otherwise assimilated into wealthy Mexican landowning families, exploiting the existing paternalistic labor system. But discharged soldiers and other adventurers wreaked violence upon the Mexican lower classes.

Various American interlopers attempted this dual strategy, of paternal and competitive herrenvolk, during the brief occupation of northern Mexico, with little success. Guerrilla warfare on the part of the peasantry and the rapacity of the American volunteers heightened racial and class tensions, and made an accommodation between the Anglo conquerors and the Mexican gentry impossible—an arrangement resisted by the lower orders of the American army *and* by the Mexican peasantry.

A typical but unusually affecting early impression of Mexico is that of H. Judge Moore, a South Carolina private. As he waited on Lobos Island to participate in the landing and siege at Veracruz he contemplated the nearby beaches on a moonlit night: "I have been in sight of their shores so long that I am getting very impatient for a nearer peep. I should like to go over if I could claim the promise made to Abraham that my seed should possess the land. I have read of a Rich Widow who lives at Matamoras and has a carriage and fine pair of mules, that I would have no objection to meeting her by the banks of the Rio Grande."[2]

The Arkansas Regiment: Paternalist and Competitive Herrenvolk

The Arkansas volunteer sergeant, John Palmer, seized upon Moore's vision and, with considerably better prospects than Moore, worked to make it a reality. Palmer tried to assimilate himself into the Mexican elite. He was an educated "gentleman," although without means, and he had a long-standing acquaintanceship with some of the wealthiest landowners in the state of Coahuila. He attempted precisely the sort of assimilation through which enterprising Anglos acquired power and privilege in Texas and the Mexican cession.

In Parras, a small city in the state of Coahuila, Americans were received with much friendliness — at least at first. The state had a long history of squabbles with the central government over sovereignty and over its unmet demands for protection from the attacks of Indians upon ranchos and towns.

Palmer's Arkansas regiment was attached to General Wool's division, which encamped in the region of Parras in December 1846. The division had marched across the desert from San Antonio, Texas, and was destined for Saltillo to link up with General Taylor.

For Coahuilans the American military presence brought welcome relief from banditry and Indian raids. Several of the local elites, mainly large ranchers, had been educated in the United States, or were politically liberal and admirers of American institutions and progress. Northern Mexicans, or Norteños, differed considerably from their compatriots in central and southern Mexico. The states of Coahuila, Chihuahua, Sonora, and Nuevo León were geographically isolated from Mexico City and had strong ties of trade and investment with the United States. Elite Coahuilans had varying positions toward the invaders, but whatever their feelings, large landowners stayed to protect their landholdings and to sell their produce to the American army.

San Lorenzo, the hacienda of the Yvarra family near Parras, was a particularly hospitable locale for American troops passing through; the Yvarras were educated in the United States and saw themselves as enlightened and modern, abreast of North American technology and economic progress. Wool's division established a large encampment a few miles outside Parras, and, according to one officer, the "camp was constantly crowded with the beauty and fashion of the town, who visited the tents of the officers without hesitation or restraint, and the most cordial feelings and intercourse

General John E. Wool and staff, in Saltillo. Wool marched his division from San Antonio, Texas,
to Saltillo, where he linked up with General Zachary Taylor's forces in December. Wool's division
arrived in time to participate in the climactic battle of Buena Vista, in February 1847.
General Wool spent the remainder of the war in command of occupation forces
around Saltillo and Monterrey. Courtesy of the Beinecke Rare Book
and Manuscript Library, Yale University, New Haven, Conn.

were established between us."[3] Lieutenant Hughes, a topographical engi-
neer, offered lavish praise of the Yvarra family and its hacienda.

> They have important machinery from the United States for their mills,
> cotton gins, and presses; and in no part of the world have I seen better
> farming arrangements—everything is convenient, sightly, comfortable,
> and efficient. This estate is of immense extent, but of course much of it
> is not arable, and is valuable only for the rearing of stock. The cultivated
> land is devoted to the growth of corn, wheat, cotton, and fruits, and to
> the production of wine and brandy from the grape, and is justly regarded
> as one of the most celebrated vineyards in Mexico. . . .

The Messrs. [Yvarras] have attempted, but without success, to substitute our agricultural implements for the crude and primitive implements in use. The peons cannot or will not employ them . . . with their characteristic tenacity and aversion to change of habits.[4]

The Yvarras were among a handful of families that owned nearly the entire state of Coahuila and served as landlords to the majority of its inhabitants. The Sánchez Navarro family was by far the largest landholder in the state, having over time built upon the remnants of a royal encomendero grant, and maintained close control over 1,500 resident peons.[5] Seasonal laborers from Saltillo and Monclova, skilled workers, and leaseholders added their presence to a thriving agricultural community.

The occupiers, however, lumped all Mexicans below the status of hacendado together under the invidious category of "lepero." U.S. soldiers delighted in describing a mounted, armed, grizzled looking Mexican in their stereotyped depictions of the "race." This archetypal Mexican was indolent, thievish, and treacherous according to the occupiers. What they were most likely describing were the *vaqueros*, or cowboys of the North, a minority of the hacienda population, but noted for their independence, despite their often debt-bound status on the hacienda. These men made excellent guerrilla fighters, or guides for organized bodies of guerrillas.[6]

The people of the North were a transient and independent lot, most having migrated from central Mexico, in search of work, land, or mining wealth. There were few sedentary Indian villages, and the steady warfare of fierce nomadic tribes against Mexican settlements meant that there was little of the racial mixing, or *mestizaje* so common in southern regions, although lower-class migrants from the south were of various racial backgrounds.

Despite the open bigotry of the conquerors, even the lower classes presented a relatively friendly demeanor toward the Americans at first. The Americans left wounded and sick soldiers alone in the towns to recuperate, and soldiers traveled at will about the countryside, often alone. This pacific situation would change, with later incursions of volunteer and Texas Ranger companies, in 1847 and 1848.[7]

Sergeant John Palmer is mentioned in chapter 5 as casually taking frequent unauthorized leaves from his company.[8] He visited other regiments to socialize with acquaintances, but as Wool's division reached the vicinity of Parras, the main objective of his frequent excursions was San Lorenzo, the hacienda of Manuel Yvarra.

Yvarra was a classmate from St. Joseph's College in Bardstown, Kentucky. Yvarra was delighted to find Palmer among the occupying force and treated him with great hospitality. Another college acquaintance, Lorenzo Yarto, also welcomed Palmer, and the sergeant became enamored of Yarto's sister. Palmer came to have tremendous respect and friendship for the Yvarra and Yarto families, and spoke of them in loving terms; they exchanged gifts, with Palmer taking frequent long leaves from the regiment to stay on the hacienda. Of Don Manuel Yvarra, Palmer said: "Every day more and more attaches me to him and his brother. They live entirely in their Hacienda, isolated from every species of vice, and their greatest pleasure is in doing good. Indeed, I have never seen a character more to be admired, respected—loved, than Don Manuel." His Mexican friends urged him to resign from the service and settle in Parras, where he "should experience no difficulty in getting land and assistance, and . . . should make plenty of money."

Sergeant Palmer's warm sentiments toward his Mexican friends were quite different from his feelings for his volunteer comrades. He confided to an officer that "I had not found one person in the company of whom I could make a companion, and consequently was so much isolated that my position was becoming unbearable."[9]

Palmer was disgusted with the Arkansans' unprovoked marauding upon Mexican civilians, which he feared—correctly—would lead to retaliation and reprisals. When the officers of the regiment, and Palmer, a mere noncommissioned officer, dined with Don Yvarra at the hacienda there was muttering in the Arkansas ranks. A soldier of that regiment expressed resentment that private soldiers were snubbed, while officers and gentlemen fraternized with the enemy. He hinted darkly that livestock would soon be disappearing from the hacienda, which was soon the case.

When Palmer's term of enlistment neared its end in mid-1847, he determined to stay in northern Mexico and settle in Parras. By this time the welcoming attitude of his Mexican friends had cooled noticeably. They feared reprisals from the local population for their friendliness with Americans; Palmer had narrowly escaped being ambushed and killed in his comings and goings from Yvarra's estate. The impending return of Mexican sovereignty presaged retaliation against those who had welcomed the Americans. Some prominent local clergymen made the U.S. military governor particularly welcome, which had already led to retaliations by the Mexican government against their order, the Franciscans, in Mexico City. The mood of the common people of Parras became particularly resentful toward the

Americans at exactly the time Palmer was considering locating there, in June 1847.

In that month a detachment of Texas cavalry rampaged through the town, committing depredations. No less than General John E. Wool warned Palmer that he would be compromising his Mexican friends' safety by remaining in Parras. The general warned that the Yvarras and Palmer would undoubtedly feel the wrath of local partisans and of the government when the occupiers left.[10] Palmer, nonetheless, decided to take his discharge near Saltillo. General Taylor had ordered all volunteers discharged in New Orleans, where they could wreak no further depredations upon the Mexicans. Taylor personally granted Sergeant Palmer immunity from this order, in a sort of gentlemen's agreement.

Palmer was in a position, with his education and connections, to gain real benefits from the project of manifest destiny, had he not encountered resistance from nationalistic Mexicans.

The Arkansas volunteer soldiers, as well, were resentful of invidious social distinction and were in no position to gain from an accord between Mexican and American elites. More than their superiors, they enacted the nationalist and racial agendas of manifest destiny, attacking lower-class Mexicans and effectively subverting the relationships of their officers (and Palmer) with upper-class Mexicans.

The Arkansas soldiers came from a frontier slave state; one might suppose them to have harshly competitive views of race relations, based on their previous experiences with African slaves and Native Americans. Indeed, they were openly contemptuous of military discipline and committed numerous murders and robberies of Mexican people. But to volunteer soldiers serving one-year enlistments, the Mexicans themselves were but one negative referent group among several that followed them from the United States, including, mercenary wagoners and sutlers, autocratic officers, slavish soldiers, and unreliable slaves and servants.

Arkansas private Jonathan Buhoup, in his published memoirs, spoke of the widespread atrocities of the Arkansas volunteers but presented them in a deliberately veiled manner. In part, his obfuscation of this issue consisted of using racial pejoratives in speaking about his fellow volunteers. A volunteer who committed innumerable thefts and acts of violence was spoken of simply as the "Indian." In fact, so numerous were his crimes, and so intimately is the reader advised of his rationales for such activities, that the character is most likely a composite of individuals in the regiment or an alter ego of Buhoup himself. In this way the narrator distanced the "white" or noble aspects of his peers from the ignoble behavior that accompanied the regiment from San Antonio to Saltillo.[11]

In descending into the hostile and alien environment of Mexico the Arkansas volunteers took on moral attributes of a suspect race, although, in the mind of the narrator, there were logical and inevitable reasons for their so doing. Their enlistment as soldiers put them in a servile position, not normally associated with white freeman status—in violation of the terms of their enlistment. In coming to terms with this declension, Buhoup gave his fellow volunteers the cast of Native Americans, at the very least a proud and independent race—if doomed—in the American racial lexicography: he categorized Mexicans with servile African Americans. It was the "Indian" of the regiment who vowed to retaliate with theft when Manuel Yvarra snubbed the volunteers and dined with the officers and the "gentleman" Sergeant Palmer. In Buhoup's view that retaliation was immoral but inevitable when Americans were put in the unnatural role of subservience to Mexicans. In fact, theft of Yvarra's property may have been a relatively mild recourse, one of several that the Arkansas soldiers took against being placed in subservience to Mexican elites.

Lieutenant Hughes observed that one of the volunteers "became intoxicated at the hacienda of Lorenzo, near Parras, and was in the act of raising his carbine to shoot Don Manuel, its amiable and accomplished proprietor." Yvarra, showing characteristic Norteño skill with a lasso, "threw the noose over him and pinioned him by the arms, when our stalwart Arkansas cavalier became as meek and quiet as a lamb."[12]

The Arkansas volunteers lashed out downward in the class system, when those above them were inaccessible, and they found class enemies they were quite at home with. According to Buhoup, the Arkansans encountered numerous former slaves from the United States living in relatively free conditions in northern Mexico. The years of animosity between Texas and Mexico had produced a political climate in which escaped slaves were given succor by the government and by citizens. It was part of Texan lore that a black man could live like a king in Mexico, while a white man would be given the shabbiest treatment.[13]

In the town of San Rosalia the Arkansas soldiers met with a delegation of twenty Mexicans, the village alcalde, and an escaped U.S. slave, acting as interpreter. One of the soldiers claimed to recognize the latter as "once belonging to a gentleman in the State of Tennessee, and who had absconded about ten years since." This incident of recognition is highly dubious, given the length of time and distance over which the two parties had been separated; but, in any event, the crime of harboring a fugitive slave merited retribution in the eyes of the volunteers. The colonel of the regiment assured the alcalde that private property would be respected, but the men nonetheless stripped a field of sugar cane. Here again, it was the "Indian" who was responsible for initiating the theft.[14] The Arkansas soldiers saw maintenance of racial discipline as a continuation of their duties as citizens of the slave South. The democratic mandate given to volunteer soldiers also allowed them to retaliate against superior officers who violated racial codes.

On an ominous note, the "Indian," like John Palmer, was discharged in Saltillo, acting against orders without any special dispensation. This left him on the scene free to commit further depredations and to practice the social and racial logic of the occupation, which continued along the border. Discharged volunteers often found employment with the army as wagoners or employed themselves as hostlers, saloonkeepers, gamblers, and the like, and remained in the Mexican border region looking for employment or opportunity.

It is unclear whether John Palmer achieved his dream of wealth and status among the Mexican elite; this would have been an exceptional achievement in the embittered postwar environment. But, as a gentleman, he was given leave by General Wool to at least attempt to do so. The common soldiers of the regiment were forcibly removed from the country, unless, like the "Indian" they chose an illicit and uncertain career on this troubled border.

Jonathan Buhoup described an American who had actually done what Palmer dreamed of, married into a Mexican family some years before the war, and set himself up in business in the country. The Arkansas volunteers, on the march through the city of Monclova encountered "a trader from St. Louis who was doing a lucrative business there. When asked how he liked the country he replied 'Like the country! . . . that is something I never could do—but I got a right smart sprinkle of money by marrying the woman I did, and I contrive to fool these yellow fellows out of a great deal more—so I manage to live pretty comfortably.'"[15]

Americans were still coming to northern Mexico and seeking fortunes in the late 1840s but they faced outright hostility from the government and people. A German American, Henriques Muller, became a partner of the most wealthy and powerful family in Chihuahua, the Terrazas, and was able to establish a successful ranching and mining enterprise. But he was subject to forced loans and government harassment during the wars of the Reforma and the French occupation.[16]

A "Scientific" View of Herrenvolk Democracy

Adolphus Wislizenus, a surgeon in a Missouri volunteer regiment, was a strong advocate for U.S. annexation of the northern Mexican territories including Coahuila; he called upon the Senate to annex all of Mexico north of the Sierra Madre range. He presented his views in Congress in 1848, as debate raged over how much of Mexico should be annexed. Missouri senator Thomas H. Benton submitted Wislizenus's report of his experiences in Mexico, as representing the views of an accomplished scientist, who had ventured into the theater of war and coolly assessed its land, resources, and people.

Wislizenus attached himself to a trade convoy in advance of the American armies, motivated by his own abiding curiosity and love of adventure. The physician Wislizenus was also a botanist and geologist, with sidelines in anthropology, astronomy, and horticulture. He was German-born, son of a clergyman, and, while a student, was arrested for participating in an anti-monarchist revolt.

When he attended the University of Jena, students seized the army barracks at Frankfurt and waited for a popular uprising that never happened. As one of the perpetrators Wislizenus was jailed briefly, but fled to Switzerland and completed his medical studies. In 1836 he settled in St. Louis, along with many other German political refugees. He became a country physician and went on an exploring expedition into the northern Rocky Mountain regions in 1839. Ever restless, he took to the trail again in 1846, this time for Santa Fe.[17]

Wislizenus presented a detailed and pragmatic view of the states of New Mexico and Chihuahua in his Senate report—not just that of a disinterested scientist, but one with a clear vision toward economic exploitation

In Santa Fe the trading expedition encountered news of the initial battles in northeastern Mexico, but the government and population seemed relatively untroubled by these distant events. The traders were rumored to be carrying weapons to sell to the Mexican authorities, which would have accounted for the equanimity with which they were received. Governor Armijo issued passports to proceed to Chihuahua, and those wishing to go went on their way, having paid duties and transacted business in Santa Fe.

Arriving at the city of Chihuahua in August, their reception was less sanguine. According to Wislizenus, a "crowd of ragged loafers and vagabonds received us at the entrance as 'Tejanos' (Texans) the usual abusive appellation to Americans." War excitement was high, with reports of the American army's advance arriving daily. Recruits drilled in the streets; the pro-war party in the state abruptly took control of the governorship and began production of cannon and ammunition. Wislizenus put up in the "American hotel," and the handful of Europeans and Americans in the city banded together against taunts and threats. Wislizenus tried to remain above the fray. "Paying no more attention to those warlike preparations than I could help, I pursued, in the meanwhile, the scientific object of my excursion to Chihuahua by collecting plants, examining the geological character of the surrounding country, and making in the yard of my dwelling barometrical and astronomical observations."[18]

Soon, however, news arrived in Chihuahua that Colonel Kearney and his regiment had captured Santa Fe. Residents organized a demonstration against the Americans, openly preparing an assault on the hotel with the avowed purpose of lynching the enemy nationals. It was a long and tense day for Wislizenus and the other Americans. By evening, a mob assembled in front of the hotel and began singing patriotic songs and stoning the door of the building. The four Americans inside loaded their weapons "and resolved to defend themselves to the last." Failing to gain entry into the hotel, the Mexicans earned only Wislizenus's contempt: "A Mexican mob is not that short, offhand, killing affair that it is in the 'far west' of the United States," he said; "it is rather an uproarious meeting, a somewhat irregular procession, arranged with a certain decency, and executed more from love of plunder than thirst of blood."[19]

It is not clear who or what was plundered here. The Mexicans earned the scorn of the pugnacious doctor by acceding to the rule of law and dispersing when the authorities finally intervened. Wislizenus expressed open admiration for lynch law, and a belief that that the community must act vigorously, decisively, and brutally on behalf of community decisions. Of course, it was important that the "best" men in the community were privy to these decisions, not just the "vagabonds" and "loafers." The doctor criticized the governor for acting indecisively in the affair, first allowing, then suppressing the mob.

In the view of Wislizenus, the Mexicans' lack of ruthlessness was an indictment of their whole political system, and the Mexicans' fitness to maintain it. As an adopted citizen, this middle-class German showed considerable alacrity in adopting the ways of the expansionist perimeter of the United States.

But perhaps his lessons had been learned earlier, in Frankfurt, when "the people" failed to rally to the student cause. Wislizenus's experience in Germany left him contemptuous and distrustful of popular movements, but American expansion, safely in the hands of commercial and military elites, could not be derailed by those lacking the political savvy to support it. If there was a reformist side to Wislizenus's outlook, it is that he saw some potential for "enlightening" the propertied classes in Mexico, allowing them a role in maintaining stability and progress.[20] But his personal and class prejudices led him to approve of whatever organized violence might be necessary to commence this "enlightenment."

The authorities of Chihuahua city placed Wislizenus and the other Americans in internal exile at a small, desolate village ninety miles west of the capital. They spent a bleak winter and spring waiting for the arrival of Colonel Stephen Kearney's regiment. Wislizenus joined the Missouri volunteers as a surgeon, and traveled with them east to meet up with Taylor's army near Saltillo. Following in the wake of General Wool's army through the states of Coahuila and Nuevo León, he noted the utter devastation—buried corpses and charred villages—that was the uniform condition of the country that the army had traversed. Wislizenus strenuously approved of the campaign of killing and burning by American soldiers and camp followers. The principle of reprisal justified these depredations, he said, and cited a few instances of American soldiers and wagoners whose mutilated bodies had turned up outside of army camps.[21]

The Peace Settlement and Annexation Plans

As Dr. Wislizenus testified before Congress the war was winding down; commercial interests and many expansionists in the government pushed for annexation of most or all of Mexico. In order to appraise the relative success of manifest destiny in northeastern and central Mexico, it is not necessary to make any imaginative leap to envision what might have been. The outlines of a project of colonization and absorption had already been laid by Americans on the scene and in Washington.

By the middle of 1847 American generals and politicians realized that Mexico might maintain an indefinite guerrilla war despite the conquest of its major cities. American military and political leaders worried about extri-

TABLE II *Aggregate American Forces in Mexico,*
January 1848

OFFICER	PLACE	REGULARS	VOLUNTEERS	AGGREGATE
Gen. Scott	Central Mexico	17,101	15,055	32,156
Gen. Taylor*	Northern Mexico	3,937	2,790	6,727
Gen. Price	New Mexico	255	2,902	3,157
Lt. Col. Powell	Fort Kearny, ON THE OREGON ROUTE		477	
Gen. Mason	California	216	803	1,019
Total		21,509	22,027	43,536

Source: *Congressional Globe,* 30th Cong., 1st sess., 1848, 17:88.

* *Temporarily commanded by General Wool.*

cating themselves from an unpopular war. Major General Robert Patterson suggested, in July 1847, that an army of 40,000 "rank and file" be placed in the field, with additional civilian auxiliaries to administer the cities. Effective strength of the army at this time, from California to Veracruz, was about 28,000 (with many more sick or on garrison duty). Political support for the war was tenuous and declining as the war dragged on, but Mexican state power had effectively disintegrated, and competing military factions made it impossible to negotiate a conclusive peace treaty.

In early 1848 the Polk administration sent Congress legislation providing for an additional 10,000 regulars and 20,000 volunteers for an indefinite occupation of Mexico. The disposition of American forces at the end of 1847 reflected the heavy recruiting of that year. The figures in table 2 give a snapshot of the army at the height of the war, with strikingly reduced numbers of one-year volunteers, great numbers of them having completed their service or been discharged. Contrast these figures with the aggregate numbers in table 1, which reflect the large but ephemeral surge of volunteering earlier in the war.

Democrat Lewis Cass presented the administration's proposal, a second ten-regiment bill, to an unenthusiastic Senate. Unlike the ten-regiment bill of 1847, it never succeeded in Congress. The midterm election of 1846 had dealt a serious blow to Polk's party, but the new Whig congress did not take

TABLE III *Population of North Mexican States*

STATE	POPULATION
Chihuahua	160,000
Sonora	130,000
New Mexico	70,000
Upper California	35,000
Lower California	5,000

Total	400,000

Source: U.S. Senate, *Memoir of a Tour to Northern Mexico*, 85.

office until December 1847, by which time the major campaigns of the war were finished.[22] But in early 1848 enthusiasts for annexation pled their case vigorously in Congress, with very specific plans for managing the people and lands beyond the boundaries of the Treaty of Guadalupe Hidalgo. The debate in January over the raising of additional regiments provided a forum for various annexation plans,

At this time Senator Thomas H. Benton submitted Wislizenus's plan for annexing everything north and west of Laredo, including all of Baja California. This plan would acquire for the United States some 300,000 Mexican citizens, over and above the 100,000 encompassed in the Guadalupe Hidalgo cession (see table 3).

Dr. Wislizenus (and presumably Benton) wanted this territory, despite fears of acquiring a large alien population. Wislizenus thought this was a manageable balance of territory and people, and stressed the relative disorganization and ineffectuality of the residents of this region. Wislizenus extolled the uplift and progress annexation would extend to Mexicans.[23] Ultimately, U.S. capitalism would solve the quandary posed by Dr. Wislizenus by expanding American investment, industry, and markets far beyond national boundaries, thus obviating the "problem" of providing citizenship rights to culturally alien peoples. It would also exploit those "foreigners" as alien labor in its occupied lands, where citizenship was denied them.

Senator Archibald Sevier of Arkansas supported the bill for additional soldiers and was strongly for acquiring as much of Mexico as was politically feasible. Some months previous, Sevier traveled to Mexico City as a negotiator in the treaty discussions.[24] In his view soldiers and settlers could handle Mexico much as they had subdued the Indian population of the United States: "three fourths" of the Mexican population were no more or less than Indians, according to Sevier. "What shall we do with these Indians? Will we allow them to vote, or to be represented? I would do neither; I would treat them as we do our own Indians—give them agents and laws, and kindness, and education. They are a degraded race in Mexico—they could be made less so under our administration."[25]

According to the senator from Arkansas, the remaining quarter of the Mexican population, the "white" population, was more problematic, but could be dealt with in the same way as European immigrants to the United States. They would be subject to naturalization laws and an oath of allegiance. Sevier acknowledged the potential for resistance from the educated, nationalistic population and dismissed it as insignificant. "If, however, they will stab and assassinate," he said "there is a remedy in this country for such abuses, and that remedy grows in Kentucky and Missouri, which is vulgarly called 'hemp.'"[26]

Sevier had a very simplistic notion of Mexican society, but it closely paralleled the views of his constituents, at least those of the soldiers of the Arkansas volunteer regiment. The kind of frontier justice they dispensed in northern Mexico and their inflexible racial codes could flourish under Sevier's plan if the sheer numbers of volunteers were available and if their own disorganization did not defeat them.

Whig opponents, with their new congressional majority, had the chance to rebuke the president but they achieved only a resolution against the war, which passed in the House but not the Senate. The opposition managed to avoid seeming unpatriotic by approving military funding but bogging down measures to widen the war. The ten-regiment bill of 1848 represented a significant expansion of the war effort. Antiwar legislators raised the specter of dangers to the race and the republic that would result from the absorption of the Mexican state, and of the all-powerful executive that would emerge from such a gigantic military venture. Senator Butler presaged the difficulties of occupation, utilizing the available human and organizational resources:

> And what is it that these [35,000 additional] troops are to be required to do? Not to fight battles. We are told they are not to fight battles. . . . The soldiers we are to raise now are not soldiers who are to be animated by the love of glory and the spirit of military adventure; their office is neither

more nor less than to be armed tax-gatherers or jailers. They are to sweep through the country, for the purpose of gathering treasures, and keeping in awe a feeble and distracted population.[27]

Butler's forebodings augured the improbability of American volunteers acting as the organized agents of the state. The "tax-gathering" and "sweeping through the country" that would go on under such a system could not have been handled by poorly organized volunteers. The political machine necessary for a genuine occupation would have required the broad support of the American middle classes, and an imprimatur of moral authority from the religious and intellectual establishment. These groups were beginning to see a potential evangelizing mission in Mexico by the end of the war and might have signed on to an occupation conceived in benevolent, paternalistic terms. The Whig Party and its leading thinkers had, over the years, acquiesced in Indian removal, and they were able to cope with slavery, with some dissension.

It was not ingrained racism or a fear of corruption that kept the United States from extending its political and economic tentacles permanently into Mexico. Those Americans who took part in the occupation of Mexico encountered a sovereign, culturally distinct people, willing to defend their own national identity. The task of reducing this population by the sword would have required a tremendous national political will and a consistent line of justification from political and religious elites. An extended campaign of rapine and murder, such as was the policy of Texas, would have caused deep rifts in the American political classes, and even among soldiers of ordinary backgrounds, conscientious objections to this sort of campaign were already evident during the war.[28]

Annexationists like Secretary of State James Buchanan and Secretary of the Treasury Robert Walker disliked the Treaty of Guadalupe Hidalgo as much as "no territory" Whigs in Congress. The political standoff, and the demands for more men and funding, however, gradually made the treaty more acceptable to both sides. President Polk threw his influence decisively behind the treaty, in late February 1848, when he had two compatible objectives within his grasp.

First, he demanded that the Wilmot Proviso, or any version thereof be excluded from the peace settlement, viewing it as an insult to the South. He also rejected Article X of the treaty, which called for recognition of all Mexican land titles in the ceded territories and Texas, even those that were incomplete under Mexican law. This was the status of much of the land held by most Mexican natives, due to disputes involving indigenous, royal, and national land titles, and the slowness and instability of Mexican bureaucracies.[29] Texas courts had already invalidated many Mexican land titles, and Article X might have reopened cases against Anglo usurpers.

Sustaining both of Polk's objectives—deletion of Article X and suppression of Free-Soil amendments—the Senate passed the treaty, squeezing between the objections of competing factions. Congressman John Quincy Adams, the former president and leader of the "no territory" advocates, collapsed on the floor of the House and died during debates over the treaty. Thus was removed one of the rallying points of opposition. The Senate ratified the treaty in March, with most northerners voting in opposition.[30] Annexationists did not see the treaty as the final word on acquisition of Mexican territory, and the years before the Civil War saw numerous schemes to extend U.S. sovereignty into Mexico and the Caribbean Basin, including armed invasions of northern Mexico by privately organized armies, or filibusters.

CHAPTER 8

Free Soil and the Heritage of the Citizen-Soldier

Some connections between the Free-Soil political movement of 1848–52 and the experiences of the Mexican War soldiers are obvious, such as the dispute over whether to allow slavery in territory conquered from Mexico. But further ties between the soldiers' war and the ensuing political shift toward antislavery existed and are worth exploring.

The Free-Soil Party was one of the most successful third-party movements in American political history, diverting large numbers of voters from the Democratic and Whig parties. The party's brief popularity played a pivotal role in both the demise of Whiggery and the birth of the Republican Party. The central goal of Free Soil was prevention of the expansion of slavery to territory outside the existing slave states. Free Soil fully encompassed the preexisting racism of the North (and may actually have given greater expression to northern Negrophobia), but it presented a decided obstacle to the system of slavery. Like the movement in opposition to the Mexican War, Free Soil has been viewed by historians in the light of the middle-class politicians and writers who spoke for the movement. However, the experience of Mexican War soldiers and their contribution to the outcome of the war were a strong determinant of postwar politics and society, regardless of what northern politicians and economic leaders were doing and thinking.

Soldiers returning from the Mexican War rejected the arbitrary use of power they had experienced in the army. The politics of free soil, while far from rejecting racism, opened a space for a dialogue about political rights apart from strictly racial hierarchies. Men who had been in central and northeastern Mexico witnessed a distinctive national culture, not simply an extension of the racial hierarchies they previously understood. Many came to realize they were fighting a nation, not a race. This obstacle to expansion destroyed any rationale of military service in defense of democracy.

In the East, free-soil ideals, and the Free-Soil Party, became a posthumous rationale for the war, modifying but not annulling manifest destiny. Dreams of land for soldiers and workers remained very much alive in eastern politics, but remained a symbolic gesture.[1] In the Mexican War the United States acquired a vast hinterland riddled with unfree labor arrangements—indentures, peonage, slavery—based on a proliferation of racial distinctions.

The foremost historian of the Free-Soil movement has said that "Despite its universalistic vocabulary, the idea of free labor had little bearing on the actual conditions of non-whites in nineteenth-century America."[2] This discourse of rights, in turn, had only limited impact on the racialist ways in which Americans thought about labor. The military experience of Mexican War soldiers from the North turned their thinking not so much toward the problem of racial domination but toward the evils of caste and excessive subordination—and insubordination—of the military kind.

For these soldiers, unaccountability of both the leaders and the led were intolerable. As we shall see, some soldiers turned their backs on military herrenvolk, having seen few tangible rewards.

Mexican War Soldiers and Free Soil

A regular army volunteer, Orlando John Hodge of Ohio, changed his views about work and democracy while serving in Mexico. Hodge signed up as a recruit in the Tenth U.S. Infantry in April 1847. This was one of the new regular army units authorized by Congress for the duration of the war. Hodge euphemistically referred to it as the "Tenth U.S. Volunteers," semantically mitigating some of the onus of regular service. The officers of the Tenth were almost exclusively from New York and New Jersey, but the regiment recruited across Ohio and Indiana.

John Hodge served in northeastern Mexico in the aftermath of the battles of Monterrey and Buena Vista. Hodge coped with the disease and boredom of camp life; he contracted typhus and was wounded in the leg in a guerrilla raid. His captain was one of Polk's political appointees, with no military training, but who nonetheless quickly got into the spirit of the regular army. Hodge wrote that "Lieutenant [Stephen] Powers our Capt. now or acting as such is one of the most abusive men in the whole regiment. . . . This morning I heard he nearly killed a man that was at work because he did not work fast enough." Hodge also witnessed the execution of three deserters from his regiment and a fatal duel among two regimental officers.

STUDYING POLITICAL ECONOMY.

A Free-Soil view of presidential politics, 1848. This cartoon portrays Whig candidate, Zachary Taylor, as a violent buffoon, tarnished by his bloody exploits against the Seminoles in Florida and in the Mexican War. In this view, antislavery interests within the party are ludicrously ineffectual, and Taylor, a Louisiana slaveowner, seems to be fomenting racial warfare. Courtesy of the American Antiquarian Society, Worcester, Mass.

Hodge was sickened by the crimes his comrades-in-arms committed against the local populace; he thought their behavior unmilitary and uncivilized. His letters indicated that there was more criminal behavior on the northern front than was generally known and that the good reputation of the new regiments of the regular army was a falsehood: "This regiment has gained everlasting renown upon the Rio Grand having used the Mexicans so well and also having other ways behaved well; so much for the truth."[3] The new regiments were thrown into service hastily in the spring of 1847 and had some of the worse qualities of the volunteer service—political officers, untrained recruits—along with the dictatorial structure of the regular army.

Although Hodge objected to abuse of power by his superior officers, he applauded the branding and whipping of a deserter from his company as "a hard but fair punishment." The crowning irony of Hodge's wartime service was that he was forced to change his name to receive his army disability pension. Hodge was entitled to a pension due to his leg wound, but a clerical mistake in his enlistment papers had him as Orlando John rather than John Orlando, his given name.[4] Hodge legally changed his name to conform to the mistake.

Hodge enlisted in a war widely criticized as serving the interests of slavery and did not seem to have any strong political commitments previously: it is somewhat surprising to find Hodge firmly in the ranks of Free Soil before the peace treaty was even signed.

John Hodge had a brother who was a sailor in the Mexican War; although the two men's experiences and outlook were widely different, neither received much in the way of reward for his service. The correspondence between John Hodge and his brother Alfred reveals something about the evolution of both their thinking about race and the politics of conquest. John and Alfred Hodge were orphaned in the early 1840s; they were raised by educated and religious family and friends. Both were sent out at a young age to work as printer's apprentices, John in Cleveland and Alfred in Buffalo. Both enlisted in the military for the duration of the Mexican War, Alfred Hodge as a seaman in the U.S. Navy. During the war he sailed around the Horn to Mazatlan and San Francisco.

In a letter to Alfred, John Hodge effusively praised the progress of the Free-Soil Party in the state of Massachusetts, enthusing "Glory to Mass. and may they live and stir up the hot buds of universal liberty!" Alfred responded with surprise and disdain to his brother's transformation:

[Senator Joshua] Giddings your abolition nigger of Ohio says our army in Mexico is nothing but an armed band of ruffians and pirates waging war on a peaceable and inoffencive people. [A] man calling himself an American and with such sentiments as these the damn scoundrel ought to be burnt alive.[5]

And in a later letter, Alfred offered further abuse:

It is a pity you were not sent to the Syracuse Convention where you could have lent the niggers (black and white) a hand to curse the Country, the Constitution, Washington, Bunker Hill & c. . . . I might fill the whole of these pages with the same sentiments but which is the use of spending time where Free Soilism has got as deep a hold as it has of you.[6]

John and Alfred continued their rancorous correspondence into the early 1850s. John Hodge became active in the Know-Nothing and later the Republican Party. He was an employing printer in Chicago in the late 1850s and engaged in various profitable business endeavors in Connecticut and Ohio.

Alfred, like his brother, reacted with distaste to indiscipline in the military. At San Francisco, in the summer of 1848, volunteers and sailors deserted in droves and headed for the gold fields. Entire warships were left unmanned. Hands were making twelve to sixteen dollars a day panning for gold. Alfred Hodge prided himself on fulfilling his enlistment and getting honorable discharge papers, though he scouted the diggings while still in the navy.

Alfred's negative experiences during the war were chiefly with unruly volunteers. He was witness to a mutiny of Colonel Stevenson's New York volunteers; nineteen men from that regiment were imprisoned on his ship.[7] For Alfred the promises of manifest destiny were fulfilled in an uncannily programmatic way. He finished his enlistment in California, easily the choicest fruit of the conquest, at the height of the gold rush. The taking of northern California was merely a political formality with a few small military engagements. The United States quickly established sovereignty and economic control over California, Anglos outnumbering Mexicans within two years.

Alfred Hodge sensed the ripeness of California and its suitability as an American outpost. Approaching San Francisco he wrote, "Monterey looks once more like yankee land, the first wood land I have seen since I left N. York. I am inclined to think that Jonathan will have none but timber land or else we would have had the whole of [Mexico]."[8]

And yet Alfred Hodge's experience in California did not exactly bear out this impression of fruit ripe for the picking. By the mid-1850s he was back in Ohio, after having failed as a merchant in the gold mining regions. His lack of capital, professional credentials, or political connections left him struggling and homesick.[9]

John Hodge experienced occupation duty and racial governance in Mexico as a personal disaster. He was thrown in with whites whom he felt were degraded by their unrestricted control over Mexicans. He also personally experienced a kind of contractual bondage, in which men of no better social standing than himself exercised abusive power over him. Seeing his comrades beaten and seeing those same comrades rape and pillage civilians was no doubt a part of his political sea change. The rewards of his service were sickness and injury — hardly offsetting a land bounty and a tiny pension.

When his fellow soldiers committed atrocities upon Mexicans and, in turn, officers exercised arbitrary authority over common soldiers, John Hodge saw these two phenomena as inextricably linked. Immediately after the war he became active in the Free-Soil Party and subsequently joined the Know-Nothing Party, once again analyzing social problems in terms of the corrupting influence of a servile people — European immigrants. Alfred Hodge admired the values of military service but by and large they did not apply to life in California. The military structure of that conquered province, quickly degenerated into a speculative free-for-all.

Homecomings

Free-Soil Stirrings in New York

John Hodge was both a Free-Soil man and a Mexican War soldier; during the Mexican War these categories represented divergent social groups. By 1848, however, Free-Soil politics had brought out some common ground between these groups, and the return of the volunteers created great dissension within the political coalition that had backed the war.

Democratic prowar meetings continued in New York City but with increasing discord and disruption from National Reformers and Working Men. With Mexican resistance faltering, the question of war objectives became the central issue. The united front of support for the war was fragmenting, and the strong-arm tactics of the Democratic gang leader Isaiah Rynders were barely enough to keep one such meeting, in February 1847, in line.

THINGS AS THEY ARE.

The spoils of manifest destiny: violence in the gold fields. This view shows Zachary Taylor succeeding James Polk as president in 1848, with Polk winging off to California. Taylor's militarism and Polk's treachery seem to have yielded up a bounty of violence and greed. Courtesy of the American Antiquarian Society, Worcester, Mass.

The Working Men's faction and the National Reform Association gained the podium at a Democratic Party meeting in Vauxhall and read a series of resolutions voicing a willingness to volunteer, if the sponsors of the meeting—wealthy and influential Democrats—also pledged to go. The dissidents also called for election of officers in the new regiment, and that "the pay . . . be equally divided among the officers and men."[10]

These interlopers at the war meeting echoed the radicalism of Mike Walsh, but they injected antislavery and homestead demands. This reappearance of the National Reform Association, along with Wilmot Proviso activists, at this moment in the war is significant.

Congress had just passed the Bounty Land Bill, providing 160-acre land bounties for soldiers. This homestead provision for soldiers was in keeping with the NRA's ideas of smallholders' democracy and gave a free-soil tint to the war.

The excitement among northern Democrats for Free Soil in the latter part of the war put quite a different face on the situation. If this was to be a war for homesteaders, in new lands that would have a white Anglo majority, then it offered fulfillment to various agrarian movements of the past decades. Unfortunately, homesteading was a symbolic promise of this war rather than a reality. National Reformers—and western homestead advocate Thomas Hart Benton—tried to make the land grants inalienable, to be used only by the soldiers. The omission of this condition from the 1847 bill and subsequent bounty and homestead acts frustrated any realization of smallholders' democracy.[11] The National Reform Association had little to offer workers in the way of genuine access to landed self-sufficiency, but the coalition of this middle-class movement with radical workingmen sowed dissension among the northern Democracy.

In February 1848, with the Mexican armies subdued and the capital occupied, Texas senator Sam Houston spoke to another "Great War Meeting" in New York. Houston waxed rhapsodic about Americans' drive to tame the wilderness, watering it with their blood, and becoming one with the land. On the other hand, he spoke of the civilizing mission of the Anglo-Saxon in elevating the Mexican and bringing him under American law and civilization.

As the "Great War Meeting" broke up, squabbles erupted between pro- and anti–Wilmot Proviso partisans, "each calling the other a d——d traitor, and a general outbreak was momentarily expected, which, however, did not take place."[12]

But Tammany Hall was soon forced to acknowledge political dissent among New York Democrats and to stanch the bleeding of party men to Free Soil. The First New York Regiment returned from its campaigns in central Mexico in July 1848 to a large and enthusiastic reception in New York City.

The changes in the political climate since the volunteers' departure were evident in the fact that John Van Buren, son of the former president, and a leading Free-Soil Party politician, gave the main address at the welcoming ceremony. He eulogized the living and fallen heroes with solemn rhetoric. The ceremony sought closure on the epic and tragic struggles of the war.[13]

In his eagerness to foster a new political movement that would include loyal Democrats, Van Buren glossed over the corruption of the First New York Regiment's officers. Many of the New York volunteers returned broken in health, starved, and cheated out of their pay and bounties. Free-Soilers looked to make peace with whatever segments of the Tammany constituency they could, and they were not prepared to challenge the politicians who had profited from the volunteer enterprise. The power of the New York Democracy was too entrenched and the crimes of colonels John D. Stevenson and Ward Burnett went unchallenged. The sad plight of the New York soldiers became a marginal issue, certainly marginal to Free-Soil Democrats.

Mike Walsh kept the issue of soldiers' rights alive in Congress, to which body he was elected in 1852. Walsh had been left behind by Free Soil, remaining firmly in the proslavery "Hunker" wing of the Democratic Party. In 1854 Walsh decried the lot of the returned volunteers as "a penury, and degradation, a wretched death, and a pauper's grave."[14] A coterie of these ruined men remained objects of charity for years afterward, and the newspapers issued periodic appeals for private aid to the veterans.[15]

New Yorkers in California: Broken Promises
The New York Regiment that set out for California, with promises of a personal stake in conquered land, fared even worse than the First Regiment. Having reached California, it was denied opportunities for land and status, and many of the regiment's soldiers were shipped back to New York City in chains.

Stevenson's men were mustered out in October 1848, and those who had not already deserted or been confined for mutiny headed immediately for the gold diggings.[16] In the winter of 1848–49, as prospectors returned from the hills to winter in San Francisco, many of the hopeful quickly found themselves broke and homeless. Discharged volunteers and other property-less men banded together for plunder in San Francisco and the surrounding areas. As the statehood convention got underway, the armed band terrorized the city, even going so far as to form "a battalion which publicly manoeu-vered on Portsmouth Square." Francis Lippitt, a former captain of the New York Regiment and by 1849 a prosperous San Francisco lawyer, remarked upon the menacing behavior of the volunteers. Lippitt noted that the band, led by Jack Powers, a soldier from his own company, "consisted chiefly of the worst elements of the mustered out volunteers."

Lippitt joined the Vigilance Committee that organized to put down the brigands. He reminisced in 1902 that "The squad which I led found and cap-tured Sam Roberts, the chief. In the prosecution and conviction of the ring-leaders I took a leading part. Those convicted were deported on the frigate Savannah. The others had fled."[17]

The Vigilance Committee rallied three more times during the 1850s to put down insurgencies against the San Francisco elite, as well as enforcing its own version of civic peace through lynch law. The uprisings, in 1853 and 1856, included among their leaders emigrant New York gang leaders Tom Hyer, "Yankee" Sullivan, and the pugilist Chris Lilly. The core of the rebel-lious New York volunteers had been broken in the 1849 clampdown: Private James Lynch of the New York regiment claimed that none of his comrades were among the 1853 gang. The gang leaders from New York and a largely Irish rank and file mobilized against a hard-fisted mercantile elite, which was quite willing to personally repress lawlessness.

At the peak of violence in 1856 a secret committee of thirty-three formed with 6,000 "volunteers" to put down the gangs. Defying the governor, the Vigilance Committee entrenched itself in "Fort Gunnybags" and ruled the city under martial law for three months. Attorney Lippitt served the com-mittee as soldier and prosecutor. In his memoirs he boasted, "The leading ruffians had been arrested, kept confined, and received every one of them, a fair trial. Those who were convicted of capital crimes were hanged, and the lesser criminals deported, not to return on pain of death, and for sev-eral years afterward San Francisco was one of the best governed cities on the globe."[18]

Gang leader "Yankee" Sullivan was said to have committed suicide in Fort Gunnybags.[19] Thus ended this experiment in street-level patronage politics. San Francisco's merchant elite did not need any intermediaries to deal with its white laborers, nor did it feel it owed them much patronage. They would

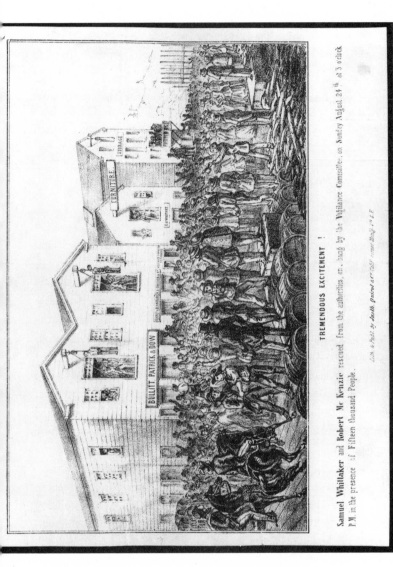

TREMENDOUS EXCITEMENT !

Samuel Whittaker and **Robert Mc Kenzie** rescued from the authorities, and hung by the Vigilance Committee, on Sunday August 24th at 3 o'clock P.M. in the presence of Fifteen thousand People.

Lith. & Publ. by Justh Quirot & Co. 151 Montg^y Montg^y S. F.

The Vigilance Committee administers lynch law, San Francisco, 1851. Middle-class California pioneers took decisive action to rein in lawless elements of the mustered-out Mexican War soldiers and subsequent waves of immigrants. In August 1851, the Vigilance Committee seized two convicted robbers and arsonists from the city jail and summarily carried out their executions. The committee acted as the virtual government of San Francisco during the 1850s in defiance of the Democratic state and city governments. (Soulé et al., Annals of San Francisco, 237.) Courtesy of the Beinecke Rare Book and Manuscript Library, Yale University, New Haven, Conn.

tolerate white workers who channeled their violence downward in the class and race structure. A few of the New York volunteers did establish independent smallholdings, but they were a distinct minority, as a chronicler of the regiment reported:

> 'Tis sad to contemplate how few of those adventurous youths and brave pioneers benefited themselves as they had the opportunity offered. A few are at this day [1882] wealthy, but the majority of the survivors are little more than earning a livelihood, and there are, no doubt, among them some who are in destitute circumstances, but the greater part of the men who were discharged in 1848 have ceased to exist, except in the memory of their old comrades and others who in California's early days were numbered among her pioneers.[20]

Return of the Massachusetts Regiment: "Almost Ashamed"

Massachusetts had one of the strongest Free-Soil political movements, and a few years after the war Free-Soilers and the Democrats combined their efforts in a coalition ticket. This went some way toward creating a cross-class coalition, focused on antislavery and, to some extent, labor reform. Those who fought in Mexico were not instantly transformed into heroes of the Free-Soil movement, but they were offered the chance to repudiate the politicians who had used them so harshly.

The Massachusetts Regiment had not seen the hard fighting that the First New York had. In fact, it had been confined to occupation duty, first in Matamoros and then in the rear of General Scott's drive to Mexico City. Combat service tended to put even a corrupt and derelict officer in a more favorable light with his men. But the Massachusetts volunteers harbored a long list of grudges against Brigadier General Caleb Cushing and his staff.

In 1847 Massachusetts Democrats had nominated him for governor, in absentia, under the slogan "Cushing, a well-fed soldiery, —our country against the world!"[21] The cruelty and hard usage meted out against the regiment had been widely publicized in the Boston press and began to take hold. When the Massachusetts volunteers returned in person bearing accusations, the political fallout for Cushing was considerable.

With the ratification of the peace treaty in June 1848, the Massachusetts Regiment began its long journey home, by steamboat to New Orleans, up the Mississippi, and east by riverboat and rail. Observers at Cincinnati,

Buffalo, and Albany noted that the Massachusetts soldiers were shockingly ragged and sickly. The regiment had marched and countermarched a total of 1,400 miles in Mexico. It numbered 459, having been reduced from its original 640 in January 1847, by deaths, discharges, sickness, and desertion—despite the regiment having taken on recruits steadily during the war.[22]

As their train pulled into Worcester, Massachusetts, the soldiers' appearance excited indignation from the press and scorn from many observers who had little sympathy with them to begin with. Worcester attorney James Henry Hill noted their arrival on July 19. "All hands of course were at the depot of the Western road to see them. Some delay was had" but finally a train arrived

> with the looked for freight—nine long cars crammed. And without exception the most sorry sight I ever looked upon. It certainly beggared all description. Dirty and filthy, ragged and half naked, I question whether you could solicit in the whole length and breadth of our ancient Commonwealth an equal number of men, that when collected would present so melancholy and wo-begone an appearance. The appearance of the officers was better but even they looked as if they had seen hard service. A better commentary upon war and glory, I'll vouch for it than could be furnished by the most zealous peace man in Christendom.

Hill had a further encounter with a volunteer over a week later, when he

> took passage in the evening stage up [to Barre, Mass.] Had for a fellow passenger up one of the Massachusetts Regiment of Volunteers—not a great man when he started—and if we may judge from his conversation not grown much since. He will probably have the satisfaction of being a Lion for two or three days in return for his many months of toil and privations. A poor reward it would be for most people.[23]

A solid Whig, Hill held antiwar opinions in line with the party papers in Worcester and Boston. He was extremely reluctant to take the plunge into Free Soil, as a majority of Worcester voters would do. He maintained the condescending attitude that his class and his party had formed toward the volunteers.

A Whig journal in Worcester, however, expressed sympathy for the volunteers, examining them in the light of the newspaper's own recent conversion to the Free-Soil Party. Affirming that he had never seen such a ragged and sickly band, the editorialist perceived as well a "moral squalidness" that had infected the men in their iniquitous career in Mexico. There were however, some manly and upright exceptions to this general rule, and "to such we gave our quick, spontaneous meed of honor, and to the rest our heartfelt pity and sudden disgust." There was furthermore, some hope that those not degraded by the war would learn from its horrors. "If false notions of patriotism and glory and liberty seduced them to Mexico," the editorial trumpeted, "juster views, the wisdom of sad experience and broader observation, will persuade them to fight, with more than physical bravery, a holier battle, with the glorious war cry of 'FREE SOIL AND FREE MEN.'"[24]

This was a fanciful interpretation of the political condition of the volunteers but certainly reflective of their discontents with the leadership that had brought them to their current state. The final encampment of the regiment was in Brighton, Massachusetts, to which place tens of thousands of the curious swarmed and listened to widespread tales of the soldiers' disaffection with their officers.

The homecoming excitement came to a head with a parade of the volunteers, and a reception at Fanueil Hall, Boston, on Saturday, July 22. Some 200 to 250 of the returned soldiers were permitted to parade with arms to the hall. One report said that number was determined by the number of muskets available. Some observers claimed that the officers picked the most politically reliable elements of the regiment for this honor. They turned out to be far from docile, nonetheless. The haggard volunteers, observers remarked, looked striking compared with the accompanying militia units with their polished buttons and plumage. At the banquet General Edmands, the leader of a civilian militia, admitted that he was "almost ashamed of the display of gala dresses exhibited by his own command." Doing homage to the volunteers, Edmands could not forbear from stating that he did not himself "feel called upon to volunteer, . . . but he honored those who had responded to the call."

Colonel Isaac Wright, commander of the regiment, spoke as the friend of the common soldier. He garnered considerable applause by noting the contrast between the departure and the reception of the regiment. He remarked that "we have troops of friends here, where before the number was small. We rejoice at the change, which has been effected, and will not inquire too curiously into the cause of that change." He also noted that the newspapers were shedding "crocodile tears" over the condition of the regiment but were doing precious little to raise money for its relief.

Colonel Wright cast oil upon the waters, but with General Cushing's appearance at the podium they began to boil. The volunteers and others of the assembled militiamen and guests greeted Cushing with groans, hisses, and cries of "Turn him out!" Cushing went on determinedly, but his remarks were barely audible beyond the first few tables around the podium. The beleaguered general finally blustered that the demonstration was mean and cowardly, and "humbly referred to himself as one of 20,000 returning volunteers." He took his seat without further comments.[25]

The gubernatorial election went badly once again for candidate Cushing, although he remained a politically influential figure in the state, due largely to his strong connection to the national Democratic Party. He served as U.S. attorney general under Franklin Pierce. Cushing remained within the conservative wing of the Democracy, until the outbreak of the Civil War, serving in the last days of the Buchanan administration as envoy to South Carolina secessionists.[26]

Soldiers resented the imperious General Cushing more than they did corrupt and brutal regimental officers, holding as he did the reins of patronage in his own hands. Aloof and censorious, he inspired hatred far more than did the drunk and slovenly company officers. Massachusetts men, like other American volunteers, would seek to fulfill democratic ideals in volunteer organizations they maintained after the Mexican War.

The Irish Militias

The importance of volunteer military service had been driven home to Boston Irish Americans and was not forgotten, even though they were legally disbanded by the antiimmigrant Know-Nothing Party in the mid-1850s. With the dissolution of the Boston militias, and the loss of sponsorship from middle-class patrons, the ideals of Irish nationalism did not disappear; rather, the militias were submerged for a time in semicivil institutions, without the ceremony of formal militias. "The Columbian Artillery became the Columbian Literary Association, while the Sarsfield Guards became the Sarsfield Union Association, and their balls, picnics, and lectures suffered no loss in popularity."

The disillusionment of the Boston Irish with the Democratic Party in the 1850s, as the party coalesced with the Free-Soil Party, enabled the ascendant Republicans to build patronage ties with Irish political figures. These ties and the nationalism—both for the United States and Ireland—brought huge numbers of Irish into Massachusetts national guard units. The Ninth

Massachusetts, for example, was an Irish regiment that formed very early in the Civil War and fought "from Bull Run to Appomatox": these units became ripe recruiting grounds for the Irish nationalist Fenian movement.[27]

As was in evidence to a much greater extent in New York City, social and political clubs, gangs, militias, fire departments, and target clubs were part of an enmeshed web of male-dominated social life. The activities of these groups cut across ethnic lines; such voluntary associations, however informal, had their own internal hierarchies based on class, but also bravado and fighting skills. In New York City, as in Massachusetts, some veterans came through the war unbowed, with a sense of accomplishment and pride. The political strength of the Irish in New York City, as compared with that in Boston, and the extent to which they had distinguished themselves on the battlefields in Mexico contributed to the strength and endurance of the Irish militias in New York, holding out against the attacks of nativists.

The Sixty-ninth Regiment of New York Militia proudly bore its green uniform, surviving intact the Know-Nothing years. The Sixty-ninth proffered a controversial snub to Edward, Prince of Wales, on a royal visit to New York in 1860. There was an outcry in the press and in the legislature to disband the regiment, but the approach of civil war placed its services in demand once more. Its green banner flew side by side with the stars and stripes throughout the Civil War.[28]

The Subsequent Career of the Citizen-Soldier

The Civil War promoted a dialogue about citizenship, nationalism, and republicanism. An important group within the Union, and to some extent the Confederate, armies adopted a broad vision of republicanism, joining the causes of liberating Ireland and protecting the United States. Irish nationalists broadened their base of support; unlike the Young Ireland movement, Fenianism drew strong support among Irish workers in the United States, Ireland, and Britain.[29]

Northern volunteers had to shed some of the cultural and racial parochialism of the Mexican War era and fight for a national cause. The secession of the Confederate states disabused Union soldiers of notions of the glory of independent Texas-style republics, established on the backs of servile races. Northerners fought for many reasons, but almost universal among them was the desire to preserve the Union, with its Constitution and legally established forms.

At its inception, the Civil War seemed to beckon to the citizen-soldier, in the same way as had the Revolution, and perhaps more than had the Mexican War; white men, from both the North and South, were called forward to defend republic and home, which were in imminent peril. Both Abraham Lincoln and Jefferson Davis issued drafts upon the states for militiamen, 75,000 three-month volunteers in the North, and 100,000 to serve for twelve months in the South. These drafts were quickly oversubscribed, as were calls in the North for more militia and supplements to the regular army in May. Congress followed Lincoln's initial call with authorization for 1 million three-year volunteers. In addition some of the northern states called out two-year volunteers. Out of this hodgepodge of enlistments there soon developed a regularized national system on both sides, including conscription, and more standardization of conditions, terms, and duration of service. Three years became the standard term of service in the North. Of 700,00 men who enlisted by early 1862 only 90,000 were three-month volunteers, and many of these reenlisted for three years. Conscription called out only 6 percent of the total Union enlistment, but there, as in the South, it pressured many more men to volunteer to avoid the disgrace of being drafted.

This mass mobilization swept away many of the vestiges of state militia traditions and practices. Out of approximately 1,780 volunteer regiments that served the Union cause, only 15 had continuous existence before the war. The decrepit remnants of the old volunteer militias were completely reorganized in the Civil War mobilization, although individual companies often had continuous organization and solidarities from the prewar era. Only those regiments with a unique group identity, usually ethnic, were strong enough to forward their services at the outset of the war. These included the Irish Sixty-ninth of New York, and German regiments in Washington, D.C., and Missouri.[30]

State volunteers, at first, relied on a combination of state, private, and federal sources of funds and equipment, as had been the case in the Mexican War. This was an insurmountable obstacle to a massive national mobilization, and the efforts of Secretary Edward M. Stanton and Quartermaster General Montgomery Meigs soon brought about a centralized disbursement of funds and provisions. A major accomplishment of this system was to make universal the blue U.S. army uniform, reducing disastrous incidents of friendly fire which plagued the Union in the early months of the war. The blue uniform had been a badge of shame for Mexican War volunteers; it quickly became an honorable symbol of national service in the Civil War.

The Confederate government was not as assiduous nor as able to adopt standardized uniforms, and its soldiers retained the ragtag look of Mexican War volunteers.

The Union and the Confederacy dealt their most devastating blows to the old volunteer system when they established examination boards for volunteer officers, relegating community approbation and elections secondary to professional qualifications. The defeat at Bull Run prompted Congress to scrutinize the competency of its officer corps, and over the next few months hundreds of officers were discharged or resigned rather than face the boards.

The practice of electing officers ended in the North by 1863. It continued a bit longer in the South, largely due to the better quality of volunteer officers. The Confederacy dispersed its regular army officers throughout the volunteer regiments, having no regular force of its own.[31]

With regular line and field officers, volunteer units often encountered the disciplinary standards and methods of the regular army. Bucking and gagging and other painful and humiliating rituals were often imposed on volunteers. In a significant change from the Mexican War, volunteer deserters were subjected to summary executions. Hundreds of deserters were shot or hung in public rituals in front of their comrades. These were only a small percentage of the hundreds of thousands of men, North and South, who deserted, but the sanctions against desertion were unmistakable; they were not negotiated as in Mexican War volunteer units.

Regiments continued to form based on town and region, despite the attrition within existing regiments. This created bodies of raw recruits rather than dispersing them among seasoned veterans. Volunteers still measured the value of their military service in terms of the esteem of their comrades and communities.[32]

As in the Mexican War, and in perhaps any other war, long, painful marches were part of the routine, as was a regimen of disease and boredom in camp. Civil War soldiers engaged in atrocities against civilians, both in foraging for supplies and as antiguerrilla warfare. Union soldiers destroyed entire towns to retaliate for sniping incidents, and rebel guerrillas mercilessly plundered pro-Union areas of the South.[33] The Civil War encompassed a bitter and protracted guerrilla war, making atrocities against civilians inevitable. As for random and uncoordinated attacks by detached bodies of soldiers, the circumstances and rationales were obviously different than in the Mexican conflict.

The Confederate soldier maintained the spirit and rationales of the Mexican War volunteer much more than his northern counterpart. Once again southerners went to war for white freedom and nonwhite servility, in a defensive rather than an expansive context. A young physician from a border state joined a Confederate regiment and wrote that "We are fighting for our liberty, against tyrants of the North who are determined to destroy slavery."[34] Southerners were also fighting for land — their own — with a population that was overwhelmingly rural.

It was the North that would actually grant some homesteading privileges to its soldiers. Southern politicians had been strongly opposed to a homestead act before the Civil War, seeing that western population expansion was going overwhelmingly to the free states. The Homestead Act of 1862 was the capstone of the free-soil movement of the preceding decades, providing opportunities for citizens of the upper Mississippi Valley region to claim new lands, despite the powerful advantage it offered to large speculators.

The Spanish-American War: Resurgent Manifest Destiny
In 1898, the government appealed once again to American volunteers to act as liberators in Latin America. The Spanish-American War recreated a volunteer mobilization, drawing on regiments and companies from American communities, with promises of heroism for the conquering citizen-soldiers. As in the Mexican War a small core of regular soldiers did the strategic fighting, while a far larger body of volunteers provided a core for the political mobilization around the war. Unlike the Civil War, state National Guard units kept their own loose disciplinary structure, with election of officers once again standard practice. The community base of individual companies reinforced the loose disciplinary structure, with hometown newspaper correspondents reporting on the conduct of the officers toward the men. As in 1846, these officers were community elites, who had a hand in organizing and supplying National Guard companies, and deference, tempered by a social veneer of equality, held the regiments together. The campaigns in Cuba were hard-fought but brief, with fewer than 400 American battlefield casualties. It was the "most popular" of the United States's foreign wars, with support garnered from across the political spectrum. Even Socialists and Progressives applauded the ostensible goals of aiding the Cuban republicans against their Spanish colonizers.[35]

One significant change in the post-Emancipation era was that African Americans were allowed a role in this war from the start, albeit in segregated regiments. The U.S. Army had created four black regiments in the aftermath of the Civil War (with white officers) and these were quickly mobilized; three additional black regular regiments were formed under the assumption that blacks had "immunity" to tropical diseases. Their fighting role enhanced African American pride over what they hoped would be a war to create a multiracial republic.[36] The Jim Crow legislation of the 1890s had codified racial discrimination, and it was carried abroad with the army. African American soldiers took on something of the role of Irish and German soldiers in the Mexican War, with insults and violence heaped upon them by white civilians and soldiers, and their racial affinity with the enemy was used to cast doubt upon their patriotism.[37]

White soldiers had less at stake than blacks. Few white soldiers went with expectations of personal conquest or aggrandizement. Most went in hopes of acquiring reputation and standing back home, although white supremacist rhetoric pervaded the conversation of the soldiers and the prowar propaganda. Absent were Mexican War dreams of land and personal conquest. Cuba was to become the fiefdom of wealthy sugar planters; there was no serious talk of homesteading or citizen-conquerors. Soldiers had come to accept the role they resisted so fiercely in the Mexican War, that of waged soldiers. They sought respect, recognition, and negotiation of their terms of service. As the citizen-soldier was subsumed to bourgeois values, he lost the romantic luster of freebooter. He was still entitled to racial privilege, both in the invaded lands and within his own army, but the state imposed some legal limits on his privilege. These restrictions were as much on his right to accept nonwhites as social equals, partners, and even superiors, as it was on his right to wreak violence on them.

Conclusion

In the twentieth-century, the American military moved sharply toward a corporate status, distinct from the broader society and polity. The government narrowed or eliminated any negotiation of terms of service, and directed soldiers away from competing loyalties. A standing, regular army was the result, ready for deployment against external or internal enemies, including rebellious American workers. Working-class internationalism was deeply suspect and a matter for the intervention of police or military authorities.[38]

A more porous boundary between civil and military life in the nineteenth century allowed freer discussion of political issues and choices about service as a matter of course within the army. The abolition of section and community as bases of the national military stripped these smaller units of decisive influence in international politics. "The tragedy of American diplomacy," as enunciated by William Appleman Williams, was precisely this artificial constriction of "domestic politics" to a limited range of issues and alternatives. "Empire as a way of life" expanded frontiers and economic power, but built a fortified wall between citizens of empire and the ideas and movements beyond that frontier.[39]

The informal structure of the Mexican War military had also lent itself to manipulations of "popular" politics; political and economic elites turned popular sovereignty into a synonym for racist brutality and wanton usurpation. In 1846 U.S. national elites placed their most restless and desperate citizens upon the throat of Mexico; these men "voted" to conquer and loot, finding themselves in a situation where this behavior was encouraged. But many individuals reacted in their own ways to the plan of manifest destiny; even those who chose to support its program took it in unexpected directions, and this was possible with the republican ideals underlying the volunteer army. The lack of scale, organization, and resources that hampered early U.S. imperialism allowed for greater individual and communitarian imperatives, to the extent that individuals and groups simply stood firmly by the promises of democracy made to them by recruiters.

Historians have seen the Mexican War as a decisive moment for American nationalism, creating a continental nation, and a hinterland for a burgeoning capitalist heartland.[40] But it is more particularly a historic moment in the creation of an American empire rather than nation, encompassing proliferating hierarchies of race and social class, establishing the basis for oligarchic rule based partly on landed wealth. The anthropologist Benedict Anderson doubts whether "even the most messianic of nationalists dream of a day when all the members of the human race will join their nation in the way that it was possible, in certain epochs, for, say, Christians to dream of a wholly Christian planet."[41]

There were clearly national objectives in the Mexican War, but also messianic racial and republican visions, and an individualistic spirit of empire that suggest both empire and revolutionary republicanism. These contrary impulses bring up perplexing questions about just what sort of "nation" the United States really was, in the European conception of the word. Of even greater moment to the present work is Anderson's observation that racism is founded in "ideologies of class rather than in those of nation: above all in claims to divinity among rulers and to 'blue' or 'white' blood." Nationalism, on the other hand, is concerned with historical destinies.[42] These historical destinies can include empire; however, in the European sense, racial caste and servitude are located outside the nation-state, in an overseas colonial setting. The United States, from its inception as a society, faced the challenge of maintaining republican egalitarianism and racial servitude within its national boundaries. The success of the creole class in the United States in maintaining this dual system, and the dismal failure of other New World creole elites led to the boundless confidence of 1846, with its headlong program of conquest and "liberation." The powerful and unpredictable mixture of racial supremacism, Jacksonian republicanism, evangelical Christianity, and European romanticism that Americans of this era carried in their heads produced a contingent and idiosyncratic national effort.

The diversity of personal and group goals in this war, and in this era of American history, made for a poor nationalism, yet for an interesting, lively (and violent) republic. In a war and an era riven with conflict, the making and writing of history involved, and involves, many contradictory strands, and any one line of narrative is monotonous and deceptive. The proponents of manifest destiny, trying to encompass the diverse and conflicting factions in the nation, needed to set national destiny in the most superlative of terms.

Thomas Hart Benton, for example, prophesied the infinite expansibility of the "fee-simple empire"—that is, American values and commerce based solidly on widespread property holding. Benton predicted that the American empire would sweep around the world to Asia, and bring enlightenment and change. Walt Whitman also predicted the "liberation" of "venerable priestly Asia." These impossible pronouncements of national messianism were both a stimulus and a disaster for nationalism. Such superlatives led to inevitable perceptions of failure and recriminations, as propagandists struggled to recreate national and universalistic myths. In the aftermath of the Mexican War political writers criticized Catholics in the United States and Mexico as a despotic, antirepublican element, standing in the way of American expansion

One writer of the immediate postwar years, Brantz Mayer, a former ambassador to Mexico, devoted a book to anti-Catholic screeds and lamentations on the sad moral condition of Mexico. As a diplomat and politician, he was in part responsible for the limitations that expansionism encountered; for Mayer, a reassertion of national cultural and political values was sufficient to obliterate any setbacks to American destiny. He reiterated the fantasy of racial purity and classless democracy that sustained the Mexican War effort. He contended that the United States, in its revolutionary origins, unlike Mexico had begun as a nation of equals.[43]

> All were essentially equal because all were equally forced to work for livelihood. There was no recognized class in government or society. We were all of one blood and did not fall into the error of amalgamation with Indians and negroes. We were controlled by reason and not governed by passions or instincts. We had nothing but liberty and space; soil and freedom. Our soldiers were rewarded with land; but that land was in the wilderness and exacted toil to make it productive; and thus compulsory industry diverted the minds of our political founders.[44]

The U.S. military sojourn in Mexico had presented formidable dangers: the threat of racial amalgamation, the temptation of easy wealth and land without toil: only a return to moral and political purity would keep Americans virtuous enough to resist these temptations.

Mayer's commentary was joined by a chorus of nativism in the 1850s as the Know-Nothing, or American, Party sought to purge internal corruption by attacking the Catholic Church and servile foreign labor. One prominent nativist traveled to Mexico and offered perspective on a society where republicanism had, by his lights, failed. Robert Wilson wrote a book of harsh commentary on Mexico in the 1850s, at the height of the Know-Nothing movement. He pointedly appealed to the white artisans and small manufacturers at the core of the antiimmigrant movement with denunciations of bound labor in Mexico. Wilson laid the blame for labor exploitation at the doorstep of large institutions, the church, the military, and foreign capital.

Wilson wrote of how artisans were lined up and searched as they left the foreign-owned manufactories each evening. Workers were treated as criminals and reduced to the state of paupers, while "white" men were too proud to perform manual labor. This state of affairs he blamed largely on the Catholic Church: "for the want of a little morality intermixed with his religious instruction," he said the working Mexican had become a thief and degraded the condition of labor.[45] By criticizing remote evils, Wilson raised the specter of a society dominated by large-scale corporatism, which could control labor to the detriment of the small master and artisan. Catholicism and racial subordination were almost identical in Wilson's view and were a clear threat to labor and the nation.

Mayer's and Wilson's formulas for renewal celebrated a virtuous and prosperous society of equals, where races were confined to their appropriate spaces and social divisions among whites done away with. They offered contrasting visions: of virtuous soldiers with land, and of iniquitous workers without even the tools of their trade. In retrospect the Mexican War provided the basis for this contrast: the Texas Ranger, freely seizing the land and labor of Mexicans, and the Irish soldier, without arms, forced on board the troop ship to Mexico. In between lay a great debate among soldiers about the terms of service and national destiny.

Notes

INTRODUCTION

1. See chapter 7, note 19.
2. See chapter 8, note 4.
3. See chapter 7, notes 9, 10.
4. Herrenvolk is the term for a society built on racial domination, with privileges accruing solely to the dominant race. It was introduced by the sociologist Pierre van den Berghe in his book *Race and Racism: A Comparative Perspective*; see esp. 18, 36.

   Van den Berghe enumerates two kinds of herrenvolk society, paternalist and competitive, with more democratic societies like the United States hewing to the competitive model, and notes that democratic societies often have harsher race relations than aristocratic ones. The deeply intertwined nature of race and republicanism leave the present work to take up the question of herrenvolk democracy at least as a point of departure. The idea, most trenchantly applied to American society by Edmund Morgan, in *American Slavery, American Freedom*, that American white, male equality was inherently supported by racial domination emerges sharply in the rhetoric of the Mexican War. A newer application of herrenvolk theory to colonial Ireland and to colonial and the early republican years is found in Allen, *The Invention of the White Race*, vol. 1. Historian George Rawick hypothesizes that racism emerged as a psychological by-product of the development of capitalism in the sixteenth and seventeenth centuries. He says that northern Europeans saw in Africans their own "pre-capitalist" behaviors and social organization and were driven to repress in others what they saw as their own worst instincts. Rawick, *The American Slave*, 125–32. This is one of a number of theories that see racism as developing out of psychological pressures, almost instinctively, rather than out of rational economic and political choices. Similarly, Roediger says that "whiteness was a way in which white workers responded to a fear of dependency on wage labor and to the necessities of capitalist work discipline. . . . The white working class, disciplined and made anxious by fear of dependency, began during its formation to construct an image of the Black population as 'other.'" *Wages of Whiteness*, 13–14. Barbara Fields offers an interesting contrary position, that racism is one of a range of ideological constructs, and that it has no fixed form or meaning for various individuals, or even for the same individual. "White supremacy is a slogan, not a belief," she claims. Fields, "Ideology and Race in American History," 156.

5. See esp. Merk, *Manifest Destiny and Mission*, 193.

6. Bennett was the editor of the *Herald* (New York), Beach of the *Daily Sun* (New York), and O'Sullivan of the *United States Magazine and Democratic Review* (New York), a national political and literary magazine. O'Sullivan coined the phrase "manifest destiny," as an expression of a will to dominate and absorb the nations of the Western Hemisphere.

7. Fuller, *The Movement for the Acquisition of All Mexico, 1846–1848*, 44.

8. Schroeder, *Mr. Polk's War*, 22.

9. Ibid., 46.

10. Pletcher, *Diplomacy of Annexation*, 552–55.

11. Griswold del Castillo, *Treaty of Guadalupe Hidalgo*, 44.

12. Ibid., 46.

13. Montejano, *Anglos and Mexicans*, 50–74.

14. See Lander, *Reluctant Imperialists* 17.

15. Hietala, *Manifest Design*, ix; Bauer, *The Mexican War*, 12.

16. Schroeder, *Mr. Polk's War*, 161–62. For a more detailed discussion of Polk's growing appetite for Mexican territory during the course of the war, see Graebner, *Empire on the Pacific*, 154–59, 167–69.

CHAPTER 1

1. Tomlins, *Law, Labor*, 260; Prude, *The Coming of Industrial Order*, 155–57; Dublin, *Women at Work*, 89, 207.

2. In 1850 the laborers in "manufacturing, construction, mining, transportation, and domestic service accounted for 21 percent of the total." Slaves accounted for another 23 percent of the labor force: Montgomery, *Citizen Worker*, 13. From 1820 to 1850, nonagricultural employment rose from approximately 800,000 to 3 million; agricultural workers increased from about 2 million to about 5 million. Cumulatively those employed by others increased from one-third of the population in 1820 to one-half at midcentury. Tomlins, *Law, Labor*, 259; Foner, *Free Soil, Free Labor, Free Men*, 16.

3. Josephson, *Golden Threads*, 268; *Daily Advertiser* (Lowell, Mass.), March 6 and 29, 1855.

4. Way, *Common Labour*, 10–11.

5. Ibid., 233, 254–55.

6. Roediger, *Wages of Whiteness*, 26.

7. The debate over corporal punishment in the military went back at least to the early years of the republic. The influence of President Thomas Jefferson and his followers contributed to the regulation of flogging in the army in 1806 and its elimination in 1812. Various forms of corporal punishment persisted nonetheless, and in 1833, in a general "reform" of military practices, flogging was reinstated, with a maximum sentence of fifty lashes, and only to be administered under the authority of a general court-martial. Skelton, *An American Profession of Arms*, 268–69.

8. Langley, *Social Reform in the United States Navy,* 166, 182–89. On the controversy over flogging in New England factories, see Montgomery, *Citizen Worker,* 18–19.

9. Cunliffe, *Soldiers and Civilians,* 124. Dean, "In Evident Mental Commotion," 168–70. Black soldiers in the Civil War were subjected to the same humiliating physical punishments as whites, and in addition were handcuffed when off duty, and often forced to perform heavy physical labor for the quartermaster: Berlin et. al., *Free at Last,* 529–33. Black laborers in the employ of the U.S. Army were actually flogged by white soldiers: Berlin et. al., *The Wartime Genesis of Free Labor,* 89, 113.

10. *Liberator* (Boston), November 12, 1847.

11. *Daily Eagle* (Brooklyn), August 5, 1846; Montgomery, *Citizen Worker,* 64–65.

12. Textile mills apparently retained the British system of caning refractory child workers in the mills. See Prude, *The Coming of Industrial Order,* 45. As late as 1833, the labor activist Seth Luther denounced the discipling of children in the "*whipping room of a large cotton manufactory.*" Luther, *Address on the Right of Free Suffrage,* 9.

13. McCaffrey, *Army of Manifest Destiny,* 6–7; Bauer, *Mexican War,* 18–19, 106–12; Justin Smith, *War with Mexico,* 1:142, 146.

14. Daniel Hill, "The Army in Texas," 440–43.

15. Henry, *Campaign Sketches,* 17–18; *Weekly Telegraph* (Houston), September 21, 1848.

16. Daniel Hill, "Army in Texas," 448.

17. "Filibusters" were privately financed and manned invasions of foreign (mostly Caribbean and Central American) nations undertaken by Americans. Filibustering was largely a phenomenon of the 1830s through 1850s, but reached its height in the early 1850s. See Brown, *Agents of Manifest Destiny.*

18. *Daily Picayune* (New Orleans), April 20, 1853.

19. Daniel Hill, "Army in Texas," 452–56.

20. Ibid., 450.

21. Ibid.

22. Cunliffe, *Soldiers and Civilians,* 170–71, 132–33.

23. Skelton, *American Profession of Arms,* 181, 218–19; Fayette Robinson, *An Account of the Organization of the Army,* 1:90.

24. Cunliffe, *Soldiers and Civilians,* 123. In the antebellum years an average of 20 to 21 percent of the men enlisted in the regular army deserted: McCaffrey, *Army of Manifest Destiny,* 112.

25. See, e.g., U.S. Department of War, Judge Advocate General, Court Martial Records, EE-514, 1847, RG 153, National Archives.

26. Here we see General Taylor, once again, using the volunteers as first-wave fodder, as he had in the Second Seminole War. This had the military effect of saving trained soldiers for strategic assaults, and the political effect of giving the volunteers the "glory" and "reputation" they so eagerly sought. Cunliffe, *Soldiers and Civilians,* 121.

27. *Niles' National Register* (Baltimore), November 21, 1846. This forceful defense of the regular forces was originally published in the *Mercury* (Charleston, S.C.), and is almost certainly the work of Daniel Harvey Hill, an acerbic and outspoken critic of the volunteer system. (See Daniel Harvey Hill Diary, December 4, 1846,

Southern Historical Collection.) He was one of the few regulars to maintain a consistent journalistic voice during the war, countering the general opinions of the legions of volunteer correspondents, whom Hill claimed were false and self-aggrandizing.

28. Quoted in *Voice of Industry* (Lowell, Mass.), February 26, 1847.
29. Ballentine, *Autobiography of an English Soldier*, xxvi, 23, 24, 58.
30. Ibid., 97.
31. Cunliffe, *Soldiers and Civilians*, 132–33; Zeh, *An Immigrant Soldier in the Mexican War*, 7.
32. Coffman, *The Old Army*, 139–40.
33. Ibid., 144.
34. Ibid., 143.
35. Cunliffe, *Soldiers and Civilians*, 120.
36. Prucha, *Broadax and Bayonet*, 44.
37. "A common idea of the regulars was expressed in the House by Tilden of Ohio, who described them as 'a set of puppets ... shut up without exercise and in barracks, from year's end to year's end.'" Justin Smith, *The War with Mexico*, 1:320.
38. Cunliffe, *Soldiers and Civilians*, 24.
39. Miller, *Shamrock and Sword*, 174; Cunliffe, *Soldiers and Civilians*, 123–25; Ballentine, *Diary of an English Soldier*, 28.
40. Cunliffe, *Soldiers and Civilians*, 231–40. The request for the Catholic chaplains was reportedly made by General Zachary Taylor. *Catholic Herald* (Philadelphia), June 25, 1846.
41. *Catholic Herald* (Philadelphia), August 5, 1847. The *Catholic Herald* employed yarns of military life to make its points about discrimination and hinted obliquely at the power of Catholics to retaliate. One such tale, early in the war, melodramatically highlighted the bravery and loyalty of Catholics, despite blanket discrimination. This story described an Irish soldier in the British army in India; his fellow soldiers, English and assimilated countrymen, tried to persuade the Irishman to abandon his religion, as the only route to promotion within the ranks. He steadfastly refused, recalling the admonition of his sainted Irish mother "never to blush for thy country or thy religion." The soldier died valiantly, sacrificing himself for his comrades-in-arms. Ibid., "Letters Received," June 11, 1846.
42. O'Brien, *Treatise on American Military Laws*, 59, 336.
43. *Truth Teller* (Cincinnati), April 16, 1846.
44. A characteristic figure is the Reverend Fitch Taylor, a naval chaplain during the war. He, in his memoir of that service, gratuitously libelled Catholic institutions, invoking the St. Bartholomew's Day Massacre and the Inquisition, and calling for dismemberment of the Mexican nation and the Mexican Catholic Church: *The Broad Pennant*, 157.
45. McEniry, "American Catholics," 46.
46. O'Connor, *Fitzpatrick*, 122.
47. Way, *Common Labour*, 190.

48. An intensive look at Mexican priests and their revolutionary activity can be found in William Taylor, *Magistrates of the Sacred*, chap. 1.

49. Henry, *Campaign Sketches*, 25–26.

50. Garesché, *Biography of Lieut. Col. Julius P. Garesché*, 70.

51. Ibid., 72; McEniry, "American Catholics," 99–126; Garesché, *Biography of Lieut. Col. Julius P. Garesché*, 71–74.

CHAPTER 2

1. *Daily Cincinnati Gazette*, June 2, 1846.

2. United States, Constitution, Article I, sec. 8; *Daily Cincinnati Gazette* June 5, 1846. For a detailed exposition of this point of view, see "Speech of Col. A. H. Bulloch, in the Massachusetts Legislature," *Massachusetts Spy* (Worcester, Mass.), January 27, 1847.

3. *Richmond Whig and Public Advertiser*, January 1, 1847.

4. By early 1847 new volunteer regiments, like the regular army troops could enlist for five years or the duration of the war. Before this volunteer enlistments were for twelve months.

5. *Congressional Globe* 29th Cong., 2d sess., 1847, 16: 269.

6. Pocock, *Machiavellian Moment*, 199–201.

7. Christopher Hill, *The World Turned Upside Down*, 59.

8. Ibid., 60–61.

9. Ibid., 109; Pocock, *Machiavellian Moment*, 410.

10. Pocock, *Machiavellian Moment*, 438.

11. Ibid., 441–42, 511.

12. Royster, *A Revolutionary People at War*, 47.

13. Cunliffe, *Soldiers and Civilians*, 184, 201–7.

14. Montgomery, *Citizen Worker*, 91.

15. Pocock, *Machiavellian Moment*, 535–36.

16. Ibid., 534.

17. Handlin, *Boston's Immigrants*, 187.

18. Lane, *Policing the City*, 36–37, 66, 69–70.

19. Handlin, *Boston's Immigrants*, 188–90.

20. Quoted in the *Daily Eagle* (Brooklyn), April 3, 846.

21. *Daily Chronotype* (Boston), February 24, 1848.

22. *National Aegis* (Worcester, Mass.), March 17, 1847, January 5 and 12, 1848.

23. Davis, "The Career of Colonel Pluck," 184, 186–89.

24. In rural settings, the militia experienced similar, if less obstreperous decline. The militia organization of western New York State flourished during the first four decades of the nineteenth century, facing threats of trouble along the Canadian frontier and with the complicity of powerful landholding interests, guarding against antirent farmers, who sporadically mounted protests in land office centers like Batavia and Leroy. As in Philadelphia, the resentment of appointed regimen-

tal officers and the lack of purpose drained enthusiasm and numbers of militia-men. "In 1844 Militia units participated for the last time in Batavia's Independence Day observance, with the volunteer fire companies thereafter taking their place. The fire company was almost the militia reincarnate with its musters, uniforms, organization of captains and lieutenants, companies and brigades." See Kutolowski and Kutolowski, "Commissions and Canvasses," 9–17, 35, 37.

25. A recent study of urban volunteer fire departments in the first half of the nineteenth century shows them to be remarkably like volunteer militia units in their lack of an overriding class-conscious agenda and, like the independent militia, doomed to obsolescence in the twenty years before the Civil War. Volunteer fire companies stoutly upheld the independence of the locally organized, democratically structured group of freemen and, despite their tendency to brawling and rioting, encompassed some of the wealthiest and most respectable members of urban communities. Volunteer fire companies were phased out in the late 1850s in favor of paid firefighters using expensive new steam engines and horses. As with the militias, political and economic elites preferred to deal with large, easily controllable organizations rather than a mélange of anarchic volunteer groups. Greenberg, *Cause for Alarm*, 9, 15, 39, 123.

26. Davis, *Parades and Power*, 77–78.

27. *Working Man's Advocate* (New York), October 26, 1844.

28. Ibid.

29. *Herald* (New York), July 29, 1846.

30. *Subterranean* (New York), June 13, 1846.

31. *Daily Delta* (New Orleans), February 16, 1847; *Public Ledger* (Philadelphia), February 27, 1847. In 1849 the Killers were still a cohesive militant organization. In the aftermath of the anti-British Astor Place riots in New York City, it was rumored for several days that they would be arriving en bloc to carry out further nativist violence. Moody, *The Astor Place Riot*, 207.

32. Hackenburg, *Pennsylvania in the War with Mexico*, 6.

33. Ibid., 8.

34. *American Celt* (Boston), August 31, 1850.

35. Mahon, *History of the Militia and the National Guard*, 83–84.

CHAPTER 3

1. *Mercury* (Charleston, S.C.), May 30, 1846.

2. *Daily Cincinnati Gazette*, February 9, 1847, June 23, 1846 and April 29, 1847.

3. Ibid., June 1, 1846.

4. Quoted in the *Daily Enquirer* (Cincinnati), June 1 and 4, 1846.

5. Ibid., July 4, 1846.

6. Ibid., May 22, June 4, July 8, 1846.

7. Quoted in ibid., May 22, 1846. Cincinnati had two Catholic newspapers during the Mexican War era, the *Telegraph* and the *Truth Teller*. Both were firmly in the Democratic camp and were not shy about voicing highly political sentiments.

The *Truth Teller* denounced the Mexican Catholic Church as corrupted by racial impurity and was eager to see American Catholics "reform" that body. The paper also denounced the early efforts of the Free-Soil Party, particularly its elevation of African Americans to the position of spokesmen. "We will ever rebel against their impudently thrusting themselves into any meeting of the Democracy to instruct us in our duty concerning the choice of our rulers." *Daily Enquirer* (Cincinnati) November 6, 1847, and August 19, 1848.

8. Ephraim K. Chamberlin Journal, May 25, 1847, Huntington Library.

9. *Daily Cincinnati Gazette,* June 4, 1847.

10. Ibid., June 15, 1847. Here is the breakdown for the First Ohio, according to Regimental Surgeon Chamberlin:

> On leaving Camp Washington, the 1st Ohio numbered about 800 . . .
> Of that number there have died of disease: 33
> Accidentally killed by a comrade: 1
> Murdered by Mexicans: 6
> Killed in Battle at Monterey: 16
> Do   do   Ceralvo: 2
> Resigned, discharged on Surgeon's certificate, or deserted before the
>   Regiment left New Orleans: 202
> Dishonorably discharged: 7
> Mean strength of the Regiment: 553
> The number of desertions before reaching the Brazos [the first landing place
>   outside the United States] was about fifty-six.

11. Ibid., June 4, 1847.

12. *Daily Chronotype* (Boston), June 4, 1846.

13. *Western Citizen* (Chicago), July 14, 1846.

14. Ibid.

15. Volunteer enlistment total for Illinois was 6,123, 1 in 140 of the white population; for the states of New York, New Jersey, and Pennsylvania together, volunteer enlistment totaled 5,324, 1 in 1,080 of the white population. Ellsworth, "American Churches and the Mexican War," 319.

16. *Western Citizen* (Chicago), February 16, 1847.

17. Ibid., June 17, 1846.

18. Faragher, *Sugar Creek,* 138–39.

19. The abolitionist editor Elijah Lovejoy was murdered by a proslavery mob, in Alton in 1836. Lovejoy was shot down in a hail of gunfire from the mob while attempting to defend a printing press. It is doubtful that Goff deserved sole credit for this act. Davis, *Autobiography of the Late Colonel Geo. T. M. Davis,* 58–67.

20. Chamberlain, *My Confession,* 30–31.

21. Faragher, *Sugar Creek.* This study of central Illinois documents the trend toward concentration of land and wealth in fewer hands and the resort to tenancy by newcomers and failed settlers of previous decades. See esp. 185–86.

22. *Weekly Tribune* (New York), June 27, 1846.

23. Eliza Dodd to John Dodd, May 30, 1847, John W. Dodd Papers, Beinecke Library.

24. John Dodd to Eliza Dodd, September 9, 1847, ibid.

25. Isaac Charles, New Orleans, to Jos. E. Siddall, Philadelphia, May 5, 1846, Isaac Charles Papers, Tulane University Archives.

26. *Daily Tropic* (New Orleans), May 20, 1846.

27. Isaac Charles to Joseph E. Siddall, Philadelphia, November, 18, 1847, Isaac Charles Papers, Tulane University Archives.

28. Quoted in Justin Smith, *War with Mexico*, 1:123.

29. *Daily Delta* (New Orleans), February 19, 1846.

30. H. Judge Moore Diary, January 24, 1847, Beinecke Library.

31. Ibid., May 12, 1846.

32. Ibid., May 10, 1846.

33. Anthony Sinclair, New Orleans, to George and Margaret Kistner, May 22, 1846, Antebellum Letter Collection, Historic New Orleans Collection.

34. Henry, *Campaign Sketches*, 113.

35. *Daily Delta* (New Orleans), May 8 and 10, 1846.

36. Ibid., May 8, 1846.

37. *Daily Tropic* (New Orleans), December 4, 1846, clipping in Works Progress Administration, Mexican War Collection, Louisiana State Museum.

38. *Daily Delta* (New Orleans), May 3 and 5, 1846; *Daily Tropic* (New Orleans), May 20, 1846.

39. *Daily Delta* (New Orleans), January 29 and February 27, 1847.

40. *Weekly Picayune* (New Orleans), February 1, 1847.

41. Mayor's Letter Books, January 28 and 30, 1847, New Orleans, Office of the Mayor, New Orleans Public Library; *Daily Delta* (New Orleans), January 29 and 31, 1847.

42. *Herald* (New York), July 15, 1846.

43. *Mercury* (Charleston, S.C.), October 19, 1846: source of internal quotes unknown.

CHAPTER 4

1. *Daily Herald* (New York), May 7, 1847.

2. Kemper, "James Lawson Kemper," 421.

3. Ibid.

4. Zeh, *An Immigrant Soldier*, 7.

5. Ibid., 4, 5.

6. See esp. the *Herald* (New York), January 25, 1847, for a detailed account of large-scale forced recruitment in Pittsburgh.

7. W. W. H. Davis, Cambridge, Mass., to father, Bucks County, Pa., December 15, 1846, W. W. H. Davis Papers, Beinecke Library.

8. John Augustus Bolles (1809–78), a Boston lawyer and former Massachusetts secretary of state. In 1839 the American Peace Society in Boston published his *Essay*

on a Congress of Nations, for the Pacific Adjustment of International Disputes. He presented Lieutenant Colonel Wright with a sword at the Faneuil Hall rally.

"Robert Rantoul (1805–52), a prominent Boston lawyer and Massachusetts Democrat, was appointed in 1846 United States District Attorney for Massachusetts. A reformer, he was opposed not only to the extension of slavery but also to capital punishment. 'Public attention had recently been called to his views [on the same issue] by some letters to Governor Briggs on the subject, written in February, 1846.'" Wortham, *James Russell Lowell's The Biglow Papers,* 193.

9. Fuess, *Life of Caleb Cushing,* 2:4–5, 12, 35.

10. Ibid., 38–39; *Daily Evening Traveller* (Boston), January 16, 1847; *Massachusetts Spy* (Worcester, Mass.), January 27, 1847.

11. *Richmond Whig and Public Advertiser,* May 21, 1847; *Daily Chronotype* (Boston), October 15, 1847.

12. *Massachusetts Spy* (Worcester, Mass.), January 27, 1847.

13. *Daily Courier* (Lowell, Mass.), January 23, 1847.

14. *Daily Evening Traveller* (Boston), January 25, 1847; *Herald* (New York), January 20, 1847.

15. Wortham, *James Russell Lowell's The Biglow Papers,* 62.

16. *National Aegis* (Worcester, Mass.), April 14, 1847.

17. Fuess, *Life of Caleb Cushing,* 2:36, 38–39.

18. *Daily Evening Transcript* (Boston), February 2, 1847; *Daily Chronotype* (Boston), February 6, 1847.

19. Parker, *Collected Works,* 4:37.

20. *Pilot* (Boston), July 31, 1847.

21. Ibid., May 29, 1847.

22. Ibid., January 23, 1847; *Daily Courier* (Lowell, Mass.), February 12, 1847. Father Fitzsimmons was removed from his church of Sts. Peter and Paul by Bishop Fitzpatrick in 1853 after a controversy, ostensibly over financial matters. The bishop took control of the church away from pastor and parishioners after it was rebuilt. The parishioners petitioned Rome to redress the general financial mismanagement of the dioceses and for restoration of their popular pastor. O'Connor, *Fitzpatrick's Boston,* 201.

23. O'Connor, *Fitzpatrick's Boston,* 55–56. Reverend O'Brien was commissioned by Governor Andrew as chaplain of the Irish Twenty-eighth Massachusetts Regiment in 1862 but failed to report for duty. "After investigation it was learned that Fr. O'Brien, who had a serious drinking problem for many years, had apparently wandered off. 'I judge that he is a "fallen brother,"' the adjutant general informed the governor. 'No one knows where he is.'" Ibid., 201.

24. *Massachusetts Spy* (Worcester, Mass.), February 17, 1847; *Daily Courier* (Lowell, Mass.), February 12, 1847; *Daily Evening Transcript* (Boston), February 12, 1847; *Daily Cincinnati Gazette,* February 19, 1847.

25. *Daily Evening Traveller* (Boston), July 20, 1848; Henry, *Campaign Sketches,* 59.

26. *Daily Evening Transcript* (Boston), February 16, 1847.

27. *Subterranean* (New York) May 23, 1846.

28. *Daily Courier* (Lowell, Mass.), May 22, 1846.

29. Ibid.

30. Bridges, *A City in the Republic*, 75.

31. Ibid., 77.

32. Curiously, the lack of any record of Walsh having become a U.S. citizen was not an impediment to his serving in the U.S. Congress despite Article I of the Constitution, which states that no one can be a U.S. representative without being a citizen for seven years. Ernst, "The One and Only Mike Walsh," 46, 40; Wilentz, *Chants Democratic*, 328.

33. Quoted in Wilentz, *Chants Democratic*, 332.

34. *Working Man's Advocate* (New York), May 11, 1844.

35. Ibid., April 27, 1844, January 25, 1845.

36. Ernst, "The One and Only Mike Walsh," 55–56.

37. Biggs, *Conquer and Colonize*, 23–25. Wright, as a U.S. senator, had opposed the annexation in 1844. He was passed over in the presidential nomination of that year and was not on good terms with Secretary of War Marcy or Polk. Ibid.

38. Lippitt, *Reminiscences of Francis J. Lippitt*, 61.

39. *Subterranean* (New York), June 13, 1846.

40. Ibid.

41. Spencer, *Victor and the Spoils*, 153–54, 29–30.

42. Biggs, *Conquer and Colonize*, 40.

43. *Subterranean* (New York), July 4 and 18, 1846.

44. Ibid., July 18, 1846.

45. Walsh later explained this scam in a speech he made in the New York legislature. "When the money was put into the hands of Stevenson to fit out the mock regiment which Marcy made him Colonel of . . . [the soldiers] had to take clothes that were originally made for the negro soldiery of St. Domingo, and so infamously made, that even they would not accept them. As to the jackets that Stevenson charged $5.06 for—the six cents he supposed were put on to show how peculiarly conscientious he was—[Walsh] said he took three men up into the Bowery and got them jackets made for $1.50 a piece—and they were far superior to the five dollar and six penny jackets that Stevenson furnished." *Subterranean* (New York), January 16, 1847.

46. Lippitt, *Reminiscences of Francis J. Lippitt*, 61.

47. *Subterranean* (New York), July 18 and August 1, 1846.

48. Biggs, *Conquer and Colonize*, 42–44; *Subterranean* (New York), August 1, 1846; *Herald* (New York), August 3 and 19, 1846.

49. *Subterranean* (New York), July 25, 1846.

50. Ibid., September 30, 1846; Lippit, *Reminiscences of Francis J. Lippitt*, 64; Biggs, *Conquer and Colonize*, 81. The California Regiment went by the designation of the Seventh New York Regiment, having taken up that designation from an existing militia company. The second regiment formed in New York was called the First New York Regiment, again having taken the name of a militia company. Later in

the war, the War Department changed the designation of the two regiments, to reflect their entry into the U.S. service. Therefore, for posterity, the California Regiment became the First New York Regiment, and the former First Regiment became the Second New York Regiment. Robarts, *Mexican War Veterans*, 25. I have referred to the Seventh Regiment as the California Regiment and the regiment organized subsequently, which went to Mexico City with Scott, as the First Regiment, and will continue to do so.

51. Spencer, *Victor and the Spoils*, 138; Lombard, *The High Private*, 7–9.

52. Lombard, *The High Private*, 7–9.

53. Ibid., 8–10.

54. *Massachusetts Spy* (Worcester, Mass.), January 20, 1847.

55. Ibid., 29; *Subterranean* (New York), January 16, 1847.

56. Lombard, *The High Private*, 26; U.S. House of Representatives, House Executive Document No. 24, 31st Cong., 1st sess., 1850, 6.

57. Lombard, *The High Private*, 26.

58. *Subterranean* (New York), June 19, 1847. A recent study confirms that judges in New York City had great freedom to issue summary judgments in the crimes in which working people were usually charged, and could issue verdicts and sentences as they liked. Less than 10 percent of all criminal convictions in New York during the 1840s involved jury trials; see Smith, "Circumventing the Jury," chap. 3.

59. *Subterranean* (New York), May 22, 1847; Ernst, "The One and Only Mike Walsh," 61.

CHAPTER 5

1. Reginald Horsman offers a useful discussion of how white Americans came to view Indians and African Americans as inferior, but with markedly different characteristics — and of how for white Americans these characteristics were the prototype for all race relations. *Race and Manifest Destiny*, 189–201.

2. Justin Smith, *War with Mexico*, 1:206.

3. See Johannsen, *To the Halls of the Montezumas* 49–50; and Smith and Judah, *Chronicles of the Gringos*, 317.

4. Quoted in *Sun* (Baltimore), July 1, 1846.

5. John Dodd to Eliza Dodd, July 9 and May 3, 1847, John W. Dodd Papers, Beinecke Library. Dodd reports men deserting over failure to get commissions or quartermaster's positions, although he does not mention actual desertions because of disappointment with wages.

6. Justin Smith, *War with Mexico*, 2:364.

7. A random sampling of land warrants under the 1847 act found only 26 out of 441 soldiers made claims on land rather than selling their warrants. Oberly, *Sixty Million Acres*, 92, 11. According to an article in the *Herald* (New York), July 19, 1848, many soldiers gave up their land bounties for twenty to thirty dollars; speculators in the land warrants bought from soldiers statements of power of attorney for the

mentioned sum, while the soldier was still in service (usually broke and on the spree) and were thus able to claim the warrant upon the soldier's discharge. Mike Walsh, in a speech in Congress in 1854, reiterated this complaint, saying that "the rich rascals who speculated in land warrants . . . [disposed] of their warrants for less than twenty-five dollars." *Congressional Globe*, 33rd Cong., 1st sess., 1854, 28, p. 3: 1957.

8. Mayer, *Mexico, Aztec, Spanish and Republican*, 159.
9. J. Dodd to Eliza Dodd, September 9, 1847, John W. Dodd Papers, Beinecke Library; *Daily Evening Transcript* (Boston), July 28, 1848.
10. February 9, 18, June 6, 1847, John Palmer Diary, Huntington Library.
11. Cooke, *The Conquest of New Mexico and California*, 62.
12. Giddings, *Campaign in Northern Mexico*, 81.
13. Quoted in Mahon, *History of the Militia and the National Guard*, 92.
14. Ephraim K. Chamberlin Journal, September 1846, Huntington Library.
15. Ibid., August 19, 1846.
16. *Richmond Whig and Public Advertiser*, February 5, 1847.
17. Ibid.
18. U.S. Senate, "Mutiny at Buena Vista," 69, 80, 208.
19. Ibid., 6–7, 14, 80.
20. Stanislaus Lasselle to Malenie Lasselle, November 24, 1846, Lasselle Family Papers, Indiana State Library, Indiana Division.
21. Daniel Harvey Hill Diary, October 29 and November 4, 1846, Southern Historical Collection.
22. See especially the correspondence of Lieutenant Mayne Reid of the New York volunteers, in *Spirit of the Times* (New York), March–September 1847, for examples of romanticized war correspondence.
23. *Liberator* (Boston), November 12, 1847; *Daily Chronotype* (Boston), September 15, 1847.
24. Fuess, *Life of Caleb Cushing*, 2:54, 58; *Weekly Tribune* (New York), November 13, 1847.
25. *Daily Chronotype* (Boston), September 22, 1847.
26. Giddings, *Sketches of the Campaign*, 276.
27. Ephraim K. Chamberlin Journal, June 22, 1846, Huntington Library.
28. Ibid.
29. Ibid., July 12, 1846.
30. *Daily Delta* (New Orleans), October 6, 1846.
31. Prior to the Mexican War blacks had been excluded from U.S. Army service, as stipulated by an 1820 general order. State militias also forbade blacks from service. The navy imposed a 5 percent quota system on free black enlistments, and a few blacks did serve on navy vessels in the Gulf and on the Pacific Coast of Mexico. May, "Invisible Men," 464.
32. *Daily Picayune* (New Orleans), August 5, 1853.
33. William M. Gardner, April 20, 1848, William M. Gardner Letters, Southern Historical Collection.

34. Anderson, *An Artillery Officer in the Mexican War*, 128.

35. Curtis, *Mexico under Fire*, 22.

36. Stanislaus Lasselle to Malenie Lasselle, February 10, 1847, Lasselle Family Papers, Indiana State Library, Indiana Division; Curtis, *Mexico under Fire*, 22–23.

37. "Journal of a Volunteer Officer . . .," 21, in W. W. H. Davis Papers, Beinecke Library; *Daily Cincinnati Gazette*, June 15, 1847.

38. *Daily Delta* (New Orleans), February 6, 1848; Buhoup, *Narrative of the Central Division*, 48.

39. U.S. Senate, Report of the Secretary of War, 31st Cong., 1st sess., 1849, Ex. Doc. No. 32, 44.

40. *Daily Cincinnati Gazette*, June 3, 1847.

41. *National Aegis* (Worcester, Mass.), July 26, 1848.

42. *Daily Evening Traveller* (Boston), November 3, 1847; Sargent, *Gathering Laurels in Mexico*, October 31, 1847.

43. U.S. Department of War, Adjutant General's Office, Incoming Correspondence, 1846-446 and 1848-1030, National Archives.

44. John Dodd to Eliza Dodd, May 31, 1847, John Dodd Papers, Beinecke Library.

45. John White Geary Papers, January 3, 1848, Beinecke Library; Hartmann, *Private's Own Journal*, 5.

46. John White Geary Papers, January 3, 1848, Beinecke Library; Hartmann, *Private's Own Journal*, 26. See also Ephraim K. Chamberlin Journal, June 22, 1846, Huntington Library; and Sargent, *Gathering Laurels in Mexico*, January 1, 1847.

47. *Planters' Banner* (Franklin, La.), December 30, 1847.

48. Ibid.

49. *Liberator* (Boston), March, 12, 1847.

50. *Daily Delta* (New Orleans), February 11, 1847.

51. Domenech, *Missionary Adventures in Texas and Mexico*, 69–70.

52. U.S. Department of War, Judge Advocate General, Court Martial Records, EE443, September 3, 1847, RG 153, National Archives. See also, ibid., EE382, March 7, 1847.

53. Carpenter, *Travels and Adventures*, 100.

54. Justin Smith, *War with Mexico*, 2:151; Miller, *Shamrock and Sword*, 155–63.

55. Miller, *Shamrock and Sword*, 32, 187–92; Cunliffe, *Soldiers and Civilians*, 120; Henry, *Campaign Sketches*, 249.

56. Carpenter, *Travels and Adventures*, 208.

57. Yeo and Thompson, *Unknown Mayhew*, 301–2.

58. Ibid., 312–14.

59. Justin Smith, *War with Mexico*, 318–19.

60. U.S. Department of War, Judge Advocate General, Court Martial Records, EE256, July 6, 1846; EE530, July 16, 1847, RG 153, National Archives.

61. Ibid., EE532, July 26, 1847.

62. Miller, *Shamrock and Sword*, 131.

63. Carpenter, *Travels and Adventures*, 136, 208.

64. Ibid., 217.

65. Ibid., 212–18, 227.

66. Ibid., 291.

67. *Weekly Picayune* (New Orleans), May 29 and August 7, 1848.

68. *American Star* (Mexico City), November 10, 1847.

CHAPTER 6

1. John Dodd to Eliza Dodd, October 15, 1847, John W. Dodd Papers, Beinecke Library; and *Sun* (Baltimore), June 8, 26, July 3, 1846.

2. Barbara Fields's essay on race and ideology was helpful here in realizing that one does not have to tie up contradictory impulses, and language neatly; rather, the spectrum of racist, and to some extent antiracist, behavior ranges across a given spectrum of ideology. "Ideology and Race in American History," esp. 155–57.

3. Giddings, *Sketches from the Campaign*, 324–26.

4. Ibid., 54; John Dodd, lieutenant in the Indiana regiment, also manifested this ambivalence toward the Texas Rangers, admiring their effectiveness, but criticizing in moderate terms their brutality. Dodd clearly expresses his belief in the fatally corrupt condition of the Mexican "race" and society: John Dodd to Eliza Dodd, November 28, 1847, and January 10, 1848, John W. Dodd Papers, Beinecke Library.

5. *Mercury*, March 2, 1847.

6. Robert Johannsen, the most prominent of recent historians of the Mexican War, concludes that the war did not necessarily perpetuate slavery or racism and, in fact, was an engine for nationalism. He says that the Mexican War advanced a nascent international democratizing and liberalizing mission on the part of the United States. *To the Halls of the Montezumas*, 273–97.

7. James Athon Journal, January 5, 1848, Indiana Historical Society.

8. *American Fistiana*, 32–33; Brackett, *General Lane's Brigade*, 79; *Daily Times* (New York), November 5, 1857.

9. Daniel Harvey Hill Diary, March 13, 1848, Southern Historical Collection; *Daily Times* (New York), November 5, 1857.

10. U.S. Senate, Report of the Secretary of War, 31st Cong., 1st sess., 1849, Ex. Doc. No. 32., 43–44.

11. M'Sherry, *El Puchero*, 147.

12. Daniel Harvey Hill Diary, October 17, 1846, Southern Historical Collection.

13. Giddings, *Sketches of the Campaigns*, 324. Regular army cavalrymen were also said to have been in the massacre at the Rancho Guadeloupe; they lost several of their own in the wagon train massacre. "The murder was committed, they say, by a party of Americans numbering about twenty, and was done in the night. The Murdered men were first made prisoners tied, and afterwards all shot through their heads." *Niles' National Register* (Baltimore), May 22, 1847.

14. Acuña, *Occupied America*, 17; Chamberlain, *My Confession*, 176; *Niles' National Register*, May, 29, 1847.

15. Giddings, *Sketches of the Campaigns*, 326.

16. Curtis, *Mexico under Fire*, xiv.

17. *Weekly Picayune* (New Orleans), February 1, 1847.

18. Ford, *Rip Ford's Texas*, 82.

19. Giddings, *Sketches of the Campaigns*, 232; John Palmer Diary, December 27, 1846, Huntington Library.

20. John Palmer Diary, April 8, 1847, Huntington Library; *Liberator* (Boston), April 16, 1847; McCaffrey, *Army of Manifest Destiny*, 124–25. There is a great deal of disparity in accounts of the responses to the massacre by Taylor and others. Some say that no punishment whatsoever was levied on the responsible companies. Other rumors flying about at the time had the numbers killed varying greatly. Samuel Chamberlain, in an apparently fanciful account, has the Arkansans scalping the civilians and doing Indian war dances. *My Confession*, 87–88.

21. Daniel Harvey Hill Diary, August 13, 1847, Southern Historical Collection.

22. Chance, *Mexico under Fire* 92, 21; Winfield Scott to David Connor, March 16, 1847, Thomas W. Sweeny Collection, Beinecke Library.

23. *Subterranean* (New York), June 7, 1847.

24. Lopez y Rivas, *La guerra del 47*, 135–36; Daniel Harvey Hill Diary, September 18, 1847, Southern Historical Collection.

25. Ford, *Rip Ford's Texas*, 84–85. For a slightly different version of this story, see the *Delta* (New Orleans), February 10, 1848. The trial of the bank robbers introduced a striking note of American racial "justice" and officially raised the question of whether Mexicans were "colored" in the same sense as African Americans. The court ruled in the negative.

    The *Delta* of the 10th contains the proceedings of five additional days of the military commission for the trial of eight Americans, charged with robbery and murder. The principal witness introduced was Francisco Marquas, whose testimony an attempt was made to exclude, on the ground that he was a person of color—a mulatto. "There was no evidence introduced to prove African blood in the witness, *and it was proved that he was a Mexican*. He was accordingly admitted to testify, and stated, in substance, that the burglary was committed by a party of nine besides himself; of the nine he knew Lieutenants Hare and Dutton, Sergeant Wragg, and four men named Booth, Laferture, Laverty, and Hollister. Lieut. Hare was the leader of the party. On the conclusion of the trial of Lieut. Hare, the Court did not render a verdict, and probably would not until all the trials were concluded. The trial of Lieut. Dutton was commenced." *Daily Journal* (Boston), May 20, 1848 (emphasis added).

26. Sargent, *Gathering Laurels in Mexico*, April 6, 1848; W. W. H. Davis to Jacob R. Hibbs, May 21, 1848, W. W. H. Davis Papers, Beinecke Library; Oswandel, *Notes of the Mexican War*, 559.

27. *Catholic Telegraph*, January 8, 1848.

28. Stanislaus Lasselle to Malenie Lasselle, February 10, 1847, Lasselle Family Papers, Indiana State Library, Indiana Division.

29. R. Patterson to Rev. Francis McFarland, January 1, 1848, Robert Patterson Letters, Western Reserve Historical Society.
30. Julius P. Garesché to Mrs. Blackford, February 29, 1848, Blackford Family Papers, Southern Historical Collection.
31. Ibid.
32. Ibid.
33. Oswandel, *Notes of the Mexican War*, 155, 158.
34. Hackenburg, *Pennsylvania in the War with Mexico*, 123–31; Oswandel, *Notes of the Mexican War*, 107.
35. *Freeman's Journal* (New York), May 20, 1848.
36. Samuel Chamberlin, quoted in Acuña, *Occupied America*, 17.
37. Brackett, *General Lane's Brigade*, 120.
38. Ballentine, *Diary of an English Soldier*, 167; Donnavan, *Adventures in Mexico*, 98.
39. Childs, like General Scott, went out of his way to be friendly to the higher clergymen, who were extremely nervous about the designs of Mexican liberals on the church's wealth and property. The bishop of Puebla refused to give a cent for the defense of the city and retired to his country home. After the occupation was established, he became very friendly with Childs and his officers: Lopez y Rivas, *La guerra del 47*, 128.
40. *Boston Post*, July 24, 1848.
41. Brack, *Mexico Views Manifest Destiny*, 117.
42. See Lopez y Rivas, *La guerra del 47*; and Acuña, *Occupied America*.
43. Lopez y Rivas, *La guerra del 47*, 135–36.
44. Olliff, *Reforma Mexico*, 12.
45. Reina, *Las rebeliones campesinas*, 342–44.
46. Ibid., 345.
47. Ibid., 346.
48. Wasserman, *Capitalists, Caciques, and Revolution*, 9–10.
49. Guardino, *Peasants, Politics*, 137–41.
50. Mallon, "Peasants and State Formation," 15–16.
51. Guardino, *Peasants, Politics*, 148, 158.
52. Cecil Robinson, *View from Chapultepec*, 17.

CHAPTER 7

1. Allen, *Invention of the White Race*, 23.
2. H. Judge Moore Diary, February 19, 1847, Beinecke Library.
3. U.S. Senate, Report of the Secretary of War, 31st Cong., 1st sess., 1849, Ex. Doc. No. 32, 41.
4. Ibid., 31–35.
5. Harris, *A Mexican Family Empire*, 210.
6. Ibid., 219.
7. Ibid., 43–44.

8. See chapter 5.

9. John Palmer Diary, November 7, 29, April 19, 1847, Huntington Library,

10. Justin Smith, *War with Mexico*, 2:230, 450; John Palmer Diary, April 21, and May 23, 1847, Huntington Library.

11. Buhoup, *Narrative of the Central Division*, 21.

12. U.S. Senate, Report of the Secretary of War, 31st Cong., 1st sess., 1849, Ex. Doc. No. 32.

13. See, e.g., Olmsted, *A Journey through Texas*, 325: "It is repeated as a standing joke—I suppose I have heard it fifty times in the Texas taverns that a nigger in Mexico is just as good as a white man, and if you don't treat him civilly he will have you hauled up and fined by an alcalde. The poor yellow-faced, priest-ridden heathen actually hold in earnest the ideas on this subject put forth in that good old joke of our fathers—the Declaration of American Independence."

14. Buhoup, *Narrative of the Central Division*, 41, 42.

15. Ibid., 42.

16. Wasserman, *Capitalists, Caciques, and Revolution*, 74, 87.

17. Wislizenus, *Journey to the Rocky Mountains*, biographical introduction; *Dictionary of American Biography*, 17, 430–31.

18. Apparently, the U.S. force under Stephen Kearny, which was ordered to capture Santa Fe, tried to overtake the traders and stop them from selling weapons to the Mexicans. In this effort they were unsuccessful. *Dictionary of American Biography*, 17, 431; U.S. Senate, *Memoir of a Tour to Northern Mexico*, 20, 48.

19. U.S. Senate, *Memoir of a Tour to Northern Mexico*, 49–50.

20. Ibid., 83–85.

21. Ibid., 62, 78.

22. Daniel Walker Howe refers to "the ponderous Constitution of that era," which mandated lengthy delays between election and service. Howe, *Political Culture*, 93.

23. Ibid., 84.

24. Griswold del Castillo, *Treaty of Guadalupe Hidalgo*, 182.

25. *Appendix to the Congressional Globe*, 30th Cong., 1st sess., 1848, 17: 261.

26. Ibid., 262.

27. *Niles' National Register* (Baltimore), July 17, 1847; *Congressional Globe*, 30th Cong., 1st sess., 1848, 17: 185.

28. John H. Schroeder attributes the failure of the United Sates to absorb all of Mexico mainly to elite political, religious, and intellectual opposition to the war, which hemmed in Polk's expansionists. *Mr. Polk's War*, 161–65; Reginald Horsman maintains that the grinding to a halt of manifest destiny at the Rio Grande came from a deep-seated American cultural aversion to the "racial dangers" that a close connection with Mexico would bring about. *Race and Manifest Destiny*, 240–48.

29. Griswold del Castillo, *Treaty of Guadalupe Hidalgo*, 45.

30. Ibid., 46.

CHAPTER 8

1. In 1851 and 1855 land grants were extended to virtually all individuals who had seen service in however limited a capacity in the Mexican and other wars. This included teamsters, musicians, and soldiers who had served for extremely brief periods or who had merely traveled to the scene of action. Less than one in twenty of these grants, like the 1847 land bounties, was ever taken up by the grantees; most were sold to speculators at various prices. Gates, *History of Public Land Law Development*, 271–81.

2. Foner, *Free Soil, Free Labor, Free Men*, xxvii.

3. John Hodge to Mrs. D. L. Wood, September 28, 1847, Orlando John Hodge Papers, Western Reserve Historical Society.

4. John Hodge to Mrs. D. L. Wood, September 13, 1847; John Hodge to Mrs. D. L. Wood, September 28, 1847, both in ibid.

5. Margaret H. Arnold, "Collection Description," ibid.

6. Alfred Hodge to John Hodge, July 23, 1849, and August 1, 1851, ibid.

7. Alfred Hodge to D. L. Wood, June 5, 1848; Alfred Hodge to D. L. Wood, November 25, 1848; Alfred Hodge to D. L. Wood, October 15, 1849, all in ibid. Alfred Hodge seemed to have Democratic proclivities from an early age. His brother's memoirs recount a tale of Alfred and some other youths sabotaging a Whig political rally in 1840, put up to the stunt by a local Democratic Party luminary. A log cabin had been erected in downtown Cleveland by the Whigs and was the headquarters of the Harrison presidential campaign. One night just before the election, when activities were in full swing, Hodge and his companions pulled down a canoe that was mounted atop the cabin and ran off with the flag. They successfully escaped and presented the flag to a "Locofoco" (i.e., Democrat) leader; Alfred later observed it hanging in a tavern. Hodge, *Reminiscences*, 39–40.

8. Hodge refers to "Brother Jonathan," a nineteenth-century equivalent of "Uncle Sam." According to popular accounts, George Washington wrote a series of letters addressed to "Brother Jonathan" Trumbull, a wealthy Connecticut merchant, soliciting funds for the Continental army during the Revolution. British publicists adopted this term to refer to the general population of the rebel colonies and, later, the United States. Brewer, *Dictionary of Phrase and Fable*, 89.

9. Alfred Hodge to D. L. Wood, November 25, 1848; Arnold, "Collection Description," both in Orlando John Hodge Papers, Western Reserve Historical Society.

10. *Weekly Tribune* (New York), February 27, 1847.

11. Gates, *Public Land Law Development*, 390.

12. *Daily Delta* (New Orleans), February 9, 1848.

13. Historian Frederick Merk notes that the New York *Herald* and the *Sun* were the largest circulation papers in the world, yet their staunch advocacy of taking all of Mexico quickly lost popular support when the more limited aims of the Treaty of Guadalupe Hidalgo were put forward. "Is it permissible for the puzzled historian to conclude that the Bennetts and Beaches and their like were mistaken in

believing they represented the inner thoughts of the masses; that they grossly exaggerated their sway over the masses and even over the masses in the big cities of the Atlantic seaboard?" Perhaps the *Herald* and the *Sun* et al. "were read by the masses on account of their freshness and coverage of news, on account of their sensationalism; or even because they satisfied their reader's earthy tastes, and not at all because their editorial views had deep-seated popular support." *Manifest Destiny and Mission*, 193.

14. *Congressional Globe*, 33rd Cong., 1st sess., 1854, 28, p. 3, 1957.

15. *Daily Delta* (New Orleans), January 12, 1850.

16. Lippitt, *Reminiscences of Francis J. Lippitt*, 76.

17. Ibid., 77–78.

18. Ibid., 101–4, 107; Lynch, *With Stevenson to California*, 53, 64.

19. Lynch, *With Stevenson to California*, 53.

20. Francis Clark, *First Regiment of New York Volunteers*, 21.

21. Fuess, *Life of Caleb Cushing*, 2:65.

22. *Weekly Argus* (Albany), July 30, 1848; *Weekly Tribune* (New York), July 29, 1848; *Boston Post*, July 20, 1848.

23. James Henry Hill Diary, Wednesday July 19 and 29, 1848, American Antiquarian Society.

24. Ibid., September 19, 1848; *Massachusetts Spy* (Worcester, Mass.), July 26, 1848.

25. *Boston Post*, July 24 and July 25, 1848; *Massachusetts Spy* (Worcester, Mass.), July 26, 1848.

26. Fuess, *Life of Caleb Cushing*, 2:198.

27. Handlin, *Boston's Immigrants*, 157; Montgomery, *Beyond Equality*, 95.

28. Mahon, *History of the Militia*, 86; Montgomery, *Beyond Equality*, 130.

29. Montgomery, *Beyond Equality*, 127.

30. McPherson, *Battle Cry of Freedom*, 318, 99–100; Montgomery, *Beyond Equality*, 94.

31. McPherson, *Battle Cry of Freedom*, 327; Mahon, *History of the Militia and National Guard*, 98.

32. Dean, "In Evident Mental Commotion," 168–70; McPherson, *Battle Cry of Freedom*, 326; Linderman, *Embattled Courage*, 80–88.

33. Dean, "In Evident Mental Commotion," 150–51.

34. McPherson, *What They Fought For*, 51.

35. Linderman, *Mirror of War*, 67–72.

36. Gatewood, *Black Americans and the White Man's Burden*, 41–47.

37. Ibid., 178.

38. See Goldstein, *Political Repression in Modern America*, 77–79, on Theodore Roosevelt's use of federal troops to put down mining strikes in the West in 1907–9; and Dawley, *Struggles for Justice*, 238, on the post–World War I mobilization of U.S. troops against steel strikes.

39. Quoted in Bergquist, *Labor*, 56.

40. See esp. Johanssen, *To the Halls of the Montezumas*, 214; Connor and Faulk, *North America Divided*, 43.

41. Anderson, *Imagined Communities*, 7.

42. Ibid., 149.

43. Mayer, *Mexico, Aztec, Spanish and Republican*, 157-60.

44. Ibid., 159.

45. Wilson, *Mexico and its Religion*, 283-84.

Bibliography

PRIMARY SOURCES

Manuscript Materials

American Antiquarian Society, Worcester, Mass.
  Abby Kelley Foster Papers
  John Gough Journal
  James Henry Hill Diaries
Beinecke Rare Book and Manuscript Library, Yale University, New Haven, Conn.
  Sumner C. Brooks. Army Letters
  W. W. H. Davis Papers
  John W. Dodd Papers
  Simon Doyle and James Doyle. Mexican War Correspondence
  Amos B. Eaton Letter Book
  John Freeland Letters
  John White Geary Mexican War Papers
  H. Judge Moore. Mexican War Diary
  William E. Prince. Diary, Letters, and Army Letter Book
  Joseph Rowe Smith Papers
  Thomas W. Sweeney Collection
  John D. Wilkins. Memorandum and Letters
  Henry Wilson Papers
Duke University, Special Collections, Durham, N.C.
  Fletcher H. Archer Papers and Notebooks
  Archibald W. Burns Journal
  John W. McCalla Papers
Historic New Orleans Collection, New Orleans, La.
  Antebellum Letter Collection
  Samuel Gray Letter
  James Robb Papers
Huntington Library, San Marino, Calif.
  Harvey Brown Journal
  Ephraim K. Chamberlin Journal
  Francis Lieber Papers
  Nathaniel Lyon Papers
  John Palmer Diary

Indiana Historical Society, Indianapolis
    James Athon Journal
    Hackleman-Towner Family Papers
    Trustin B. Kinder Papers
    Henry S. Lane Papers
    Benjamin F. Scribner Papers
Indiana State Library, Indiana Division, Indianapolis
    Calvin Benjamin Letters
    Lucius C. Embree Letters
    Lasselle Family Papers
    James H. McNeely Papers
    Daniel D. Pratt Letters
    Mildred K. Richardson — Dr. E. W. Beck Letters
    Richard W. Thompson Papers
    John H. Towner Book
    Thomas Williams Letter
Louisiana State Museum, New Orleans
    Letters to Cousin Collingwood
    Lewis H. Webb Diaries
    Works Progress Administration, Mexican War Collection
Louisiana State University Archives, Baton Rouge
    I. H. Charles Letters
    Hazard Company Letters
National Archives, Washington, D.C.
    United States. Department of State.
        Despatches of U.S. Consuls in Ciudad Juarez, Chihuahua, Matamoras,
            Monterrey, Tampico, Texas, and Santa Fe, 1816–59. (Examined on
            microfilm.)
    United States. Department of the Treasury.
        Collector of Customs, New Orleans. Collector's letters. Record Group 36.
    United States. Department of War.
        Adjutant General's Office. "Addison File," 1848–50. Record Group 94.
        Adjutant General's Office. General Orders, Headquarters, Mexico, 1847–48.
            Record Group 94.
        Adjutant General's Office. Incoming Correspondence, 1845–48. Record
            Group 94.
        Adjutant General's Office. Records of Garrison Courts Martial, Tampico
            Department, February 1–June 15, 1848. Record Group 94.
        Judge Advocate General. Records of the Office of the Judge Advocate General
            (Army). Court Martial Records, 1845–48. Record Group 153.
        San Patricio Microfilm. Selections from Record Group 94 and Record
            Group 153.
New Orleans Public Library, New Orleans, La.
    New Orleans. Office of the Mayor. Mayor's Letter Books, 1845–54.

Southern Historical Collection, University of North Carolina, Chapel Hill
   William Austine Letters
   Romeyn B. Ayres Diary
   Blackford Family Papers
   Borough House Books (Thomas Childs Letter Book)
   James A. Crocker Book
   William M. Gardner Letters
   John H. Green Letters
   Daniel Harvey Hill Papers
   William A. Hoke Papers
   John Kimberly Papers
   Walter Nicol Diary
   John T. Wheat Letters
Tulane University Archives, Baton Rouge, La.
   Isaac Charles Papers
   Smith, Hubbard and Co. Correspondence
   Daniel L. Winsor Papers
Western Reserve Historical Society, Cleveland, Ohio
   Orlando John Hodge Papers
   Robert Patterson Letters

Published Diaries and Memoirs

Allen, G. N. *Mexican Treacheries and Cruelties. Incidents and Sufferings in the Mexican War; with Accounts of Hardships Endured; Treacheries of the Mexicans; Battles Fought, and Success of American Arms.* . . . Boston and New York, 1847.

Allen, Lewis Leonidas. *Pencillings of Scenes Upon the Rio Grande; Originally Pub. bn [sic] the Saint Louis American, By the Rev. L. L. Allen, Late Chaplain to the La. Volunteers in the United States Service Upon the Rio Grande.* New York, 1848.

Anderson, Robert. *An Artillery Officer in the Mexican War, 1846–7; Letters of.* . . . New York and London: G. P. Putnam's Sons, 1911.

Ballentine, George B. *Autobiography of an English Soldier in the United States Army.* Ed. William H. Goetzmann. Chicago: Lakeside Press, 1984.

Barbour, Philip N. *Journal of the Late Brevet Major Philip Barbour.* . . . Ed. Rhoda van Bibber Tanner Doubleday. New York: G. P. Putnam's Sons, 1936.

Beauregard, Pierre G. T. *With Beauregard in Mexico; The Mexican War Reminiscences of P. G. T. Beauregard.* Ed. T. Harry Williams. Baton Rouge: Louisiana State University Press, 1956.

Blanchard, A. G. *Diary and Biography of Captain A. G. Blanchard, Second Louisiana Infantry Volunteers, Mexican War, May 2nd, 1846 to July 25, 1848.* New Orleans, 1848.

Brackett, Albert G. *General Lane's Brigade in Central Mexico.* . . . Cincinnati: H. W. Derby, 1854.

Buhoup, Jonathan W. *Narrative of the Central Division, or Army of Chihuahua, Commanded by Brigadier General Wool.* . . . Pittsburgh: M. P. Morse, 1847.

Carleton, James H. *The Battle of Buena Vista, with the Operations of the "Army of Occupation" for One Month.* New York: Harper and Brothers, 1848.

Carpenter, William W. *Travels and Adventures in Mexico: In the Course of Journeys of Upwards of 2500 Miles Performed on Foot, Giving an Account of the Manners and Customs of the People and the Agricultural and Mineral Resources of that Country.* New York: Harper Brothers, 1851.

Chamberlain, Samuel E. *My Confession, Written and Illustrated by. . . .* New York: Harper, 1956.

Clark, Amasa G. *Reminiscences of a Centenarian, As Told by Amasa Gleason Clark, Veteran of the Mexican War. . . .* [Bandera, Texas], ca. 1930.

Clark, Francis D. *The First Regiment of New York Volunteers, Commanded by Col. Jonathan D. Stevenson, in the Mexican War: Names of the Members of the Regiment during Its Term of Service in Upper and Lower California, 1847–1848, with a Record of All Known Survivors on the 15th Day of April, 1882. . . .* New York: Geo. S. Evans, 1882.

Cooke, Philip St. George. *The Conquest of New Mexico and California; An Historical and Personal Narrative.* New York: G. P. Putnam's Sons, 1878.

Coulter, Richard, and Thomas Barclay. *Volunteers: the Mexican War Journals of Private Richard Coulter and Sergeant Thomas Barclay, Company E, 2nd Penna. Infantry.* Ed. Allan Peskin. Kent, Ohio: Kent State University Press, 1991.

Curtis, Samuel R. *Mexico under Fire. . . .* Ed. Joseph E. Chance. Fort Worth: University of Texas Press, 1994.

Davis, Col. Geo. T. M. *Autobiography of the Late Colonel Geo. T. M. Davis . . . from Posthumous Papers.* New York: Press of Jenkins and McCowan, 1891.

Devlin, John S. *The Marine Corps in Mexico; Setting Forth its Conduct as Established by Testimony before a General Court Martial . . . for the Trial of First Lieutenant John S. Devlin of the U.S.M.C.* Washington, D.C.: Printed by L. Towers, 1852.

Domenech, Emmanuel. *Missionary Adventures in Texas and Mexico. A Personal Narrative of Six Years Sojourn in those Regions. . . . Translated from the French under the Author's Supervision.* London: Longman, Brown, Green, Longmans and Roberts, 1858.

Donnavan, Corydon. *Adventures in Mexico; Experience during a Captivity of Seven Months.* Boston: G. R. Holbrook, 1848.

DuPont, Samuel Francis. *Extracts from Private Journal-Letters of Captain S. F. DuPont while in Command of the Cyane during the War with Mexico, 1846–1848.* Wilmington, Del.: Ferris Bros., 1885.

Edwards, Frank S. *A Campaign in New Mexico with Colonel Doniphan.* London: James S. Hodson, 1848.

Elderkin, James D. *Biographical Sketches and Anecdotes of a Soldier of Three Wars, as Written by Himself. . . .* Detroit: Record Printing, 1899.

Fletcher, Calvin. *The Diary of Calvin Fletcher, Including Letters to and from Calvin Fletcher, 1817–1866.* Indianapolis: Indiana Historical Society, 1972–.

Ford, John S. *Rip Ford's Texas.* Ed. Stephen B. Oates. Austin: University of Texas Press, 1963.

Furber, George C. *The Twelve Months Volunteer, or, Journal of a Private: In the Tennessee*

Regiment of Calvary in the Campaign in Mexico, 1846-7. Cincinnati: J. A. and U. P. James, 1848.

Garesché, Louis. *Biography of Lieut. Col. Julius P. Garesché, Assistant Adjutant-General, U.S. Army.* Philadelphia: the author, 1887.

Gibson, George R. *Journal of a Soldier under Kearny and Doniphan.* Glendale, Calif.: Arthur H. Clark, 1935.

Giddings, Luther. *Sketches of the Campaign in Northern Mexico. In Eighteen Hundred Forty-Six and Seven. By an Officer of the First Regiment of Ohio Volunteers.* New York: G. P. Putnam, 1853.

Hardy, Richardson. *The History and Adventures of the Cuban Expedition, from the First Movements Down to the Dispersion of the Army at Key West, and the Arrest of General Lopéz. Also: An Account of the Ten Deserters at Isla de Mugeres.* Cincinnati, 1850.

Hartmann, George W. *A Private's Own Journal: Giving an Account of the Battles in Mexico . . . with Descriptive Scenes and a Roll of Company E, 2nd Pennsylvania Regiment. . . .* Greencastle, Pa.: Printed by E. Robinson, 1849.

Haynes, Martin A. *General Scott's Guide in Mexico, A Biographical Sketch of Col. Noah E. Smith.* Lake Village N.H.: Reprint from the *Lake Village Times*, 1887.

Henry, William S. *Campaign Sketches of the War with Mexico.* New York: Harper and Brothers, 1847.

Hill, Daniel Harvey. "The Army in Texas." *Southern Quarterly Review* 9 (April 1846): 434-57.

Hodge, Orlando J. *Reminiscences.* 2 vols. Cleveland: the author, 1902.

Kemper, James L. "The Mexican War Diary of James Lawson Kemper." Ed. Robert R. Jones. *Virginia Magazine of History and Biography* 74:4 (October 1966): 386-428.

Lane, Walter P. *The Adventures and Recollections of General Walter P. Lane, a San Jacinto Veteran, containing Sketches of the Texian, Mexican, and Late Wars. . . .* Marshall, Tex.: Tri-weekly Herald Print, 1887.

Lippitt, Francis J. *Reminiscences of Francis J. Lippitt: Written for his Family, his Near Relatives and Intimate Friends.* Providence, R.I.: Preston & Rounds, 1902.

Lombard, A. *The High Private, with a Full and Exciting History of the New-York Volunteers, and the Mysteries and Miseries of the Mexican War. . . .* New York: "Printed for the publisher," 1848.

Lynch, James. *With Stevenson to California, 1846.* Tierra Redonda, Calif.: 1896.

McLane, Louis. *The Private Journal of Louis McLane USN, 1844-1848.* Ed. Jay Monahan. Los Angeles: Danson's Book Shop, 1971.

M'Sherry, Richard. *El Puchero: or a Mixed Dish from Mexico, Embracing General Scott's Campaign, with Sketches of Military Life. . . .* Philadelphia: Lippincott, Grambo, 1850.

Moore, H. Judge. *Scott's Campaign in Mexico: From the Rendez-vous on the Island of Lobos to the taking of the City, including an account of the Siege of Puebla . . . by H. Judge Moore of the Palmetto Regiment.* Charleston, S.C.: J. B. Nixon, 1849.

Norman, Benjamin M. *Rambles by Land and Water, or, Notes of Travel in Cuba and Mexico; Including a Canoe Voyage up the River Panuco, and Researches among the Ruins of Tamaulipas.* New York: Paine and Burgess; New Orleans: B. M. Norman, 1845.

Oswandel, Jacob. *Notes of the Mexican War, 1846–47–48: Comprising Incidents, Adventures and Everyday Proceedings and Letters while with the United States Army in the Mexican War....* Philadelphia: N.p., 1885.

Preston, William. *Journal in Mexico: Dating from November 1, 1847 to May 25, 1848 by Lieutenant Colonel William Preston of the Fourth Kentucky Regiment of Volunteers.* Paris: Lecram-Servant, 192[?].

Reid, Samuel C. *The Scouting Expeditions of McCulloch's Texas Rangers: or the Summer And Fall Campaign of the Army of the United States in Mexico....* Austin, Tex.: Steck, 1935.

Robertson, John B. *Reminiscences of a Campaign in Mexico: by a Member of "the Bloody-First": Preceded by a Short Sketch of the History and Condition of Mexico....* Nashville: J. York, 1849.

Ruxton, George F. A. *Adventures in Mexico and the Rocky Mountains.* London: J. Murray, 1847.

Sargent, Chauncey F. *Gathering Laurels in Mexico: The Diary of an American Soldier in the Mexican American War.* Ed. Ann Brown James. Lincoln, Mass.: the editor, 1988.

Scott, John A. *Encarnacion; or, the Prisoners in Mexico. Being an Account of their Capture, Treatment and Travels. Also a Description of the Mexican People and Country in Connexion with the Above....* Louisville, Ky.: G. H. Monsarrat and Co.'s Steam Press, 1848.

Scribner, Benjamin F. *Camp Life of a Volunteer, A Campaign in Mexico, or a Glimpse at Life in Camp....* Philadelphia: Grigg, Elliot; New Albany, Ind.: J. R. Nunemacker, 1847.

Scenes of the War in Northern Mexico, with Pictures of Life, Manners and Scenery. New York: D. Appleton and Co., 1848.

Semmes, Raphael. *Service Afloat and Ashore during the Mexican War.* Cincinnati: W. H. Moore and Co., 1851.

Smith, Ashbel. *Reminiscences of the Texas Republic.* 1875. Reprint, Austin, Tex.: Pemberton Press, 1967.

Smith, Gustavus. *Company "A" Corps of Engineers, U.S.A., 1846–48, in the Mexican War.* N.p.: Battalion Press, 1896.

Smith, Isaac. *Reminiscences of a Campaign in Mexico: An Account of the Operations of the Indiana Brigade on the Line of the Rio Grande and Sierra Madre, and a Vindication of the Volunteers against the Aspersions of Officials and Unofficials.* Indianapolis: Chapman and Spann, 1848.

Smith, S. Compton. *Chile con Carne; or, The Camp and the Field....* New York: Miller and Curtis, 1857.

Taylor, Fitch W. *The Broad Pennant: or a Cruise in the United States Flagship of the Gulf Squadron, during the Mexican Difficulties; together with Sketches of the Mexican War....* New York: Leavitt, Trow, 1848.

Twitchell, Ralph Emerson. *The History of the Military Occupation of the Territory of New Mexico from 1846–1851 by the Government of the United States, together with Biographical Sketches of Men Prominent in the Conduct of the Government during that Period.* Denver: Smith-Brooks, 1909.

United States. Senate. *Memoir of a Tour to Northern Mexico, Connected with Col. Doniphan's Expedition, in 1846 and 1847. By A. Wislizenus, M.D.* 30th Cong., 1st sess.

Senate. Miscellaneous. No. 26. Washington, D.C.: Tippin & Streeter, Printers, 1848.

Wynkoop, J. M. *Anecdotes and Incidents: Comprising Daring Exploits . . . of the Mexican War*. Pittsburgh: 1848.

Zeh, Frederick. *An Immigrant Soldier in the Mexican War*. Ed. William J. Orr and Robert R. Miller. College Station, University of Texas Press, 1995.

Newspapers and Periodicals

American Celt (Boston)
American Star (Mexico City)
Baptist Banner and Western Pioneer (Louisville, Ky.)
Biblical Repository and Classical Review (Boston)
Boston Post
Broadway Journal (New York)
Brother Jonathan (New York)
Brownson's Quarterly Review (Boston)
Burrit's Christian Citizen (Worcester, Mass.)
Catholic Herald (Philadelphia)
Congressional Globe (Washington, D.C.)
Daily Advertiser (Lowell, Mass.)
Daily Chronotype (Boston)
Daily Cincinnati Gazette
Daily Courier (Lowell, Mass.)
Daily Delta (New Orleans)
Daily Eagle (Brooklyn, N.Y.)
Daily Enquirer (Cincinnati)
Daily Evening Transcript (Boston)
Daily Evening Traveller (Boston)
Daily Journal (Boston)
Daily Picayune and *Weekly Picayune* (New Orleans)
Daily Sun (New York)
Daily Times (New York)
Daily Tropic (New Orleans)
DeBow's Review (New Orleans)
Freeman's Journal (New York)
Free State Rally and Texan Chain-Breaker (Boston)
Gospel Banner (Augusta, Me.)
Herald (New York)
Hunt's Merchant Magazine and Commercial Review (New York)
Knickerbocker Magazine (New York)
La Patria (New Orleans)
Liberator (Boston)
Massachusetts Spy (Worcester, Mass.)

Mercury (Charleston, S.C.)
National Aegis (Worcester, Mass.)
Niles' National Register (Baltimore)
Pilot (Boston)
Planter's Banner (Franklin, La.)
Propagateur Catholique (New Orleans)
Public Ledger (Philadelphia)
Richmond (Va.) Whig and Public Advertiser
Southern Presbyterian Review (Columbia, S.C.)
Southwestern Baptist Chronicle (New Orleans)
Spirit of the Times (New York)
Subterranean (New York)
Sun (Baltimore)
True American (Lexington, Ky.)
Truth Teller (Cincinnati)
United States Catholic Magazine (Baltimore)
United States Magazine and Democratic Review (New York)
Voice of Industry (Lowell, Mass.)
Weekly Argus (Albany)
Weekly State Gazette (Austin, Tex.)
Weekly Telegraph (Houston)
Weekly Tribune (New York)
Western Citizen (Chicago)
Working Man's Advocate (New York)

Contemporary Publications

Alcaraz, Ramón, et al. *The Other Side: or Notes for the History of the War Between Mexico and the United States*. Trans. and ed. Albert C. Ramsey. New York: J. Wiley, 1850.

The American Fistiana: Showing the Progress of Pugilism in the United States, from 1816 to 1873: Embracing all the Particulars and all the Rounds of every Fight of which there is Positive Record. New York: R. M. DeWitt, 1873.

Avery, The Hon. A. C. *Memorial Address on Life and Character of Lieutenant General D. H. Hill, May 10, 1893*. Raleigh, N.C.: Edwards and Broughton, 1893.

Balbontín, Manuel. *La invasion americana, 1846 á 1849. Apuntes del subteniente de artilleria*. Mexico: Tip. de G. A. Esteva, 1883.

Bancroft, George. *Literary and Historical Miscellanies*. New York: Harper and Brothers, 1855.

Bustamante, Carlos María de. *El nuevo Bernal Díaz del Castillo o sea, historia de la invasión de los Anglo-americanos en México*. Mexico: Impr. De V. García Torres, 1847.

Capen, Nahum. *The Republic of the United States of America: Its Duties to Itself and its Responsible Relations to Other Countries: Embracing also a Review of the Late War between the United States and Mexico*. New York: D. Appleton; Philadelphia: B. S. Appleton, 1848.

Cary, Samuel. *A Sermon Preached Before the Ancient and Honourable Artillery Company, in Boston, June 6, 1814.* . . . Boston: Thomas Wells, 1814.

Castillo Negrete, Émilio del. *Invasion de los norte-americanos en México; obra histórico escrita por.* . . . 6 vols. Mexico: Imprenta del editor, 1890–91.

Channing, William E. "A Letter to the Hon. Henry Clay, On the Annexation of Texas to the United States." 1837. In *Works of William E. Channing*, 183–254. Boston: George G. Channing, 1849.

Christy, William A. *Proceedings in the Case of the United States versus William Christy: on a Charge of Having Set on Foot a Military Expedition, in New Orleans, against the Territory of Mexico in November 1835.* . . . New Orleans: Printed by D. Levy, 1836.

Claiborne, J. F. H. *Life and Correspondence of John A. Quitman, Major-General, U.S.A., and Governor of the State of Mississippi.* 2 vols. New York: Harper and Brothers, 1860.

Clapp, Rev. Theodore. *Autobiographical Sketches and Recollections During a Thirty-Five Years' Residence in New Orleans.* Boston, 1857.

Clay, Cassius M. *The Writings of Cassius Marcellus Clay: including Speeches and Addresses.* . . . Ed. Horace Greeley. New York: Harper and Bros., 1848.

Didimus, Henry. *New Orleans As I Found It.* New York, 1845.

Ellis, George E. *A Discourse Delivered in the First Church, Boston, Before the Ancient and Honorable Artillery Company, June 1, 1846.* . . . Boston: Eastburn's Press, 1846.

Exposición de una persona residente en la República Mexicana sobre la guerra que actualmente sostiene con los Estados-Unidos del Norte. Mexico: Tipografía de R. Rafael, 1847.

Farnham, T. J. *Illustrated European and American History and Biography.* . . . New York: American Family Publication Estab., 1853.

Foster, Stephen C. *Speech of Hon. Stephen C. Foster, of Maine: Delivered in the House of Representatives, April 24, 1860.* "Republican Land Policy — Homes for the Million: Give the Public Lands to the People, and you settle the Slavery Question, obliterate the Frontiers, dispense with a Standing Army, and extinguish Mormonism." Washington, D.C.: Buell and Blanchard, 1860.

Gayarré, Charles. *Romance of the History of Louisiana, A Series of Lectures.* . . . New York: D. Appleton; Philadelphia: G. A. Appleton, 1848.

Giddings, Joshua R. *Speeches in Congress.* Boston: John P. Jewett; Cleveland: Jewett, Proctor and Worthington; London: Sampson Low, Son, 1853.

Hall, Abraham Oakey. *The Mahattaner in New Orleans, or, Phases of Crescent City Life.* New York: J. S. Redfield, 1851.

Hamline, Leonidas L. "Christian Patriotism." 1841. In *Works*, ed. F. G. Hibbard, 396–413. Cincinnati: Hitchcock and Walden, 1869.

Hughes, Rev. John. *Christianity, The only Source of Moral, Social and Political Regeneration. A Sermon: Preached in the Hall of the House of Representatives of the United States, on Sunday, December 12, 1847.* New York: Edward Dunigan, 1848.

Jay, William. *A Review of the Causes and Consequences of the Mexican War.* Boston: B. B. Mussey; Philadelphia: U. Hunt, 1849.

Kendall, George W. *The War between the United States and Mexico, Illustrated.* . . . New York: D. Appleton; Philadelphia: G. S. Appleton, 1851.

Livermore, Abiel A. *War with Mexico Reviewed.* Boston: American Peace Society, 1850.

Lunt, William P. *A Discourse Delivered in the First Church, Boston, Before the Ancient and Honorable Artillery Company, June 7, 1847. . . .* Boston: Eastburn's Press, 1847.

Luther, Seth. *An Address on the Right of Free Suffrage, with an Appendix Containing the Rhode-Island Bill of Rights.* Providence, 1833.

McCarty, John. *A Thanksgiving Sermon Preached in the National Palace of the City of Mexico, on Sunday October Third, A.D., 1847. . . .* Mexico: Printed at the office of the *American Star*, 1847.

McGee, Thomas D'Arcy. *A History of the Irish Settlers in North America, from the Earliest Period to the Census of 1850.* Boston: Office of the *American Celt*, 1851.

Mayer, Brantz. *Mexico, Aztec, Spanish and Republican: A Historical, Geographical, Political, Statistical and Social Account of that Country from the period of the Invasion by the Spaniards to the Present Time. . . .* 2 vols. Hartford: S. Drake, 1851.

New York City. Board of Aldermen. *Proceedings of the Boards of Aldermen and Assistant Aldermen, Approved by the Mayor. . . .* Vol. 14. New York: Casper C. Childs, Printer to the Common Council, 1847.

Norman, B. M. *Rambles by Land and Water . . . in Cuba and Mexico. . . .* New York: Paine and Burgess; New Orleans: B. M. Norman, 1845.

O'Brien, John. *A Treatise on American Military Laws, and the Practice of Courts Martial; with Suggestions for their Improvement.* Philadelphia, 1846.

Olmsted, Frederick Law. *A Journey through Texas; or, A Saddle-Trip on the Southwestern Frontier, with a Statistical Appendix.* 1860. Reprint, New York: B. Franklin, 1969.

Parker, Theodore. *The Collected Works of Theodore Parker. . . .* Ed. Frances P. Cobbe. Vol. 4. London: Trübner, 1863.

Perry, J. A. *Travels, Scenes and Sufferings in Cuba, Mexico and California, Illustrated with Engravings: Thrilling Adventures of a New Englander.* Boston: Redding, 1853.

Ripley, Roswell S. *The War with Mexico. By R. S. Ripley, Brevet Major in the United States Army, First Lieutenant of the Second Regiment of Artillery, Etc.* 2 vols. London: Sampson Low; New York: Harper and Brothers, 1850.

Roa Bárcena, José María. *Recuerdos de la invasion norteamericana (1846–1848).* Mexico: Editorial Porrúa, 1947.

Robinson, Fayette. *An Account of the Organization of the Army of the United States. . . .* 2 vols. Philadelphia: E. H. Butler, 1848.

Roll of the Members of the Military Company of Massachusetts, now Called the Ancient and Honorable Artillery Company of Massachusetts, with a Roster of the Commissioned Officers and Preachers, 1638–1694. Boston: Alfred Mudge and Son, 1895.

The Rough and Ready Annual: or Military Souvenir. New York: D. Appleton, 1848.

The Rough and Ready Songster: Embellished with Twenty-five Splendid Engravings, Illustrative of the American Victories in Mexico, By an American Officer. New York: Nafis and Cornish, [1848].

Scott, John M. *Address to the Pennsylvania Volunteers Returned from Mexico: Delivered July 24, 1848 at Philadelphia.* Philadelphia.: C. Sherman, printer, 1848.

Smith, Ashbel. *An Oration Pronounced before the Connecticut Alpha of the Psi Beta Kappa at Yale College, New Haven, August 15, 1849.* New Haven: B. L. Hamlen, 1849.

Smyth, Rev. Thomas. "The Relation of Christianity to War, and the Portraiture of a

Christian Soldier, A Discourse delivered on occasion of the First Commencement of the Citadel Academy." Walden, 1869. Reprinted in *Complete Works of Rev. Thos. Smyth*, ed. J. Wm. Flinn, 5:351–77. Columbia, S.C.: R. L. Bryan, 1908–12.

Soulé, Frank, John H. Gihon, and James Nisbet. *Annals of San Francisco: containing A Summary of the History of the First Discovery, Settlement, Progress, and Present Condition of California....* New York: D. Appleton, 1855.

Thomas, E. *Covenant Breaking and its Consequences: The Present Posture of Our National Affairs in Connection with the Mexican War....* Rossville, Ohio, 1847.

United States. House of Representatives. House Executive Document No. 24, 31st Cong., 1st sess., 1849.

United States. Senate. "Message from the President of the United States in answer to a resolution of the Senate calling for the proceedings of the court of inquiry convened at Saltillo, Mexico, Jan 12, 1848, for the purpose of obtaining full information relative to an alleged mutiny at Buena Vista, about the 15th August, 1847." 30th Cong., 1st sess. Washington, D.C., 1848.

———. Report of the Secretary of War, Communicating, In compliance with a resolution of the Senate, a map showing the operations of the army of the United States in Texas and the adjacent Mexican states on the Rio Grande; accompanied by astronomical observations, and descriptive and military memoirs of the country. March 1, 1849. 31st Cong., 1st sess., 1849. Ex. Doc. No. 32.

Wilson, Robert A. *Mexico and its Religion: with Incidents of Travel in that Country during Parts of the Years 1851–52–53–54....* New York: Harper and Brothers, 1855.

Wislizenus, F. A. *A Journey to the Rocky Mountains in the Year 1839.* Saint Louis: Missouri Historical Society, 1912.

Wright, Henry C. *Dick Crowninshield, the Assassin, and Zachary Taylor, the Soldier: the Difference Between Them.* Hopedale, Mass.: Non-Resistant and Practical Christian Office, 1848.

SECONDARY SOURCES

Books

Acuña, Rodolfo. *Occupied America: A History of Chicanos.* 2d ed. New York: Harper and Row, 1981.

Albion, Robert G. *The Rise of New York Port, 1815–1860.* New York: Charles Scribner's Sons, 1939.

Allen, Theodore. *The Invention of the White Race.* Vol. 1, *Racial Oppression and Social Control.* London: Verso, 1994.

Anderson, Benedict. *Imagined Communities: Reflections on the Origin and Spread of Nationalism.* London: Verso, 1991.

Baker, Jean. *Affairs of Party: The Political Culture of Northern Democrats in the Mid-nineteenth Century.* Ithaca: Cornell University Press, 1983.

Baudier, Roger. *The Catholic Church in Louisiana.* New Orleans: A. W. Hyatt Stationary Mfg. Co., 1939.

Bauer, K. Jack. *The Mexican War, 1846–1848*. New York: Macmillan, 1974.

Bemis, Samuel Flagg. *The Latin American Policy of the United States: An Historical Interpretation*. New York: Harcourt, Brace, 1943.

Bergquist, Charles. *Labor and the Course of American Democracy: US History in Latin American Perspective*. London: Verso, 1996.

Berlin, Ira, Barbara Fields, et al., eds. *Free at Last: A Documentary History of Slavery, Freedom and the Civil War*. New York: New Press, 1992.

Berlin, Ira, Steven F. Miller, et al., eds. *The Wartime Genesis of Free Labor: The Upper South*. Series I, Vol. II, *Freedom: A Documentary History of Emancipation, 1861–1867*. . . . Cambridge: Cambridge University Press, 1993.

Berstein, Iver. *The New York City Draft Riots: Their Significance for American Society and Politics in the Age of the Civil War*. New York: Oxford University Press, 1990.

Biggs, Donald C. *Conquer and Colonize: Stevenson's Regiment and California*. San Rafael, Calif.: Presidio Press, 1977.

Blue, Frederick J. *The Free Soilers: Third Party Politics, 1848–54*. Urbana: University of Illinois Press, 1973.

Bodo, John. *The Protestant Clergy and Public Issues, 1812–1848*. Princeton: Princeton University, 1954.

Brack, Gene M. *Mexico Views Manifest Destiny, 1821–1846: An Essay on the Origins of the Mexican War*. Albuquerque: University of New Mexico Press, 1975.

Breen, Matthew P. *Thirty Years of New York Politics: Up-to-Date, With Illustrations*. New York: the author, 1899.

Brewer, E. Cobham. *Dictionary of Phrase and Fable*. Philadelphia: J. B. Lippincott, 1899.

Bridges, Amy. *A City in the Republic: Antebellum New York and the Origins of Machine Politics*. Ithaca: Cornell University Press, 1984.

Brown, Charles H. *Agents of Manifest Destiny: The Lives and Times of the Filibusters*. Chapel Hill: University of North Carolina Press, 1980.

Coffman, Edward M. *The Old Army: A Portrait of the American Army in Peacetime, 1784–1898*. New York: Oxford University Press, 1986.

Connor, Seymour V., and Odie B. Faulk. *North America Divided: The Mexican War, 1846–1848*. New York: Oxford University Press, 1971.

Cummins, Light T. and Glen Jeansonne. *A Guide to the History of Louisiana*. Westport, Conn.: Greenwood Press, 1982.

Cunliffe, Marcus. *Soldiers and Civilians: The Martial Spirit in America, 1775–1865*. Boston: Little, Brown, 1968.

Davis, Susan G. *Parades and Power: Street Theatre in Nineteenth-Century Philadelphia*. Philadelphia: Temple University Press, 1986.

Dawley, Alan. *Struggles for Justice: Social Responsibility and the Liberal State*. Cambridge, Mass.: Belknap Press, 1991.

Dictionary of American Biography. New York: Knopf, 1923.

Dolan, Jay P. *The Immigrant Church: New York's Irish and German Catholics, 1815–1865*. Baltimore: Johns Hopkins University Press, 1975.

Dublin, Thomas. *Women at Work: The Transformation of Work and Community in Lowell, Massachusetts, 1826–1860*. New York: Columbia University, 1979.

Faragher, John M. *Sugar Creek: Life on the Illinois Prairie.* New Haven: Yale University Press, 1986.

Foner, Eric. *Free Soil, Free Labor, Free Men: The Ideology of the Republican Party before the Civil War . . . With a New Introductory Essay.* Oxford: Oxford University Press, 1995.

Foner, Philip. *U.S. Labor Movement and Latin America: A History of Workers' Response to Intervention.* Vol. 1, *1846–1919.* Critical Studies in Work and Community Series. South Hadley, Mass.: Bergin and Garvey, 1988.

Freidel, Frank. *Francis Lieber, Nineteenth-Century Liberal.* Baton Rouge: Louisiana State University Press, 1947.

Fuess, Claude M. *The Life of Caleb Cushing.* 2 vols. New York: Harcourt and Brace, 1923.

Fuller, John D. P. *The Movement for the Acquisition of All Mexico.* Baltimore: Johns Hopkins Press, 1936.

Gates, Paul W. *History of Public Land Law Development.* Washington, D.C.: U.S. Government Printing Office, 1968.

Gatewood, Willard B. *Black Americans and the White Man's Burden, 1898–1903.* Urbana: University of Illinois Press, 1975.

Goldstein, Robert J. *Political Repression in Modern America: 1870 to the Present.* Cambridge, Mass.: Schenkman Publishing; New York: Two Continents Publishing, 1978.

Graebner, Norman A. *Empire on the Pacific: A Study in American Continental Expansion.* New York: Ronald Press, 1955.

Greenberg, Amy S. *Cause for Alarm: The Volunteer Fire Department in the Nineteenth-Century City.* Princeton: Princeton University Press, 1998.

Griswold del Castillo, Richard. *The Treaty of Guadalupe Hidalgo: A Legacy of Conflict.* Norman: University of Oklahoma Press, 1990.

Guardino, Peter F. *Peasants, Politics, and the Formation of Mexico's National State: Guerrero, 1800–1857.* Stanford: Stanford University Press, 1996.

Hackenburg, Randy W. *Pennsylvania in the War with Mexico: The Volunteer Regiments.* Shippensburg, Pa.: White Mane, 1992.

Handlin, Oscar. *Boston's Immigrants: A Study in Acculturation.* Rev. and enl. ed. Cambridge, Mass.: Belknap Press, 1959.

Harris, Charles H. *A Mexican Family Empire: The Latifundio of the Sánchez Navarros, 1765–1867.* Austin: University of Texas Press, 1975.

Heitman, Francis B. *Historical Register and Dictionary of the United States Army . . . to March 2, 1903.* 2 vols. Washington, D. C.: Government Printing Office, 1903.

Herrera Serna, Laura, ed. *México en guerra (1846–1848): Perspectivas regionales.* Mexico, D. F.: Museo Nacional de las Intervenciones, 1997.

Hietala, Thomas R. *Manifest Design: Anxious Aggrandizement in Late Jacksonian America.* Ithaca: Cornell University Press, 1985.

Hill, Christopher. *The World Turned Upside Down: Radical Ideas during the English Revolution.* Middlesex: Penguin Books, 1975.

Horsman, Reginald. *Race and Manifest Destiny: The Origins of American Racial Anglo-Saxonism.* Cambridge, Mass: Harvard University Press, 1981.

Howe, Daniel W. *The Political Culture of the American Whigs*. Chicago: University of Chicago Press, 1979.

Johannsen, Robert W. *To the Halls of the Montezumas: The Mexican War in the American Imagination*. New York: Oxford University Press, 1985.

Josephson, Hannah. *The Golden Threads: New England's Mill Girls and Magnates*. New York: Duell, Sloan and Pearce, 1949.

LaFeber, Walter. *The New Empire: An Interpretation of American Expansion, 1860–1898*. Ithaca: Cornell University Press, 1963.

Lander, Ernest M. *Reluctant Imperialists: Calhoun, the South Carolinians, and the Mexican War*. Baton Rouge: Louisiana State University Press, 1980.

Lane, Roger. *Policing the City: Boston, 1822–1885*. Cambridge, Mass.: Harvard University Press, 1967.

Langley, Harold D. *Social Reform in the United States Navy, 1798–1862*. Urbana: University of Illinois Press, 1967.

Linderman, Gerald F. *Embattled Courage: The Experience of Combat in the American Civil War*. New York: Free Press; London: Collier Macmillan, 1987.

———. *Mirror of War: American Society and the Spanish-American War*. Ann Arbor: University of Michigan Press, 1974.

Lopez y Rivas, Gilberto. *La guerra del 47, y la resistencia popular a la ocupación*. Mexico City: Editorial Nuestro Tiempo, 1976.

Lott, Eric. *Love and Theft: Blackface Minstrelsy and the American Working Class*. New York: Oxford University Press, 1993.

McCaffrey, James M. *Army of Manifest Destiny: The American Soldier in the Mexican War, 1846–1848*. New York: New York University Press, 1992.

McPherson, James M. *Battle Cry of Freedom: The Civil War Era*. In *The Oxford History of the United States*, ed. C. Vann Woodward. New York: Oxford University Press, 1988.

———. *What They Fought For, 1861–1865*. Baton Rouge: Louisiana State University Press, 1994.

Mahon, John K. *History of the Militia and the National Guard*. In Macmillan Wars of the United States Series, ed. Louis Morton. New York: Macmillan, 1983.

Mallon, Florencia E. *Peasant and Nation: The Making of Postcolonial Mexico and Peru*. Berkeley: University of California Press, 1995.

Merk, Frederick, with the collaboration of Lois Bannister Merk. *Manifest Destiny and Mission in American History: A Reinterpretation*. Cambridge, Mass.: Harvard University Press, 1963.

Miller Robert R. *Shamrock and Sword: The Saint Patrick's Battalion in the U.S.-Mexican War*. Norman: University of Oklahoma Press, 1989.

Montejano, David. *Anglos and Mexicans in the Making of Texas, 1836–1986*. Austin: University of Texas Press, 1987.

Montgomery, David. *Beyond Equality: Labor and the Radical Republicans, 1862–1872*. New York: Knopf, 1967.

———. *Citizen Worker: The Experience of Workers in the United States with Democracy and the Free Market during the Nineteenth Century.* Cambridge: Cambridge University Press, 1993.

Moody, Richard. *The Astor Place Riot.* Bloomington: Indiana University Press, 1958.

Morgan, Edmund. *American Slavery, American Freedom: The Ordeal of Colonial Virginia.* New York: Norton, 1975.

Niehaus, Earl F. *The Irish in New Orleans, 1800–1860.* Baton Rouge: Louisiana State University Press, 1965.

Norton, Wesley. *Religious Newspapers in the Old Northwest to 1861: A History, Bibliography and Record of Opinion.* Athens: Ohio University Press, 1977.

Oberly, James W. *Sixty Million Acres: American Veterans and the Public Lands before the Civil War.* Kent: University of Ohio Press, 1990.

O'Connor, Thomas H. *Fitzpatrick's Boston, 1846–1866: John Bernard Fitzpatrick, Third Bishop of Boston.* Boston: Northeastern University Press, 1984.

Olliff, Donathon C. *Reforma Mexico and the United States: A Search for Alternatives to Annexation, 1854–1861.* University: University of Alabama Press, 1981.

Palladino, Grace. *Another Civil War: Labor, Capital and the State in the Anthracite Region of Pennsylvania, 1840–1868.* Urbana: University of Illinois Press, 1990.

Pletcher, David M. *The Diplomacy of Annexation: Texas, Oregon, and the Mexican War.* Columbia: University of Missouri Press, 1973.

Pocock, J. G. A. *The Machiavellian Moment: Florentine Political Thought and the Atlantic Republican Tradition.* Princeton: Princeton University Press, 1975.

Prucha, Francis. *Broadax and Bayonet: The Role of the United States Army in the Development of the Northwest.* Madison: Historical Society of Wisconsin, 1953.

Prude, Jonathan. *The Coming of Industrial Order: Town and Factory Life in Rural Massachusetts, 1810–1860.* Cambridge: Cambridge University Press, 1983.

Rawick, George P. *The American Slave: A Composite Autobiography.* Vol. 1. Westport, Conn.: Greenwood Press, 1972.

Reeves, Jesse S. *American Diplomacy under Tyler and Polk.* Baltimore: Johns Hopkins Press, 1907.

Reina, Leticia. *Las rebeliones campesinas en México, 1819–1906.* Mexico City: Siglo Veintiuno, 1980.

Richardson, James F. *The New York Police, Colonial Times to 1901.* New York: Oxford University Press, 1970.

Rives, George L. *The United States and Mexico, 1821–1845: A History of the Relations between the Two Countries. . . .* 2 vols. New York: Charles Scribner's Sons, 1913.

Robarts, William H. *Mexican War Veterans: A Complete Roster. . . .* Washington, D. C.: Brentano's, 1887.

Robinson, Cecil, trans. and ed. *The View from Chapultepec: Mexican Writers on the Mexican-American War.* Tucson: University of Arizona Press, 1989.

Roediger David. *The Wages of Whiteness.* New York: Verso, 1991.

Rogin, Michael P. *Subversive Genealogy: The Politics and Art of Herman Melville.* New York: Alfred A. Knopf, 1983.

Rosenberg, Charles E. *The Cholera Years: The United States in 1832, 1849, and 1866; with a New Afterword.* Chicago: University of Chicago Press, 1962, 1987.

Royster, Charles. *A Revolutionary People at War: The Continental Army and American Character, 1775–1783.* Chapel Hill: University of North Carolina Press, 1979.

Sandweiss, Martha A., Rick Stewart, and Ben W. Huseman. *Eyewitness to War: Prints and Daguerreotypes of the Mexican War, 1846–1848.* Fort Worth, Tex.: Amon Carter Museum, 1989.

Saxton, Alexander. *The Rise and Fall of the White Republic: Class Politics and Mass Culture in Nineteenth Century America.* London: Verso, 1990.

Schroeder, John H. *Mr. Polk's War: American Opposition and Dissent, 1846–1847.* Madison: University of Wisconsin Press, 1973.

Shea, John D. G. *History of the Catholic Church in the United States.* . . . 4 vols. New York: J. G. Shea, 1886–92.

Shenton, James P. *Robert John Walker: A Politician from Jackson to Lincoln.* New York: Columbia University Press, 1961.

Skelton, William B. *An American Profession of Arms: The Army Officer Corps, 1784–1861.* Lawrence: University Press of Kansas, 1992.

Smith, George W., and Charles Judah. *The Chronicles of the Gringos: The U.S. Army in the Mexican War, 1846–1848: Accounts of Eyewitnesses and Combatants.* Albuquerque: University of New Mexico Press, 1968.

Smith, Justin H. *The War with Mexico.* 2 vols. New York: Macmillan, 1919.

Spencer, Ivor D. *The Victor and the Spoils: A Life of William L. Marcy.* Providence: Brown University Press, 1959.

Stout, Joseph A. *The Liberators: Filibustering Expeditions into Mexico, 1848–1862 and the Last Thrust of Manifest Destiny.* Los Angeles: Westernlore Press, 1973.

Taylor, William B. *Magistrates of the Sacred: Priests and Parishioners in Eighteenth-Century Mexico.* Stanford: Stanford University Press, 1996.

Thornton, J. Mills. *Politics and Power in a Slave Society: Alabama, 1800–1860.* Baton Rouge: Louisiana State University Press, 1978.

Tomlins, Christopher. *Law, Labor, and Ideology in the Early American Republic.* Cambridge: Cambridge University Press, 1993.

van den Berghe, Pierre. *Race and Racism: A Comparative Perspective.* 2d ed. New York: Wiley, 1978.

Wasserman, Mark. *Capitalists, Caciques, and Revolution: The Native Elite and Foreign Enterprise in Chihuahua, Mexico, 1854–1911.* Chapel Hill: University of North Carolina Press, 1984.

Way, Peter. *Common Labour: Workers and the Digging of North American Canals, 1780–1860.* Cambridge: Cambridge University Press, 1993.

Wilentz, Sean. *Chants Democratic: New York City and the Rise of the American Working Class, 1788–1850.* New York: Oxford University Press, 1984.

Wortham, Thomas, ed. *James Russell Lowell's The Biglow Papers [First Series]: A Critical Edition.* Dekalb: Northern Illinois University Press, 1977.

Yeo, Eileen, and E. P. Thompson. *The Unknown Mayhew.* New York: Pantheon, 1971.

Ziegler, Valarie H. *The Advocates of Peace in Antebellum America.* Bloomington: Indiana University Press, 1992.

Articles and Dissertations

Boyett, Gene W. "Money and Maritime Activities in New Orleans during the Mexican War." *Louisiana History* 17 (1976): 413-29.

Chevalier, François. "The North Mexican Hacienda: Eighteenth and Nineteenth Centuries." In *The New World Looks at Its History: Proceedings of the Second International Congress of Historians of the United States and Mexico*, 95-107. Austin: University of Texas Press, 1963.

Davis, Susan G. "The Career of Colonel Pluck: Folk Drama and Popular Protest in Early Nineteenth-Century Philadelphia." *Pennsylvania Magazine of History and Biography* 109:2 (April 1985): 179-202.

Dean, Eric T. "In Evident Mental Commotion: Post-Traumatic Stress and the Civil War." Ph.D. diss., Yale University, 1996.

Ducrest, Jerome S. "New Orleans Commerce, 1830-1860." M.A. thesis, Louisiana State University, 1926.

Ellsworth, Charles S. "American Churches and the Mexican War." *American Historical Review* 45 (January 1940): 301-26.

Ernst, Robert. "The One and Only Mike Walsh." *New-York Historical Society Quarterly* 36 (1952): 43-65.

Fields, Barbara. "Ideology and Race in American History." In *Region, Race and Reconstruction: Essays in Honor of C. Van Woodward*, ed. J. Morgan Kousser and James M. McPherson. 143-77. Oxford: Oxford University Press, 1982.

Gilley, B. H. "'Polk's War' and the Louisiana Press." *Louisiana History* 20 (1979): 5-23.

Gorn, Elliott. "'Goodbye Boys, I Die a True American': Homicide, Nativism, and Working-Class Culture in Antebellum New York City." *Journal of American History* 74 (September 1987): 388-410.

Hinckley, Ted C. "American Anti-Catholicism during the Mexican War." *Pacific Historical Review* 31 (May 1962): 121-37.

Huston, John R. "Land and Freedom: The Anti-Rent Wars, Jacksonian Politics, and the Contest over Free Labor in New York, 1785-1865." Ph.D. diss., Yale University, 1994.

Kutolowski, John F., and Kathleen Smith Kutolowski. "Commissions and Canvasses: The Militia and Politics in Western New York, 1800-1845." *New York History* 63:1 (January 1982): 5-38.

Lucassen, Jan. "The Other Proletarians: Seasonal Labourers, Mercenaries and Miners." *International Review of Social History* 39 suppl. (1994): 171-94.

McEniry, Blanche M. "American Catholics in the War with Mexico." Ph.D. diss., Catholic University of America, 1937.

Mallon, Florencia. "Peasants and State Formation in Nineteenth-Century Mexico: Morelos, 1848-1858." In *Political Power and Social Theory: A Research Annual*, vol. 7, ed. Maurice Zeitlin. 1-54. Greenwich, Conn.: JAI Press, 1988.

May, Robert E., "Invisible Men: Blacks and the U.S. Army in the Mexican War." *Historian* 49 (August 1987): 463-77.

————. "Young American Males and Filibustering in the Age of Manifest Destiny: The United States Army as Cultural Mirror." *Journal of American History* 78:3 (December 1991): 857.

Montgomery, David. "Wage Labor, Bondage, and Citizenship in Nineteenth-Century America." *International Labor and Working-Class History* 48 (Fall 1995): 6–27.

Nash, Gary B. "The Hidden History of Mestizo America." *Journal of American History* 82:3 (December 1995):941–65.

Reilly, Tom. "A Spanish-Language Voice of Dissent in Antebellum New Orleans." *Louisiana History* 23 (1982): 325–39.

Rogan, Bernadette. "Louisiana's Part in the Mexican War." M.A. thesis, Tulane University, 1939.

Shearer, Earnest C. "The Carvajal Disturbances." *Southwestern Historical Quarterly* 55 (1951): 201–30.

Smith, Bruce P. "Circumventing the Jury: Petty Crime and Summary Jurisdiction in London and New York City, 1790–1855." Ph.D. diss. Yale University, 1996.

Strausberg, Stephen F. "Indiana and the Swamp Lands Act: A Study in State Administration." *Indiana Magazine of History* 73 (Spring 1972): 191–203.

Urban, Chester S. "A Local Study in Manifest Destiny: New Orleans and the Cuba Question during the Lopez Expeditions of 1849–1851." *Louisiana Historical Quarterly* 22 (1939): 1095–1167.

Winston, James E. "New Orleans and the Texas Revolution." *Louisiana Historical Quarterly* 10:3 (July 1927): 317–54.

Acknowledgments

This book owes its existence to the generosity, labor, and faith that various individuals and institutions have bestowed upon its author. Jon Butler gave much encouragement in reading and critiquing drafts of this project from its earliest stages. David Montgomery was there from the beginning and provided a vast amount of help and advice at every step along the way. Alexander Saxton was more than generous in providing guidance in turning a sprawling dissertation into a book. David Roediger read an early draft and provided useful advice. Mark Weiner read the manuscript and supplied thoughtful comments.

Robert May and Richard Griswold del Castillo provided a great deal of insightful commentary in the final stages of revision. Brian MacDonald and Ron Maner, at the University of North Carolina Press, did a fantastic job with copyediting and project management. David Perry, editor-in-chief at the UNC Press, provided moral support and practical advice. Ellen Foos contributed a thorough proofreading.

Susan Froetschel, of the Bass Writing Program at Yale, helped me to write with some clarity and style; that I still have a great deal to learn is by no means her fault. Marian MacDonald gave from her wealth of experience and sympathy during the early years of this project.

The Mellon Foundation gave financial support, providing grants for a semester's research and travel, and a year-long writing grant. The American Antiquarian Society bestowed a two-month resident fellowship and much moral and intellectual support. Almost every member of the Society's staff made a personal effort to make this book a better and more thoroughly researched piece of work, particularly Joanne Chaison, Tom Knoles, and Russell Martin.

The Huntington Library also provided a resident fellowship in the summer of 1996; the Huntington is an oasis for scholarship. Peter Blodgett was very helpful in steering me through its excellent manuscript resources for this project. A grant from the Beinecke Library at Yale gave me an opportunity to spend a summer immersed in its outstanding Mexican War collections. Thanks to George Miles for his help at the Beinecke.

Special thanks to Mary and Joseph Foos for their help and patience. No professions of gratitude could ever repay Lisa and Judith Foos. They have undergone several relocations and dislocations while I stole odd moments from my career as an academic migrant laborer to write this book. What was stolen from them I will endeavor to repay again and again.

Index